KOREAN POLITICS

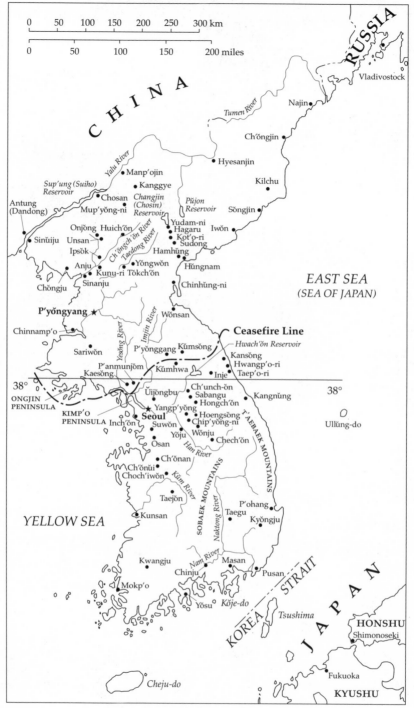

KOREA

KOREAN POLITICS

The Quest for Democratization
and Economic Development

John Kie-chiang Oh

Cornell University Press

Ithaca and London

First Published 1999 by Cornell University Press
First printing, Cornell Paperbacks, 1999

Printed in the United States of America

Library of Congress Cataloging-in-Publication Data

Oh, John Kie-chiang, 1930–
    Korean politics : the quest for democratization and economic
development / John Kie-chiang Oh.
        p.   cm.
    Includes bibliographical references and index.
    ISBN 0-8014-3447-5 (cloth : alk. paper). — ISBN 0-8014-8458-8
(pbk. : alk. paper)
    1. Democracy—Korea (South) 2. Korea (South)—Politics and
government—1988- 3. Korea (South)—Economic conditions—1960-
I. Title
JQ1729.A15043   1999
320.95195—dc21   98-36484

Cornell University Press strives to use environmentally responsible suppliers and materials to the fullest extent possible in the publishing of its books. Such materials include vegetable-based, low-VOC inks and acid-free papers that are recycled, totally chlorine-free, or partly composed of nonwood fibers.

Cloth printing   10   9   8   7   6   5   4   3   2   1
Paperback printing 10   9   8   7   6   5   4   3   2   1

This book is dedicated to my wife, who has managed to build

an academic career while sharing an eventful and

fruitful life with me for forty years,

to our three children and their spouses,

and to our six grandchildren.

CONTENTS

CHRONOLOGY AND LIST OF TABLES

ACKNOWLEDGMENTS

This book is being completed in the thirty-sixth year of my academic career, which took a full-time administrative path for twelve years. Because this book is a sequel, at least in my mind, to my *Korea: Democracy on Trial*, also published by Cornell University Press, in 1968, I realize anew that I have been concerned about democracy for a long time. I am still grateful to the Social Science Research Council and the American Council of Learned Societies, whose grants supported my earlier research into democracy in Korea.

I began my research for this book during my sabbatical in 1989–1990 on resigning from the post of Academic Vice President of the Catholic University of America. This political scientist wanted to learn something about the Korean economy; and I was a visiting senior fellow at the Korea Development Institute. I am grateful to Dr. Cho Soon, then Vice Premier for economic affairs, for interceding on my behalf with the then-President of the Institute, Dr. Koo Bon-ho, who made my study at the campuslike setting of the Institute not only possible but also enjoyable. I would also like to express my appreciation to Chairman Kim Joo Jin of the Anam Group for providing me with start-up support for this project.

I am thankful for the research grants from Catholic University of America toward the end of this project. I am also grateful to Dr. Dennis L. McNamara, Y. H. Park Professor of Korean Studies at Georgetown University, for inviting me to some of his Korean studies conferences, where a few of my ideas were tested and enriched. Professors David I. Steinberg of Georgetown University and Baek Im-hyŏk of Koryo University generously shared their thoughts and publications with me. Dr. Kim Yŏng-kuk,

Professor Emeritus of political science of the Seoul National University, and Lee Kiwon, former Vice President of the Academy of Korean Studies, were also helpful to me during my stay in Seoul.

My gratitude goes to Dr. Ilpyong J. Kim, Professor Emeritus of political science of the University of Connecticut, and Dolores Mulligan of the University of Maryland for reading my manuscript. I am thankful to Dr. Sung Y. Kwak of Howard University for his help with economic statistics. I must express my special thanks to Dr. Cho Sung Yun and Dr. Kim Joobong, both of the Library of Congress, for their always cheerful help. Dr. Kim Kook Kan of Philadelphia and David A. Parker of the Korean Information Center also helped me graciously. I am grateful to Dr. Cheong Y. Lee, President of Green Computer Systems, for keeping my word processor functioning, though not without a few moments of panic. It has been a great pleasure to work with Roger Haydon of Cornell University Press. I should also thank many others who are too numerous to mention in a brief acknowledgment.

Finally, this book could not have been written without the loving support and encouragement of my wife, Dr. Bonnie Bongwan Oh, Distinguished Research Professor of Korean Studies at Georgetown University.

JOHN KIE-CHIANG OH

Potomac, Maryland

KOREAN POLITICS

Introduction

On February 25, 1998, for the first time in half a century of turbulent politics, Korea experienced a peaceful transfer of power. Kim Dae-jung was inaugurated as the fifteenth president of the Republic of Korea on a rare smog-free and sunny morning in Seoul. It was a historic landmark: an orderly transfer of power from a long-entrenched ruling camp to the opposition was accomplished at a simple inaugural ceremony. If a basic test of democracy is the ability of the people to "kick the rascals out" through free and fair elections, South Koreans passed this test fifty years after the establishment of the republic in 1948.

The celebration launching a "government for the people" was subdued, however, because of the economic cataclysm that had occurred in the late fall of 1997. The financial crisis had led to a $57 billion bailout agreement with the International Monetary Fund (IMF), announced on December 3, just before the presidential election on December 18. Seemingly evaporated overnight was the vaunted "miracle on the Han" that had been triggered in the mid-1960s. The sustained quest for economic growth and development came to a screeching halt, and the country now faced the daunting task of implementing drastic reforms in the industrial–financial sector.

Thus two epochal events occurred almost simultaneously. Just when the quest for democratization reached an important turning point, economic meltdown stunned the nation. The economy appeared to have passed the danger of a sovereign insolvency by the time of the launching of the new government. However, a new, minority president, who had garnered 40.3 percent of the votes, together with a minority coalition in the national legislature now confronted an unprecedented economic crisis. Whereas the rapid economic growth had been initiated by a "strong government" headed by a former army general, Park Chung Hee, the economic turmoil was faced by a civilian government that was likely to be prone to deadlock. The political and economic transformations in South Korea ushered in an era of a vastly different relationship between the government and the economic sector.

Since the end of World War II, political and economic transformations of South Korea have been extraordinary, not only in Korean history but also in comparison with many other Asian nations. When Korea was freed from Japanese colonial domination in 1945 the southern half of the peninsula was in search of a new political identity; the new Republic of Korea was then one of the poorest nations in the world. The 1948 constitution made democracy the founding ideology of this new republic that soon would experience breakdowns in its republican system. By the end of the 1980s, however, sweeping changes in South Korean politics had occurred, including the reinstitution of a direct presidential election in response to massive popular demands for "democratic reforms." The simultaneous and impressive growth in gross domestic product made South Korea one of the "mini dragons" of Asia. In 1993 a "civilian and democratic"[1] government was reborn. These remarkable transformations were hailed by many as the "democratization" of the country's authoritarian past coupled with the "development" of her economy, despite the many ups and downs.

Until 1948 Korean politics had been anything but democratic, although populist, protodemocratic teachings spread among the peasantry for a brief period. The Chosŏn dynasty was terminated in 1910, only to be replaced with domination by imperial Japan. An American military government ruled South Korea until a "democratic" republic was hurriedly inaugurated. In terms of economic life, most Koreans in a mountainous peninsula had endured agrarian lives of genteel poverty for millennia and continued to do so until the mid-1960s, when the government of the Third Republic launched ambitious economic growth programs. Rapid and spectacular economic growth indeed occurred and was generally sustained until the mid-1990s; per capita annual income was less than $100 when the Korean republic was inaugurated but surpassed $10,000 by 1995. Meanwhile, until the late 1980s "democracy" had remained an often illusory but persistently recurring political aspiration. After long

[1] From *munmin* in Korean. This compound term is not mentioned in Yi Hŭi-sŭng, *Kuk'ŏ daesajŏn* (The Complete Dictionary of the National Language), 4th ed. (Seoul: Minjung sŏrim, 1988). It is obvious that *mun* means civilian, as distinguished from *mu*, or *military*, and *min* is an abbreviation of *minju*, or *democracy*. However, *munmin* is usually translated *civilian*.

and often uneven contests between authoritarian forces and democratic elements, a duly elected government was reestablished when the Seventh Republic was launched, replacing military-dominated regimes that had ruled for three decades, since 1961. Korea may be said to be undergoing important if sometimes "constrained"[2] democratic transitions and moving toward some early democratic consolidation.[3]

This book looks at the political and economic evolution of South Korea, including significant relationships or "interplays"[4] between South Korea's politics and its economy. The book engages in largely chronological analyses of politics and the economy, with an emphasis on the former. In a sense, this is a sequel to my *Korea: Democracy on Trial.*[5] That book discusses the difficult process of the hurried transplantation of some aspects of Western democracy on the inhospitable Korean political culture, as well as the challenges faced by "democratic" politics in South Korea until they were terminated by the military *coup d'état* of 1961. This book expands that scope by adding an economic dimension. It also expands the time span covered. This book briefly discusses relevant cultural, political, and economic aspects of traditional Korea in a way symbolized by the *Tonghak* ("Eastern Learning") movement while updating other material.

Democratization and economic development serve as the theoretical framework for selecting materials included in this book. For example, certain protodemocratic ideas of the Eastern Learning movement that originated in Korea in the nineteenth century are seen as relevant. The Seoul Olympiad of 1988 merits but a passing mention, however, inasmuch as the authoritarian regime in place at the time dared not use draconian measures against its democratic opponents while worldwide media attention was being focused on Korea. Of course, there have long been other significant pressing concerns for Korea such as security, reunification, and various external factors. They, too, deserve some comments here. However, it is essentially a study of domestic politics as they bear on the two key issues, democratization and economic development.

To the extent that such concepts as authoritarianism, democratization, and economic development have theoretical contents, this book includes

---

2 Juan J. Linz and Alfred Stepan, *Problems of Democratic Transition and Consolidation* (Baltimore: Johns Hopkins University Press, 1996), pp. 151–65. Guillermo O'Donnell, Philippe C. Schmitter, and Laurence Whitehead, eds., *Transition from Authoritarian Rule* (Baltimore: Johns Hopkins University Press, 1988), Chap. 1.

3 Larry Diamond, "Rethinking Civil Society: Toward Democratic Consolidation," *Journal of Democracy* 5, no. 3 (1994), pp. 4–17. Juan J. Linz and Alfred Stepan, "Toward Consolidated Democracies," *Journal of Democracy* 7, no. 2 (1996), pp. 14–33.

4 David C. Cole and Princeton N. Lyman, *Korean Development: The Inter-play of Politics and Economics* (Cambridge, MA: Harvard University Press, 1971).

5 John Kie-chiang Oh, *Korea: Democracy on Trial* (Ithaca, NY: Cornell University Press, 1968).

such elements. There has been no dearth of theoretical tomes and admirable attempts at model building regarding authoritarianism, democracy, and economic developments in different countries and times. This book will thus benefit from insightful theories, paradigms, and models, such as those of democratic transition and consolidation or developmental states, when they are clearly illuminating and explanatory. However, this is largely an empirical–historical study of the highlights of political evolutions and of economic development in South Korea. It is neither an attempt at breaking new theoretical ground nor an effort to fit the Korean example into some particular theoretical framework or model.

A few key concepts need brief delineation at the outset, however, for the dual purposes of indicating the meanings of these terms and to suggest some yardsticks by which to gauge the process and degrees of democratization, as well as economic growth and development in Korea. Democracy here means a philosophy of political organization and functions in which major public policies are decided and executed by public officials (leaders or decision makers) subject to popular control through periodic elections conducted on the principle of individual autonomy and under conditions of political freedom.[6] This definition suggests that democracy has not only the usual political and institutional aspects but also societal and functional dimensions. When applied to an Asian society, such as Korea today with its heavy residues of authoritarianism and elitist structures, this definition implies an essential equality of individuals not only through the political formula of one person, one vote but also functionally in freely exercising that political right, or what some call "democratic autonomy."[7]

Without adequate economic and social autonomy, formal political rights alone would not always free an individual from various types of coercions, say, by families or employers or the state. This definition of democracy presupposes the presence of at least minimal economic autonomy to exercise the political right; the attainment of economic autonomy presumes that a large enough majority partakes tangibly in the benefits of economic growth to make those people not only politically but also economically autonomous to participate in the democratic process.[8] The def-

---

[6] This definition falls somewhere between the narrow concept formulated by Joseph Schumpeter, *Capitalism, Socialism, and Democracy* (London: Allen and Unwin, 1942), p. 260, and a broader concept advocated by David Held, *Models of Democracy* (Stanford, CA: Stanford University Press, 1987), p. 271.

[7] Georg Sorensen, *Democracy and Democratization* (Boulder, CO: Westview Press, 1993), p. 10. Held, *Models of Democracy*, p. 285.

[8] Robert A. Dahl, *Policarchy: Participation and Opposition* (New Haven, CT: Yale University Press, 1971), pp. 48–104; Robert A. Dahl, *A Preface to Economic Democracy* (Cambridge, MA: Polity Press, 1985), p. 60.

inition thus agrees with the view that the higher the socioeconomic level of a country, the more likely it will be a democracy, and further that "the more well-to-do a nation, the greater the chances that it will sustain democracy."[9]

In a consideration of conditions leading to and sustaining democracy in Korea, socioeconomic groups including entrepreneurs, the middle class, and the workers would prove relevant. Generally, in democratizing Western societies the middle class and the industrial workers, for instance, have favored democracy, whereas traditional landowners have opposed it. In an observation of the roots of democracy one observer concluded that "a vigorous and independent class of town dwellers has been an indispensable element in the growth of parliamentary democracy. No bourgeoisie, no democracy."[10] South Korea has seen a rapidly urbanizing society with a rapid expansion of the middle class since the mid-1970s. "Civil society" has emerged, though whether it has reached a stage of having dense "networks at multiple levels of society"[11] remains to be seen.

It is also proposed to bear in mind the questions of legitimacy of the governing authorities and the effectiveness of various regimes. The perception that a given government is appropriate and proper is important in the stability of most societies. It is particularly so for a democratizing society and especially in Korea, where there exist heavy residues of the Confucian idea that leaders must be legitimate. Effectiveness pertains to "the basic functions of government as defined by the expectations of most members of a society."[12] Questions of legitimacy and effectiveness appear often to be tied; for example, even a legitimate government may lose its legitimacy if the regime is incapable of functioning, just as an illegitimate regime may become acceptable if it proves to be effective, and may purchase legitimacy by such prolonged performance.

Matters that hinder the democratization of Korea include traditional political cultures, authoritarianism, elitism, regionalism, and militarism—both old and new. The all-too-frequent absence and betrayal of "trust,"[13] particularly public or vertical trust in institutions and authorities, likewise have been serious issues. "Trust" here simply means the condition in which

[9] Seymour Martin Lipset, "Some Social Requisites of Democracy: Economic Development and Political Legitimacy," *American Political Science Review* 53, no. 1 (1959), p. 75.

[10] Barrington Moore, Jr., *Social Origins of Dictatorship and Democracy* (Boston: Beacon Press, 1966), p. 418.

[11] Larry Diamond, "Rethinking Civil Society: Toward Democratic Consolidation," *Journal of Democracy* 5, no. 3 (1994), p. 15.

[12] Lipset, "Social Requisites," p. 86.

[13] Robert D. Putnam and Eric M. Uslander, "Democracy and Social Capital," and Ronald Inglehart, "Trust, Well-Being, and Democracy" (papers presented at the Conference on Trust and Democracy, Georgetown University, November 1996). Francis Fukuyama, *Trust: The Social Virtues and the Creation of Prosperity* (New York: Free Press, 1995), Chap. 2.

someone expects the likelihood of another to fulfill his or her normal obligation. It must be emphasized, however, that there have been exceptionally acute problems in Korea, due largely to the divisiveness within the peninsula since 1948. A war, rebellions, and economic difficulties—"three types of crisis in the life of a democratic nation"[14]—have been largely attributable to the hostile division that persists in Korea to this day.

Democratization here means the continuous process of changes toward more democratic politics. Economic development is distinguished from economic growth. Development means more than growth, particularly in a society such as Korea that aspires to democratize. Historically growth in some sectors such as heavy industries or armaments could be commanded for a relatively short term, usually with high sociopolitical costs, in countries including Nazi Germany and the Soviet Union. However, it has been abundantly clear, from China to North Korea, that economic growth in selected sectors or particular regions could not produce overall economic development.

In a society in which aspirations for both liberty and equality are evidently becoming stronger, economic growth alone will not suffice. This is particularly so in a country such as Korea where rapid growth seems to be concentrated in narrow sectors of the economy and much of the spectacularly visible wealth produced by that growth is perceived to be monopolized by a relatively small number of individuals or by largely family-owned business conglomerates, or *chaebŏl*.

With the heightened desire for economic equality along with political liberty, it is evident that the concept of "equity"[15] is becoming increasingly important among Korean experts on economy and politics in defining economic development in Korea today. Simply put, according to these Korean experts economic development means "high growth with equity."[16] Equity, according to one such expert, means a "socially acceptable degree of 'fairness' in the system of capital accumulation, resource use, and provision of opportunities." Fair opportunities are synonymous with "incentive systems" for all economic actors, including the workers, in the long-term process of economic development "to serve the people rather than the people serving development."[17] In this view, economic and so-

---

[14] Clinton L. Rossiter, *Constitutional Dictatorship: Crisis Government in the Modern Democracies* (Princeton, NJ: Princeton University Press, 1948), pp. 6–13.

[15] Irma Adelman and Cynthia Taft Morris, among others, disaggregated the concepts of growth, equity, and development, in *Economic Growth and Social Equity in Developing Countries* (Stanford, CA: Stanford University Press, 1973).

[16] Song Byung-Nak, *The Rise of the Korean Economy* (Oxford: Oxford University Press, 1990), p. 172.

[17] Cho Soon, *The Dynamics of Korean Economic Development* (Washington, DC: Institute for International Economics, 1994), p. 74.

cial justice mean not only reasonably fair income distribution but also due attention paid to such important social services as fair access to education, to housing, and to medical care. These are some aspects of "economic democratization" that elevate "procedural, political democracy" to what some Korean scholars call "real democracy."[18] This is why the question of economic "development" has become a key issue in South Korea only in recent decades and promises to remain important in the near future.

Democracy or development is an idealized stage to be attained after a prolonged process of evolution. Thus democracy and development are both processes and goals. Cynics in various schools would question even the applicability of the term *democracy* to Korea, just as some question the existence of democracy in Japan today. "Democratization" in South Korea has occurred only recently, and for a relatively brief period as compared to the evolution of Western democracy and even the long history of Korea. As in many other countries, democratization in Korea faces a difficult future and even potential breakdowns. Economic growth and development in Korea are recent phenomena; the nation also faces numerous challenges, both domestic and international, as was abundantly clear in various IMF-related crises of the late 1990s. However, few will challenge the proposition that democratization and economic development remain the two central questions in Korea for the foreseeable future.

The transliteration of Korean names and terms in this study generally conforms to the McCune-Reischauer Romanization System, with a number of notable exceptions such as the spellings of Syngman Rhee, Park Chung Hee, Kim Young Sam, and Seoul. Many Koreans, including this author, began romanizing place names and their own names before they became familiar with the McCune-Reischauer system, and I do not want to tamper with these spellings, which are so widely accepted. For the sake of consistency, Korean family names will precede given names (e.g., Kim Dae-jung instead of Dae-jung Kim).

In such a look at largely contemporary events as this, one runs the risk of unintentionally offending the particular sensitivities, convictions, or loyalties of individuals or groups. I disavow any interest whatever in making a case for or against any individuals, alive or deceased, or groups; I have made my best effort at maintaining scholarly objectivity with the data known to me at this writing.

[18] Choi Jang-jip, *Hanguk hyŏndae chŏngch'iŭi kujowa pyŏnhwa* (The Structure and Changes in Contemporary Korean Politics) (Seoul: Kkach'i, 1989), pp. 255–70. Similar views are discussed in Pak Tong-so and Kim Kwang-ung, *Hangukinŭi minju chŏngch'i ŭisik* (The Democratic Political Consciousness of the Korean People) (Seoul: Seoul National University Press, 1989), pp. 9–10.

✪

CHAPTER 1

Traditional Society

Because contemporary Korean politics and economy are built on the foundations of traditional Korea (Korea through the end of the Yi dynasty, which was terminated in 1910 by Japanese colonial rule), it is necessary to touch briefly on relevant highlights of Korean history.[1] Traditional Korea had an unusual cohesion and continuity in a small and clearly delineated peninsula within the relatively stable geopolitical environment of Asia. Within the peninsula traditional Korean society was tightly knit, allowing few deviations from the prevalent political and socioeconomic norms. Traditional political and economic patterns were pervasive within the small nation and lasted through the first decade of the twentieth century with only minor changes. It is said that when you scratch a contemporary Chinese there emerges a Confucian Chinese. To the extent that this observation is valid, it is equally true that even today, beneath a relatively thin veneer of the contemporary Korean, there lies a "traditional" Korean.

The Agrarian Economy and Class Structures

Korea was an agrarian society for millennia. Most Koreans today can locate their agrarian and rural roots if they look back as few as two generations. In the agrarian economy even the special production of goods and

---

[1] Fine Korean history books in English include Carter J. Eckert et al., *Korea Old and New: A History* (Seoul: Ilchokak New Publishers, 1990); William E. Henthorn, *A History of Korea* (New York: Free Press, 1971); and Andrew C. Nahm, *Korea: Tradition and Transformation* (Seoul: Hollym, 1988).

commerce dealt in such items as ginseng, tobacco, cotton, and fish, and the dominant "industry" until the recent past was boat-building for river merchants to transport these and similar goods to all reaches of, for instance, the Han River in central Korea. Artisans and craftsmen produced both exquisite objets d'art and utensils, such as the ceramics and ceremonial vessels that are highly valued even today, for the enjoyment and use by the aristocracy. The vast majority of the common people, however, led lives barely above a subsistence level. It was only in the last half of the nineteenth century and during the Japanese colonial period, that landed aristocracy and wealthier merchants accumulated the wealth that was the basis of a rudimentary form of a "capitalist" economy.[2]

The most defining and lasting legacies of traditional Korea—legacies that affect Korean politics today—were in political, intellectual, and cultural arenas. Until 1910 Korea had a monarchical system of government, with some variations in elite structures and nomenclatures. Kings ruled the country with the assistance of well-entrenched elite groups that concerned themselves with the administration of the nation. In the Silla dynasty, which unified Korea in 668 A.D., for example, most nobles came from rigidly stratified aristocratic families. The court and the aristocracy established a tightly centralized government, and those people enjoyed vast privileges and wealth while the common people were increasingly impoverished and some of them were even reduced to slavery. The Koryŏ dynasty (936–1392) largely remained an aristocratic society with a centralized power structure. Although the Koryŏ elites subscribed to Confucianism as the orthodox doctrine for governance, they also accepted Buddhism for their spiritual tranquility and salvation after death. Buddhist monasteries gradually became large and powerful landowners during Koryŏ thanks to donations to temples by the royal court and aristocratic families of tax-free lands.

The Chosŏn dynasty was established in 1392 by a military commander, Yi Sŏng-gye. This last Korean dynasty, sometimes called the Yi dynasty, lasted until 1910. Yi was effectively supported by the neo-Confucian literati in inaugurating this new dynasty. Without the military Yi could not have seized power, and without the literati he could not have established legitimacy for his new regime.[3] The question of legitimacy for the regime, which captured power through a military coup d'etat, was important then and remains so today. Once the Yi regime had been consolidated neo-Confucianism became the state teaching, and civilian scholar

---

[2] Carter J. Eckert, *Offspring of Empire: The* Koch'ang Kims *and the Colonial Origins of Korean Capitalism, 1876–1945* (Seattle: University of Washington Press, 1991), pp. 7–17.

[3] Martin Deuchler, *The Confucian Transformation of Korea* (Cambridge, MA: Harvard University Press, 1992), pp. 126–28.

officials who passed state examinations based largely on the mastery of Confucian classics became extremely powerful. Buddhism was largely discredited, and temple lands were seized in sweeping land reforms launched by the new regime.

From about the tenth century on, the concept and system of *yangban* (literally, two groups) of officials had existed in Korea. It was in the Chosŏn period, however, that the *yangban* system was formalized. The term is frequently used to this day, now meaning, roughly, a learned gentleman. Originally, however, the term meant two separate groups of officials lined up before the throne, civil on one side and military on the other.

Until the end of the Yi dynasty, civil and military officials had distinct existences and levels of importance. Because there was a prolonged period of relative peace in Korea during the Chosŏn dynasty, and following the Confucian tradition of looking down on soldiers, military officials were normally subservient to civilians. Initially Korean officials attained their positions through the merit system of state examinations administered at various levels, as was usually the case in China, where the system originated. Subsequently, however, some Korean monarchs began arbitrarily appointing men of their choice without the benefit of examinations. During the Yi period eligibility for state examinations was legally limited to *yangban* descendants as the *yangban* system became a recognized structure. Both of these modifications negated important aspects of open competition and social mobility based on merit, making the system of recruiting government officials increasingly more arbitrary, manipulative, ascriptive, and corrupt. Those attaining *yangban* membership, always a tiny portion of the population, monopolized prestige, power, and wealth.

Below the "aristocracy" of those actually attaining government positions, and their family members and relatives who claimed aristocratic status, were the *chungin* (middle men). The concept of the middle class apparently originated early in traditional Korea. These were originally the permanent professional-clerical staff of ministries and offices in Seoul. Along with clerks in some 350 counties, which constituted local administrative units in the Yi period, as well as the professional military officers in these units, the *chungin* constituted the middle layer of the population. They were mostly from humble social origins and performed practical functions such as clerical assistance in the central government, tax collection, assessing and supervising *corvee* (forced labor) and performing skilled work in dam construction and disaster relief projects. Most members of this class had undertaken some book learning.

While members of the *yangban* class mastered Confucian classics and argued endlessly about them, the *chungin*, who were slightly more numerous than the *yangban*, acquired practical and professional knowledge

and skills. Because they were not strictly bound to the Confucian orthodoxy and its tightly prescribed social order during the roughly five hundred years of the Chosŏn dynasty, some members of this stratum were
more open than aristocrats to nonorthodox teachings. One such teaching
was Catholicism, which was introduced through China beginning in the
early seventeenth century and ending only when it was suppressed at the
beginning of the nineteenth century. While intense, high-level controversies regarding "Western learning" subsequently raged among the *yangban*
factions, some *chungin* also had early exposure to rudimentary forms of
Western astronomy, calendars, commerce, mathematics, science, and technology. When the Chosŏn dynasty and its rigidly aristocratic class began
rapidly faltering toward the end of the nineteenth century, it was the middle class that proved pragmatic and aggressive. Despite the prevailing
view that merchants were the lowest social stratum in the old Korea, the
chungin became more skilled and thereby successful in the emerging commercial activity. Some became entrepreneurs as Japan colonized Korea.
More important, after World War II "democracy" and social mobility provided a highly favorable setting for their skills, energy, and connections.
Running enthusiastically in countless elections, members of the *chungin*
became probably the single most significant political class in Korea.[4]

Below the middle layer were a vast number of commoners, including
farmers, artisans, merchants, and the *ch'ŏnmin* (despised people). Farmers
constituted the largest segment of the population, probably more than three-
fourths of it in the Chosŏn period, and in the traditional hierarchical view
farmers followed only the *yangban* as farming was said to be the foundation
of society. Next came the many craftspeople, potters, carpenters, and the
like, who produced useful items largely with their hands, something that
scholar–officials would not do. As daily commodities ranging from cloth
and woven baskets to earthenware proliferated, a large number of peddlers
became the forerunners of today's businessmen. Lower down the hierarchy,
butchers, dog catchers, grave-diggers, and shoemakers constituted the bulk
of *ch'ŏnmin*, the "despised" people. Finally, a relatively small number of
slaves existed until the end of the Yi period.

Throughout the era, the court and the *yangban* constituted a tiny minority of the population, while the middle stratum probably fluctuated
but was not large in number. Commoners, including a larger number of
farmers, seem to have constituted more than four-fifths of the total population that toiled and supported the *yangban* officials and those who directly served them. Because more than five hundred years of Yi-era Korea
were largely settled and stable, the class distinctions also remained

---

[4] Gregory Henderson, *Korea: The Politics of the Vortex* (Cambridge, MA: Harvard University Press, 1968), pp. 46–53.

largely fixed and usually unbreachable. Some social mobility existed, but this was the exception rather than the rule. For about five centuries most Koreans accepted their social status with apparent resignation.

Some Legacies of Confucianism and *Tonghak* (Eastern Learning)

Confucianism became the state ideology of the Chosŏn dynasty, whose scholar officials sought to legitimize the military coup-like seizure of the declining Koryŏ throne by General Yi Sŏng-gye. Buddhism, which enjoyed official patronage during the Koryŏ period, was largely displaced by the essentially secular teachings of Confucianism. Most Buddhist temples and monks were banished to remote mountains without their land holdings, which had been confiscated by the new regime. Paradoxically, the lives of the monarchy, court officials, and *yangban* scholars were hardly stable, relaxed, or peaceful. It was partly because of the awareness of the Confucian tradition that the monarch and his officials had to be virtuous to retain the mandate to rule and that *minsim* (the mind of the people) reflected the mandate of Heaven. The Confucian tradition had given rise to the concept of "justifiable revolutions" when rulers were not virtuous and ceased to be models. When dynastic overthrows occurred, however, they were not accompanied by any systematic or political reforms that affected the rights of the common people. When Yi Sŏng-gye and his followers ousted the Koryŏ dynasty, a new ruling clique forcibly replaced the old, but the old ruling and class patterns remained in place.

Confucian heritage. Confucianism gave rise to a large number of prescriptions and proscriptions. It prescribed *samgang* (three bonds) and *oryun* (five relationships) in all human relationships. The latter dealt with relationships between ruler and subject, father and son, husband and wife, elder and younger brothers, friend and friend. The most important, the first three of these relationships, or the "three bonds," were vertical, hierarchical, strict, unequal relationships of loyalty, filial duty, and submission. Even the fourth relationship, between elder and younger brothers, prescribed order (*sŏ*), and only the fifth dealt with trust (*sin*) between friends on an equal level. The Confucian concept of trust in a tightly stratified Korea, however, applied among friends of the *yangban* class; the lower-class people did not socialize with members of the *yangban* and were not accorded the dignity of being trusted. Unquestionably, the *samgang* were authoritarian, which suited the monarchists. It was true that "Confucian scholars were taught that remonstration against an erring monarch was a paramount duty" of a loyal and principled official and that many "promising political elites gave their lives"[5] in protest against an irascible tyrant. The question remains whether such courageous acts were ultimate expressions of loyalty to the king or whether such "memorials" were submitted "to protect the right to free speech."[6] On balance there was little that was protodemocratic in the Confucian tradition during the Chosŏn period.

The central axis of Confucian political philosophy was formed by the closely intertwined concepts of loyalty and filial piety. Loyalty, of course, governed the relationship between the ultimate ruler (and his scholar–officials) and the monarch's subjects. The people had to be loyal and obedient to the monarch and his officials, who were supposedly appointed on a meritocratic basis from among the scholars who passed the rigorous state examinations. In the Confucian, bifurcated view of society from the time of Mencius,[7] the common people had to follow the dictates of the exalted officials, who putatively possessed superior intellectual ability and virtue. However, the relationship between the rulers and the people was sporadic and remote, whereas that between parents and children was daily and proximate. Thus in Koreans' daily lives, whether in the king's palace or in an ordinary household, filial piety was the primary virtue, the key to a harmonious family, which in turn was the basic unit of a peaceful society. Such a nation ultimately depended on self-regulation and the diligent performance of one's proper roles.

According to *The Great Learning* of Confucianism:

What is meant by "In order rightly to govern the state, it is necessary first to regulate the family," is this:—It is not possible for one to teach others, while he cannot teach his own family. Therefore, the ruler, without going beyond his family, completes the lessons for the state. There is filial piety:—therewith the sovereign should be served. There is fraternal submission:—therewith elders and superiors should be served. . . . The ruler must himself be possessed of the good qualities, and then he may require them in the people. He must not have the bad qualities in himself, and then he may require that they shall not be in the people. . . . When the ruler . . . is a model, then the people imitate him.[8]

Therefore, the key legacies of Confucianism in Korea were authoritarian, paternalistic, and family-centered, legacies that are visible in that country today. Most Koreans still look to their leader, the president, for key deci-

[5] Kim Dae-jung, "Is Culture Destiny? The Myth of Asia's Anti-Democratic Values: A Response to Lee Kuan Yew," *Foreign Affairs* 73, no. 6 (1994): p. 192.

[6] Ibid.

[7] Cho Lee-Jay, "Ethical and Social Influences of Confucianism," *Economic Development in the Republic of Korea: A Policy Perspective,* ed. Lee-Jay Cho and Yoon Hung Kim (Honolulu: East-West Center Book distributed by the University of Hawaii Press, 1991), p. 559.

[8] James Legge, trans., *The Four Books* (Taipei: Culture Books, 1970), pp. 23–27.

sions and Korean chief executives have played extraordinarily defining roles in Korean politics and government. Family ties in Korea still constitute the central element in the lives of Koreans and their organizations, particularly in the economic sector, where family-owned and -operated conglomerates predominate. Every member of the family must be diligent in fulfilling his or her role. Families become extended, and what is done in the interests of the families—including nepotism and even corruption—is often overlooked by "upright" people. According to *Confucian Analects:* "The Duke of Sheh informed Confucius, saying, 'Among us here are those who may be styled upright in their conduct. If their father has stolen a sheep, they will bear witness to the fact.' Confucius said, 'Among us, in our part of the country, those who are upright are different from this. The father conceals the misconduct of the son, and the son conceals the misconduct of the father. Uprightness is to be found in this.'"[9]

In the early Chosŏn period the neo-Confucian doctrines of Chu Hsi (Chuja in Korean) became dominant. Chuja maintained that "behind the Universe stood the Supreme Ultimate which controlled the operation of the two universal elements of *yin* and *yang* which manifest their 'will' through the five elements of fire, water, wood, metal and earth."[10] In neo-Confucian Korea the monarch was at the epicenter of a relatively small, centralized, and tightly controllable universe. He was not only the temporal ruler, but also the chief sage, responsible to Heaven for the political, moral, and ethical tones of his realm. In this setting the doctrines of the Chu Hsi, or *sŏngni*, school of Confucianism were made the basis of the curriculum in the National Confucian Academy, the center of Confucian orthodoxy.

One of the key tenets of Chu Hsi-ism was the mutual interaction of the inseparable universal principles of *i* (or *li*), which is often translated as "reason," and *ki* (or *ch'i*), which is frequently translated as "vital force." These can be looked on as opposing principles, *i* representing such intangibles as logic or moral principles, and *ki* including activity or substance. Clearly these were highly abstract concepts that were beyond concrete or scientific proof. Because various other elements of neo-Confucianism were also capable of engendering widely different interpretations and, more importantly, because the outcomes of these interpretations were tied directly to *yangban* scholars' appointments to government positions and thus to their fortunes, factionalism among these scholar–officials was inevitable, rampant, and bitter. Various factions formed alliances and counteralliances in intolerant and uncompromising struggles. When the monarch himself was directly involved in these controversies, as was

[9] Ibid., pp. 306–7.
[10] Nahm, *Korea*, Chap. 4.

sometimes the case, factionalism became a life-or-death struggle among *yangban* scholars and officials.

While the court and the *yangban* officials were preoccupied with vacuous controversies over futile theoretical issues, factional struggles intensified. It should not be surprising that governance of the country was neglected. Furthermore, as politics became faction ridden and less based on the merit principle, corruption was pervasive, from the very top down to the level of local tax collectors, usually at the expense of the powerless and the poor. Worse still, a series of famines, floods, and epidemics swept across the peninsula, and by about 1800 Korea was racked by revolts large and small. The peasants, who had been forced by corrupt local officials to bear increasing tax burdens often starved by the time of *ch'unkungki* (spring starvation periods), by which time they had exhausted the foodstuffs they had retained after paying the heavy taxes. One of the most bloody revolts occurred in 1812: the rebellion led by Hong Kyŏng-nae, a disgruntled *yangban*. The revolt was joined by peasants, merchants, and even some discontented local government officials. However, the government was capable of mobilizing a large force that outnumbered the three thousand rebels. As a result, in utter desperation the peasants and other lower-class people turned with increasing frequency to the "new religions" that offered them hope. However, Korean Catholics who followed the teachings of "the Lord of Heaven,"[11] which were brought to Korea from China in the late 1780s and spread among farmers in central Korea,[12] were ruthlessly persecuted and eliminated as believers in an alien Western teaching.

Legacies of the *Tonghak*. At this juncture, it was a revolutionary indigenous cult, *tonghak* (Eastern Learning) that attracted a huge following among the downtrodden. The followers of *Tonghak* initiated the first nationwide peasant uprising in Korean history and, simultaneously coupled with international politics around the Korean peninsula, played a decisive role in the demise of the Chosŏn dynasty.

Aspects of *Tonghak* tenets had what might be called populist or protodemocratic inspiration relevant to contemporary ideas in Korean politics. The relevance is reflected, among other places, in the writings of at least two important but disparate political figures in Korea, Park Chung Hee and Kim Dae-jung. Park led the first successful military coup in contemporary Korea in 1961 and then served as president of the re-

---

[11] Kang Wi Jo, *Christ and Caesar in Modern Korea: A History of Christianity and Politics* (Albany: SUNY Press, 1997), p. 2.

[12] Han Woo-keun, *The History of Korea* (Honolulu: University of Hawaii Press, 1970), pp. 316–20.

public from 1963 to 1979. He wrote in his memoirs that he was "a son of a *Tonghak* rebel," and strongly suggested that his "military revolution" of 1961 was a manifestation of the spirit of the *Tonghak* rebels.[13] Kim, a determined opposition leader who tenaciously championed "democracy" and was an unsuccessful presidential candidate three times before his victory in 1997, wrote that "the indigenous *Tonghak* was a democratic ideology that motivated some 500,000 Korean peasants to revolt against an oppressive government in 1894."[14] A number of scholars also share the belief that the native teaching was significant and of relevance to contemporary South Korean politics,[15] particularly to the *minjung* (roughly, the common people) movement of the 1970s and 1980s. One scholar wrote that the "*Tonghak* discourse has been strikingly present oriented: although the revolution occurred in another century, it is easily discussed as a legacy that continues to incite *minjung* consciousness and action."[16]

Tonghak was originated in 1860 by Ch'oe Che-u (1824–1864), an illegitimate son of a local squire and thus destined never to be a *yangban*-official. *Tonghak* was a syncretic revealed religion that incorporated various elements of neo-Confucianism, Catholicism, Buddhism, Taoism, and Shamanism. What was revolutionary about the teachings were four closely interrelated key articles of the faith: *si ch'ŏnju* (serve heavenly master), *in nae ch'ŏn* (man and Heaven are one), *sa in yŏch'ŏn* (treat people as though they are heaven), and *tongkwi ilch'e* (all revert to one body). Toward the end of the decaying Chosŏn dynasty these propositions logically and explicitly dictated the political principle of *poguk anmin* (protecting the nation and securing the well-being of the people).[17]

The *Tonghak* incantation begins with the term *si ch'ŏnju*,[18] which has been interpreted in various ways by *Tonghak* leaders. Ch'ŏnju (heavenly master) was a term used by Korean Catholics; Catholicism was, and still is, known as *ch'ŏnjukyo* (literally, the teaching of the heavenly master). It

[13] Pak Chŏng-hŭi (Park Chung Hee), "Naŭi sonyŏn sichŏl" (My Boyhood), *Pirok: hanguk ŭi daet'ong nyŏng* (Hidden Records: The Presidents of Korea) ed., Wolgan Chosŏnbu (Seoul: Chosŏn Ilbosa, 1993), p. 512. Park also made the same statement repeatedly to Choi Duk Shin, head of the *Ch'ŏndokyo*, the name *Tonghak* organizations adopted after 1905. Interviews with Choi in Seoul, July 1970.

[14] Kim Dae-jung, "Asia sik minjujuui" (Asian style democracy), *Sin Dong-a* (December, 1994): p. 230.

[15] For example, Carter Eckert, Ki-baik Lee, Young-ik Lew, Michael Robinson, and Edward W. Wagner, *Korea Old and New: A History* (Seoul: Ilchogak, 1990), pp. 214–21.

[16] Nancy Abelmann, *Echoes of the Past, Epics of Dissent: A South Korean Social Movement* (Berkeley: University of California Press, 1996), p. 27.

[17] Yi Ton-hwa, *Ch'ŏndokyo ch'anggŏn-sa* (The History of the Inauguration of the Teaching of the Heavenly Way) (Seoul: Ch'ondogyo Central Headquarters, 1933), pp. 42–8. Kim Yong Choon, *Oriental Thought* (Springfield, IL: Charles C. Thomas Publishers, 1973), p. 98.

[18] *Ch'ŏndokyo kyŏngjŏn* (The *Ch'ondogyo* Scriptures) (Seoul: Ch'ondogyo Central Headquarters, 1973), p. 34.

is clear that Ch'oe Che-u had been exposed to Catholic terminologies by the 1860s or was even a "crypto-Catholic."[19] Even before the advent of Catholicism, however, Koreans had long been familiar with the seldom-defined concept of heaven, as in China. However, the Korean vernacular for heaven was *hanul*, which also meant the sky.

In any case, Ch'oe Che-u declared that for him *si ch'ŏnju* meant not just helpless man serving an omnipotent but distant Heaven. Rather, any human, not only men but women—an astounding departure from the previously male-centered tradition—possessed "the divine spirit within and infinite energy without." It was a novel concept that a human being embodied the essential element of the divine and that a human could bear Heaven within him- or herself. This startlingly revolutionary notion logically led to that of *in nae ch'ŏn* (man and Heaven are one), a dictum that was emphasized in 1888 when the second *Tonghak* leader, Ch'oe Si-hyŏng, published the *Tonggyŏng taejŏn*[20] (The Canon of Eastern Scriptures). That idea boldly declared that a human being is equal to Heaven.

Though the Koreans had long used the term Heaven, until this *Tonghak* declaration Heaven had been infinitely above and beyond earth and man. By this three-character declaration, *in nae ch'ŏn*, *Tonghak* leaders equated Heaven and man without even positing a single intermediary such as a son of Heaven, a monk, a sage, or a shaman. By unqualifiedly equating man with Heaven, this *Tonghak* concept elevated man to a heavenly value for the first time in Korean history. The concept completely negated all the class distinctions that had condemned peasants and other lower-class people to lives of worthlessness and indignity for generations.

Because a man or a woman equals Heaven, then, it naturally followed that each and every person, regardless of parentage or position, had to be treated as though he or she were Heaven itself, or *sa in yŏch'ŏn*. It was further declared that all humans ultimately fused into one eternal body or *tongkwi ilch'e*. Ch'oe Che-u clearly rejected the idea that some ascended to Heaven while others descended to hell. Instead, he believed that every human being—regardless of birth, class, or gender—would find happiness within the one eternal and universal being. It was a uniquely egalitarian view. Further, this was not to be a remote and uncertain Heaven but the actual dwelling place of all people, human society, or the *chisang ch'ŏnguk* (the Heaven on earth). It was not otherworldly; it was definitely of this world. It was startlingly good news to all lowly people who had fatalistically accepted for millennia their lives as hopeless.

Millenerian

[19] Susan S. Shin, "*Tonghak* Thought: The Roots of Revolution," ed., The Korean National Commission for UNESCO (Seoul: Sisa yŏngu-sa Publishers, 1983), p. 205.

[20] Ch'oe Si-hyŏng, Tonggyŏng Taejŏn (The Canon of Eastern Scriptures) (Seoul: Chŏndo-gyo Headquarters, no date).

To achieve a Heaven on earth, the first task had to be the practical and political stage of protecting the Korean nation that was threatened internally by greedy and oppressive officials and externally by marauding Western aggressors and Japan. Thus *poguk anmin* (protecting the nation and securing the well-being of the people) was necessary. *Tonghak* leaders were thoroughly convinced that politics and ethics in dynastic Korea were corrupt beyond redemption and that external menaces could not be countered by the court and *yangban* officials.[21]

In the fifth passage of his *"Kwŏnhakka"* (Songs to prompt learning) Ch'oe wrote that "righteous people should firmly unite to achieve the goal of *poguk anmin.*" The message was clear: the "righteous people" of the nation must rise up and overthrow the old monarchical and elite-dominated order and establish a new government that would be capable of protecting the nation and establishing a new order. Ch'oe apparently could not detail his political programs at the time, fearing that the authorities would persecute him and his followers for doing so. However, the revolutionary concept of the righteous people who would unite to correct the wrongs perpetrated by unjust and oppressive authorities took root in Korean political consciousness and was to have significant consequences in both the short and the long run.

Rebellions and the Fall of the Chosŏn Dynasty

Some *Tonghak* teachings were written in *han'gŭl*, the Korean alphabet readily understood by the commoners and women, whereas Chinese characters were used in the court and in *yangban* circles. As Ch'oe's teachings rapidly gained popularity, three southeastern provinces were engulfed in rebellions by peasants who considered themselves righteous. In a monthlong rampage in the spring of 1862 several thousand peasants wearing white headbands swarmed through southern villages and cities, killing not only government soldiers and officials but also local landlords and wealthy merchants. By the time the superior government forces had wiped out the ragtag *Tonghak* rebels, the latter had swept through dozens of cities and villages.

Ch'oe was arrested the following year. He was charged specifically with preaching of the existence of an ultimate being superior to the king and that his doctrine was identical to the Catholic belief in *ch'ŏnju* (heavenly master). Ch'oe was executed in April 1864 as a subversive. Ch'oe's martyrdom, however, did not stop the spread of *Tonghak* among the poor

[21] Interviews with Choi Duk Shin in Seoul, July 1970.

and downtrodden, who were only further incensed by the execution of their leader.[22] Another revolt was launched in 1871.

> The peasants occupied the county office, seized weapons, distributed illegally collected tax rice to the poor. . . . The peasants rallied around Chŏn Pong-jun and other local Tonghak leaders. . . . They tied multicolored cloths around their heads and waists, and armed themselves with the few rifles, swords and lances they had seized, but mostly with bamboo spears and cudgels.[23]

Meanwhile the Korean government's treasury emptied owing to both its efforts to contain the widespread revolts and the breakdown of the taxation system in a country racked with unrest. As the taxation base shrank, those still effectively under government control were taxed to the utmost.

Under these circumstances, the *Kabo Tonghak* Rebellion of 1894 had both national and international consequences. Tens of thousands of "righteous" peasants engaged in a full-scale rebellion mostly in the southwestern provinces of Ch'ungch'ŏng and Chŏlla. Unable to crush the waves of *Tonghak* rebels who threatened to topple the enfeebled central government, the Chosŏn court requested Chinese military assistance. The subsequent dispatches of Chinese troops to suppress the *Tonghak* rebels and the landing of uninvited Japanese troops in Korea, allegedly to counter the Chinese, eventually led to the Sino-Japanese War that resulted in the Japanese annexation of Korea by 1910. From another perspective, the common people of Korea had a dramatic and massive—if bloody and abortive—initiation to grassroots political action, driven by a belief system that demanded the correction of political wrongs.

Throughout Korean history there have been small-scale and isolated rice riots and other antigovernment disturbances. However, they were all quite unlike the massive—though intermittent—mobilization of the "righteous" people for more than thirty years, from 1862 to 1894. In the past ethical, religious, and ideological justifications had been the monopoly of the elite—never affecting the lives of the masses. For the first time, *Tonghak* provided the motivating force to the righteous people. It may not be claimed that *Tonghak* founders were the first democrats of Korea, but from the perspective of Korean history they may be seen as protodemocrats. It cannot be denied that *Tonghak* teachings held the first identifiable embryo of what may be called "populist" concepts. These ideas included revolutionary views on human dignity for all, essential equality between men and women, social and economic justice for the lower classes, and a national commonweal for all. Their contemporary significance cannot be minimized.

---

[22] Paek Se-myong, *Tonghak sasang kwa Ch'ŏndokyo* (The *Tonghak* Ideologies and the Teaching of the Heavenly Way) (Seoul: Tonghak-sa, 1956), p. 139.

[23] Eckert et al., *Korea Old and New*, pp. 217–18.

Japanese Colonial Domination

The Japanese colonial rule of Korea that formally began in 1910 can be divided into the following three eras: the military rule of the 1910s; the period of "cultural rule" following the March First Independent Movement of 1919; and the militarist-fascist war period beginning in the 1930s.[24] In 1905, shortly before Korea was formally annexed to Japan, *Tonghak* was renamed *Ch'ŏndogyo* (the Teaching of the heavenly way). The rebellion of 1894 had provided a justification for the first Sino-Japanese War (1894–1895) and the Japanese colonization of Korea, the first step in the Japanese militarist expansion into the Asian mainland. Likewise, *Ch'ŏndogyo* leaders and followers, among many other influential nationalist groups, unquestionably provided a key leadership group, financial resources, and nationwide networks and mobilization for the massive March First Independence Movement[25] of 1919. It was the third "supreme leader" of *Ch'ŏndogyo*, Son Pyŏng-hui, a man of considerable charisma and stature, who was a central figure in forging a coalition among nationalist notables. These included *Ch'ŏndogyo*, many Christian churches in Korea, Buddhists and other groups, who organized the massive nationwide demonstration for Korean independence from Japan. Clearly the inspiration and initial leadership for the March First Independence Movement came from nationalist elites of various backgrounds, but it was the common people who demonstrated across the country. It was an almost spontaneous confluence of the largely conservative elite groups and the common people that together produced the massive nationalist demand for independence. As thirty-three self-anointed "national representatives" signed the declaration (and promptly surrendered to the Japanese authorities), Son Pyŏng-hui was the first to sign and affix his seal on the "Declaration of Independence," to be followed by Christians, Buddhists, and other leaders.

By 1919 *Ch'ŏndogyo* organizations were apparently solvent enough to lend five thousand won—a sizeable amount—to Christian groups to agitate and mobilize Christians in nationwide demonstrations.[26] According to *Ch'ŏndogyo* records, Son also sent 30,000 won to Korean nationalist groups in Shanghai, where a "provisional government" in exile was

---

[24] Kim Chang Rok, "The Characteristics of the System of Japanese Imperialism in Korea from 1905 to 1945," *Korea Journal* 36, no. 1 (1996): pp. 20–49. Kim Un-t'ae, *Ilbon chegukchui-ŭi han'guk t'ongch'i* (Japanese imperial rule of Korea) (Seoul: Pagyŏng-sa, 1985), pp. 6–7.

[25] *Samil undong osipchunyŏn kinyŏm nonmunjip* (Collected Essays on the Fiftieth Anniversary of the March First Movement (Seoul: Dong-A Ilbo-sa, 1969).

[26] Chosen kenpeitai shireibu (The [Japanese] Military Police Headquarters) ed., *Chōsen san-ichi dokuritu sōyō jiken* (The Incident of the March First Independent Disturbance in Korea) (Tokyo: Reinandō shoten, 1969), p. 28.

formed, and 60,000 won to Korean nationalists in Manchuria. Such financial strength was based on the practice of more than three million *Ch'ŏndogyo* members throughout Korea who made regular donations to the organization through the practice of the *sŏngmi* (sincerity rice) system, whereby each family set aside one tablespoonful of rice per member daily to contribute to *Ch'ŏndogyo* activities.

According to various statistics on Koreans arrested by Japanese troops and police between March and December 1919, it is also clear that *Ch'ŏndogyo* believers participated in demonstrations in large numbers and constituted some 11.7 percent of those arrested—second only to Presbyterians, who constituted 12.7 percent. Son, the third *Ch'ŏndogyo* supreme leader, was also arrested. After lengthy trials with the "national representatives" and other notable demonstration leaders, was sentenced by the Japanese authorities to a three-year prison term that was suspended because he suffered a brain hemorrhage and severe complications. When Son died at age sixty-two in 1922, *Ch'ŏndogyo* ceased to be a unified and effective religious-political entity. Its demise was due in part to factional struggles among its leaders after the passing of such a charismatic and towering supreme leader.

The intellectual elitist nationalists were also split between the Right and the Left. The Right came largely from landed and learned groups who launched the *Tongnip Hyŏphoe* (Independence Club),[27] among others. The Left became the socialist groups both in Korea and abroad during the colonial period and the *Namnodang* (Southern Labor Party) after Korean liberation in 1945.[28] Though many of them sustained the hope for Korean independence during the dark decades of the Japanese rule, both the rightist and the leftist elites were essentially foreign oriented and had little or no mass base in tightly controlled Korea. Some intellectuals, including Ch'oe Nam-sŏn, who drafted the March First Independence Declaration, and Yi Kwang-su, who was the literary giant of his day, succumbed to Japanese pressure and enticements and became "collaborators."

For a brief period (1920 to 1926) during the "cultural rule" period of Japanese colonialism, *Ch'ŏndogyo* provided an important outlet to nationalist, intellectual, and literary expression in *Kaebyŏk* (Creation), a magazine affiliated with *Ch'ŏndogyo* that gave the publication a solid financial and organizational base. Articles were subject to heavy-handed Japanese censorship and publication of the journal was suspended by the Japanese thirty-two times before it was ordered to cease altogether in 1926. *Kaebyŏk*

---

[27] Ki-baik Lee, ed., *A New History of Korea*, trans. Edward W. Wagner (Cambridge, MA: Harvard University Press, 1984), p. 267.

[28] Chong Sik Lee, *Materials on Korean Communism, 1945–1947* (Honolulu: Center for Korean Studies, 1977), Chap. 3.

was an important vehicle for the development of a post-March First intellectual movement that stressed the cultural and socioeconomic development of Korean society.[29] A part of the Korean energy that erupted in the politically futile March First movement found a narrow channel of expression in the *Ch'ŏndogyo*-backed magazine. Yi Ton-hwa, a close associate of the third *Ch'ŏndogyo* leader, Son Pyong-hui, was the editor-in-chief and emphasized the role of *Kaebyŏk* as the Korean "people's voice."

Various articles in the magazine advocated the urgent transformation of Korean society through the cultivation of new values such as democracy, justice, and truth. Yi Ton-hwa's insights led him to urge urban-centered economic development as he despaired of conservative and selfish rural landowners. Considering that Korea in 1920 was decidedly rural and undeveloped, this was a surprising prescience. One noted contributor to *Kaebyŏk*, Yi Kwang-su, wrote in 1922 that the development discussed by Yi Ton-hwa would be led by the middle class, which he called the "core class," along the lines of Western democratic societies.[30] The role of the middle class or middle strata—the equivalent of the "middle men" of traditional Korea—has become a central concern in Korea today in terms of democratization and economic development.

The *Ch'ŏndogyo Ch'ŏngudang* (The Young Friends Party) was organized in September 1923 under the indigenous doctrinal concepts of *sa in yŏch'on* (treat the people as though they are Heaven) and *chisang ch'ŏnguk kŏnsol* (the establishment of Heaven on earth). The Young Friends Party was quickly paralyzed by factional strife and was driven underground with the arrest of several hundred members by the Japanese authorities in 1934 during the "militarist-fascist" period. This marked the demise of visible *Ch'ŏndogyo* activities in Korea until the end of the Japanese colonial rule. Since 1945 *Ch'ŏndogyo* has reemerged in both North and South Korea, but largely as a feeble appendage to the ruling groups.

Ch'ŏndogyo groups were not the only native forces that struggled to survive under the iron rule of the Japanese colonialists. Many Koreans, including those who fled to China, Manchuria, the United States, and the Soviet Union, labored valiantly and persistently—if no successfully—to resist Japanese domination over all aspects of Korean existence. It may be a safe generalization, however, to state that *Ch'ŏndogyo* activities typified the powerlessness and despair of native Korean political stirring—however pregnant with new aspirations for Korean future they might have been—for the thirty-six years of Japanese domination that had thoroughly debilitated Korea.

---

[29] Michael E. Robinson, *Cultural Nationalism in Colonial Korea, 1920–1925* (Seattle: University of Washington Press, 1988), pp. 57–64.

[30] Ibid., pp. 62–63.

However, the Japanese colonial period was not without some "modernizing"[31] effects on Korea, notably in the modernization and expansion of educational systems, the building of new roads, the improvement of irrigation systems, the development of other infrastructures, and the growth of light industries. On the other hand, colonial rule under the governor general of Korea, who was commissioned by the Japanese Emperor himself from among Japanese generals and admirals of the imperial military, was extremely militaristic, oppressive, and arbitrary. Even in comparison with the Chosŏn dynasty, during which the Confucian principle of virtue moderated somewhat—at least in theory—the arbitrariness of the monarchical government, "the Japanese rule of Korea was the most despotic in the history of the Korean people."[32]

Though constitutionalism—albeit a peculiarly emperor-centered version—was unfolding in Japan until the military firmly dominated the government during the war years, the Korean people were denied any meaningful experience in a constitutional government under the Japanese Governor-General. Meanwhile, the anemic Korean provisional government in exile in China, then a key locus of Korean exiles, vaguely professed to follow a "republicanism" that remained largely undefined. Many conservative exile groups found the Chinese version of republicanism under Sun Yat-sen or Chiang Kai-shek uninspiring, whereas those who found their way to the United States found American democracy appealing. Still other activist exile groups in Manchuria and the Soviet Union understandably subscribed to Marxism-Leninism as the path to Korean national independence. In any case, many Koreans on the peninsula were not even aware of the existence of these exile groups toward the end of the Japanese colonial domination.

[31] Kim Chang Rok, "Characteristics of Japanese Imperialism," p. 21. Kim Un-t'ae, *Ilbon chegukchui-ŭi han'guk t'ongch'i*, pp. 570–71.
[32] Kim Chang Rok, "Characteristics of Japanese Imperialism," pp. 43–44.

✦

CHAPTER 2

A "Democratic" Republic on Trial, 1945–1961

It was on a peculiarly traditional yet debilitated political soil that a new state was hurriedly erected in South Korea after Japanese colonial domination. As World War II ended, the southern half of the Korean peninsula was occupied by American troops and the northern half by Soviets to accept the surrender of Japanese troops.

As the American occupation began in September 1945 the Korean economy was in shambles, although the country had been spared the physical destruction to which Japan had been subjected as a target of systematic American bombing. Anything of economic value in Korea had been cannibalized to feed the increasingly desperate Japanese war machine, which was then engaged in wars in vast areas of the Asia–Pacific region including China. Further, toward the end of the war Japanese colonial administration had issued enormous amounts of bank notes to meet endless war needs; this practice of printing increasing amounts of currency as needed continued under the American military government, to meet local needs. The total amount of currency in circulation grew from 4,698 million won in July 1945 to 10,333 million won in July 1946, to 18,638 million in July 1947, and to 30,500 million by July 1948[1]—a whopping 649 percent increase in just three years. That inflation was rampant is an understatement; paper money became almost worthless.

Southern Korea had been the agricultural half of the peninsula before the country's division, producing some 63 percent of the nation's foodstuffs. It also was the location of most of the light industry and about 24 percent of

[1] Nahm, *Korea: Tradition and Transformation*, p. 352.

the heavy industry developed under the Japanese. The northern half of the peninsula was developed by the Japanese as an industrial base; almost all of the country's electric power was generated by hydroelectric plants on the Yalu and other rivers. The entire supply of chemical fertilizer in Korea came from the Japanese-established plant at Hŭngnam in the north. When that was choked off by northern authorities as the division of the peninsula hardened, farm production in the south shrank sharply, creating a serious food shortage in the south, where consumption had risen sharply after years of tight food rationing by the Japanese. Worse still, because of the shortage of electric power, most of the industries in the south came to a grinding halt just when people were eagerly seeking the daily commodities they had lacked for so long during the Pacific war.

What aggravated the economic situation in South Korea further was the influx in the first years of the division of more than 1.5 million refugees from North Korea, Manchuria, and China, as well as those who were being repatriated from Japan and elsewhere after having been forced to serve the Japanese as either soldiers or laborers. The South Korean population in August 1945 was slightly over 16 million, but it jumped to over 19 million by September 1946, and to 21 million in 1947. Starvation was not unknown among the refugees, and serious social and moral problems were reported among those who could not choose means of sustaining themselves.

The American Occupation (1945–1948) and Democratic Impulses

These desperate circumstances presented urgent challenges to the American military government, which was ill prepared to meet them. During three years of American military occupation, the Korean economy barely rose above a subsistence level. Washington dispatched economic missions to South Korea, and between 1945 and 1948 the United States provided $409 million in relief funds to South Korea. These funds from the U.S. Government Appropriation for Relief in Occupied Areas (GARIOA) are credited with preventing the starvation and deaths of many in South Korea. Shiploads of American wheat flour were imported to feed the starving, and other emergency relief goods from the United Nations Relief and Rehabilitation Agency (UNRRA), such as medical supplies and dried milk, saved the lives of thousands of children and elderly.

The rapid erosion of the wartime alliance between the United States and the Soviet Union made it increasingly difficult for the two powers to agree on the future of a divided Korea. Initially the problem was to be addressed by a U.S.–Soviet joint commission that met in Seoul, but when the meeting adjourned on May 8, 1946, without having accomplished anything of substance, hope began to fade for the abolition of the dividing line at the thirty-eighth parallel. In a larger context, the United States launched its "containment" policy explicated by President Truman on March 12, 1947. The reverberations of this policy were felt in most of the problem areas of the world, including Korea. In many ways 1947 was an important turning point in East–West relations, as well as in Korea. The joint commission remained deadlocked in the spring of 1947, so the United States government decided to bring the Korean question to the U.N. General Assembly. That body adopted a resolution on November 14, 1947, recommending that elections be held no later than March 31, 1948, "on the basis of adult suffrage and by secret ballot to choose representatives . . . and which representatives, constituting a National Assembly, may establish a National Government of Korea."[2] The resolution envisioned that the new national government would administer all of Korea and thus the problem of the division of the country would be resolved. However, Soviet occupation forces in North Korea refused to cooperate with the United Nations. The United Nations, which was then dominated by the United States, adopted another resolution on February 26, 1948, to proceed with an election in the south, resulting in the U.N.-sponsored generation election of May 10, 1948. This historic election now formalized the division of the peninsula by establishing the South Korean National Assembly, the first duly constituted legislative body of the "separate" republic, to be inaugurated with the termination of the American occupation. Unlike in Japan, where the United States had a firm policy commitment to stay and remake the former enemy nation, in South Korea the United States took an expedient course of action to end its occupation as soon as possible. The U.S. Congress had slashed defense appropriations shortly after World War II, and the U.S. armed services pressed for an early end to the Korean occupation.

Evidently anticipating an early termination of the American military government in Korea and the transfer of power to the Koreans, in May 1947 the American military government established an interim government as a counterpart to itself, but still under American advisors' effective control. It was this interim authority under American direction that appointed an initial constitution drafting subcommittee. Under an American advisor, this subcommittee was composed of Kim Yong-mu, chief justice of the Supreme Court; Kim Pyŏng-no, minister of justice; Yi In, prosecutor general; Kwŏn Sung-yŏl, vice minister of justice; Kang Pyŏng-sun, attorney; and Yu Chin-o, professor of law.[3] These Koreans had re-

---

[2] Donald G. Tewksbury, ed., *Source Materials on Korean Politics and Ideologies* (New York: Institute of Pacific Relations, 1950), p. 90.

[3] Yu Chin-o, *Hŏnpŏp kich'o hwoegorok* (Recollection of Constitution Drafting) (Seoul: Ilchogak, 1980), pp. 48–51.

ceived most of their higher education during the Japanese occupation. Yu Chin-o had graduated from the Law College of the Keijo (Seoul) Imperial University, and Kim Pyŏng-no and Yi In had studied law at the Meiji University in Japan. These three were probably the most influential drafters. Their academic backgrounds suggested little that would indicate any fervent belief in liberal, democratic constitutionalism. When this subcommittee of prominent Koreans settled down to work they consulted widely among Koreans who were emerging as leaders, such as Syngman Rhee, who favored a presidential system of government, and with American constitutional experts.

Meanwhile, debates regarding the character of the Korean government to be established became intense. For most Korean elites, including the members of the constitution drafting subcommittee, the occasion of state building at the termination of Japanese colonial domination was a golden opportunity to make a quantum leap toward modernization of Korea's polity. The drafters faced a daunting task, as Korea had not yet had a formally written constitution. Returning to the familiar dynastic form was utterly unthinkable. The old Japanese model was likewise repugnant and unacceptable. Instead, it was clear that they should adopt a system that would be compatible with the future. To most Korean intelligentsia, who were familiar with Western democratic polities, the victory of the "democratic" coalition in two world wars indicated that democracy represented the wave of the future. Establishing a democratic government might also demonstrate Korea's—or at least her elite's—cultural equality and respectability to world powers and make her acceptable to the advanced nations of the world. Furthermore, the virulent rivalry with the Communist authority in the north dictated that South Korea establish an anti-Communist government.

At this juncture an important proclamation was issued by the highest-ranking American in Korea. Just before the general elections were to be held Lieutenant General John R. Hodge, commander of all U.S. military forces in Korea, issued a "Proclamation on the Rights of the Korean People," on April 5, 1948. General Hodge had been hitherto reticent about issuing public statements on political matters, quite unlike General Douglas A. MacArthur, who apparently savored opportunities to issue lofty political declarations in Japan. The surprise Hodge proclamation declared, among other matters, that all Koreans "are equal before the law and entitled to equal protection under the law, and no privileges of sex, birth, occupation or creed are recognized. . . . Personal liberty is inviolable, and any limitations upon it are not permissible, except by virtue of law duly enacted and promulgated. . . . No person shall be deprived of life, liberty, or property without due process of law and without procedure prescribed by law."[4] The similarities between this proclamation and the U.S. Bill of Rights, as well as the chapter on the rights and duties of the people in the Japanese Constitution drafted in February 1946, were striking. Hodge declared that the basic rights of the Korean people included the freedoms of assembly, association, press, speech, and religion, regardless of gender or origin. Korean women were declared equal to men—just as in Japan under the 1947 "MacArthur Constitution"—for the first time in Korean history. Other derivative rights, such as one's right to be secure in one's domicile and the freedom from ex post facto laws, were also emphasized.

What was significant was that the full text of General Hodge's declaration was emphatically highlighted in all major daily papers in South Korea and had the effect of setting the direction of a new South Korean polity yet to be determined by the end of the American military occupation.[5] Yu Chin-o, a noted constitutional lawyer who had been a constant member of the ever-changing constitutional drafting committees, listed the Hodge proclamation among the important documents consulted by drafters of the new Korean constitution.[6] At about the same time, Colonel Emery J. Woodall, a legal officer of the American military government, was preparing his own version of a draft Constitution for Korea, which he presented to Yu. Though the Korean constitution was drafted by a small number of Koreans, it is abundantly clear that there was an enormous American influence on its spirit and letters.[7]

A "Democratic" Republic and Recurring Crises

The process of launching a brand-new and "democratic" republic needed to be accelerated as the United States had decided to end its occupation of Korea by August 15, 1948, the third anniversary of the Japanese surrender. The first formally written Korean constitution was adopted by the very first National Assembly on July 12, 1948, and promulgated five days later. The preamble to the constitution declared that the newly independent republic was determined "To establish a demo-

---

[4] *Official Gazette,* Headquarters, United States Army Forces in Korea (April 15, 1948): pp. 1–2.

[5] Kim Ch'ŏl-su, *Hanguk hŏnpŏpsa* (A History of the Korean Constitution) (Seoul: Taehak ch'ulpansa, 1988), pp. 27–28.

[6] Yu, *Hŏnpŏp kich'o hwoegorok,* p. 22. Among those involved in drafting the Korean constitution, Dr. Yu was the only one who left a memoir, which sheds light on the process of the constitution making.

[7] Tscholsu Kim and Sang Don Lee, "Republic of Korea: The Influence of U.S. Constitutional Law Doctrines in Korea," in *Constitutional Systems in Late Twentieth Century Asia,* ed. Lawrence W. Baer (Seattle: University of Washington Press, 1992), p. 303.

cratic system of government eliminating evil social customs of all kinds, to afford equal opportunities to every person and to provide for the fullest development of the capacity of each individual in all the fields of political, economic, social and cultural life." The "General Provisions" in Chapter I declared that the Republic of Korea "shall be a *democratic republic*" and that "the sovereignty of the Republic of Korea shall reside in the people from whom all state authority emanate" (emphasis added). Article 5 stated that the republic "shall be responsible for respecting and guaranteeing the liberty, equality and initiative of each individual and for protecting and adjusting these for the purpose of promoting the general welfare." The chapter also renounced all aggressive wars, placing on the military "the sacred duty of protecting the country." The constitution stipulated that no military personnel shall be appointed prime minister or minister unless he has resigned from active service, obviously emulating similar features in both the new Japanese constitution and practices in the United States.

The rights and duties of citizens of the Republic were specifically spelled out in the lengthy Chapter II, Articles 8 to 30, which enumerated the basic rights guaranteed in the first chapter. These included equality before the law; personal liberty; freedom of domicile; freedom from trespass and unlawful search; freedom of private correspondence; and freedoms of speech, press, assembly, "the right of poverty," "equal opportunity of education," and "the equality of men and women." Indeed, little fault could be found with the liberal-democratic aspects of this chapter— so far.

However, Article 28 qualified all preceding articles by stipulating that "laws imposing restrictions upon the liberties and rights of citizens shall be enacted only when necessary for the maintenance of public order or the welfare of the community." The freedoms mentioned in preceding articles were guaranteed, but with such qualifications and escape clauses elsewhere in the constitution as "except as specified by law," "except in accordance with the law," and "with the provisions of the law." Thus, when deemed "necessary" by the ruling authorities "for the maintenance of public order or the welfare of the community," all these liberties could legally be restricted.

Furthermore, Article 57 included an emergency clause: "When in time of civil war, in a dangerous situation arising from foreign relations, in case of natural calamity or on account of a grave economic or financial crisis, it is necessary to take urgent measures for the maintenance of public order and security, the President shall have the power to issue orders having the effect of law or to take necessary financial disposition, provided, however, that the President shall exclusively exercise such power if time is lacking for convening of the National Assembly."

The second paragraph of the article, however, hedged against arbitrary use of this power: "Such orders or dispositions shall be reported without delay to the National Assembly for confirmation. If confirmation of the National Assembly is not obtained, such orders or dispositions shall lose their effect thereafter and the President shall promulgate such nonconfirmation without delay."

Though the constitutional framework at first glance appeared to establish legislative supremacy in the new republic, close examination disclosed many opportunities for a strong president. Some powers normally found in the legislature were to be exercised as presidential powers through the constitutionally recognized power to issue presidential orders (Article 58).

As to the judicial branch of the new government, Chapter V stated that judges should be free from executive and legislative interference. Theoretically the judiciary was to be autonomous. In practice, however, the chief justice of the Supreme Court, who was appointed by the president with the ratification of the National Assembly, and judges of other courts appointed for a relatively short term of five years, were also made amenable to presidential direction. Questions involving the constitutionality of laws and orders were to be decided by a constitutional committee presided over by the vice president of the republic and composed of five justices of the Supreme Court and five members of the National Assembly. A two-thirds majority of the committee, which could be politically amenable to a strong president, was needed to declare a law unconstitutional. It was meant to be extremely difficult to declare any executive actions unconstitutional. Thus the "judicial review" by the courts, as evolved in the United States, was rejected in the original Korean constitution.

In the brief sixth chapter on economy the constitution declared: "The principle of the economic order of the Korean Republic shall be to realize social justice, to meet the basic demands of all citizens and to encourage the development of a balanced economy." Article 86 stipulated that the "farm land should be distributed to self-tilling farmers," in accordance with subsequent legislation. Government ownership of natural resources was discussed in the article that stated that "mineral and other underground resources as well as resources from the sea" are owned by the state. The constitution also stipulated that important enterprises with public character shall be managed by the state or the public. Transportation, communications, banking, insurance, electricity, water management, and gas supplies were specifically named as important enterprises. Thus the state was to play a prominent role in the economic management of the republic, and the constitution was not an embodiment of economic liberalism. To wit, "economic freedom of individuals" was to be guaranteed "within the limits" of the national economy to meet the "basic needs of the people."

Thus, much was made dependent on the very first president of the First Republic in shaping the government, setting precedents and the style of the operation of the government, and applying and interpreting constitutional provisions. For the new Korean Republic to face the future without some provisions for rapid and decisive executive actions would have been to ignore the realities in a divided peninsula where a hostile Communist regime, the Democratic People's Republic of Korea (DPRK), was almost simultaneously being established, on September 9, 1948.[8] However, whether the emergency and other escape clauses would destroy the "democratic" features of the Seoul government would be apparent only with time. A considerable array of constitutional weapons were entrusted to those who were to wield the executive powers of the new government, particularly the first president. Syngman Rhee was duly elected president by the National Assembly on July 20, 1948, and the Republic of Korea was formally inaugurated on the third anniversary of V-J Day. A hopeful beginning was made.

President Syngman Rhee and a crisis government. It was hoped by many that Dr. Rhee, who had spent some thirty-three years as a political exile, mostly in the United States, where he was educated at George Washington, Harvard, and Princeton universities, would lead the first republic to realize American-style "democracy." It was presumed that Rhee would have learned about democratic politics and observed American democracy in operation at close range for a few decades, and that he would conduct his presidency in the style of American chief executives. Such a hope in the euphoric days of the inauguration of the republic, however, tended to ignore the weight of the traditional political culture in Korea, Rhee's own origins and personality, and the political realities that a divided Korea was then facing. It was no exaggeration that the Korean nation was only a few wobbly steps away from her indigenous national past—the dynastic culture. From the perspective of realizing "democratic" politics, the colonial period under the Japanese was of no help. If anything, the thirty-six–year era had tended to accentuate the negative aspects of the traditional culture including superstitions, which the colonial masters encouraged because they made Korea easier to rule. Although it is undeniable that Japanese rule contributed to the development of the Korean infrastructure, the Japanese also erected a highly authoritarian and modern

[8] For an extensive comparative study of North and South Koreas see Sung Chul Yang, *The North and South Korean Political Systems: A Comparative Analysis* (Boulder, CO: Westview Press, 1994).

Phalanxes of Seoul citizens on the boulevard leading to the old central government building (top center) where the inauguration of the Republic took place. The Renaissance-style structure, dedicated in 1926, was the seat of the Japanese Government General in Korea. The dismantling of the building, which symbolized Japanese colonial rule, began on August 15, 1995, the 50th anniversary of V-J Day. (The U.S. National Archives)

bureaucratic colonial administration that did not hesitate to use the naked power of security forces and police to control the behavior of the people.

Rhee was also heir to a *yangban* family of traditional Korea that was allegedly descended from a prince of the Chosŏn dynasty. Rhee spent most of his adult life as a political exile abroad, and when he returned to Korea at the end of World War II he was a septuagenarian. At that time Rhee had

The first President-elect, Dr. Syngman Rhee, in traditional Korean garb, taking the oath of office at the inauguration of the Republic of Korea on August 15, 1948. (The Korean Information Office)

neither the experience of administering a large-scale operation nor an interest in economic matters. Like scholar–gentries of yore, he was above material concerns: as a youth in Korea, he had lacked little materially. As a political exile he had relied successfully on his considerable charisma and diplomacy for financial support for himself and his attempts at promoting Korean independence.

When Rhee was elected its first president in 1948, South Korea was a poor imitation of a nation. Rhee's immediate task was state building, erecting a functioning government. When he began to govern South Korea with its myriad accumulated problems, Rhee's behaviors quickly reverted to those of a traditional *yangban* aristocrat. Even as elected president he demanded obedience and loyalty from his appointed ministers. Rhee continually named and abruptly dismissed cabinet ministers largely to strengthen his own political control, and the tenures of his ministers were often only a few months long.

According to Clinton L. Rossiter, there are three types of crises in the life of a democratic nation: economic depression, rebellion, and war.[9] The infant republic headed by Rhee managed to face all three types just within the first three years of the establishment of the government. The economy in South

[9] Clinton L. Rossiter, *Constitutional Dictatorships: Crisis Government in Modern Democracies* (Princeton, NJ: Princeton University Press, 1948).

Korea then was one of endless despair, despite considerable aid from the United States and elsewhere. Rhee, who became a Machiavellian autocrat early in his presidency, was largely indifferent to the economic plight of ordinary people, while habitually paying lip service to the "well-being of our people," from whom he was distant. The government barely paid its bills, thanks largely to American aid programs, which covered more than one-third of the administration's budget in the early Rhee period. Rhee's appointments to economy-related ministries clearly reflected this indifference to the economy, as few of these ministers had expertise in economy or finance. However, all were obsequious to Rhee. Not surprisingly, these ministers did precious little to focus attention on the economy. There did still exist a few light industrial operations with colonial roots including textiles and food processing, but entrepreneurial initiatives received little government or social recognition or reward. When Rhee was occasionally made aware of the economic problems of South Korea, he did little more than issue an incoherent and sophomoric statement:

> What the government encourages is a free development of industries by the citizenry. However, Korean entrepreneurs are not yet investing their capital to form large economic enterprises, obliging the government to manage the economy. . . . We cannot live by agriculture alone. . . . We must discard goods made by hand and bring in machineries to mass produce inexpensive goods, which will enable us to compete with others and live better.[10]

As inflation in the wake of the Korean War became a serious matter, Rhee abruptly and unilaterally decided that the government should not continue to print more money. In an incident that revealed both his arbitrary ruling style and the "idiotic"[11] level of his knowledge of the economy, he personally ordered that the police security bureau seal off presses at the mint on February 11, 1954, the intent being to stop inflation simply and immediately. The president of the Bank of Korea, which administered the mint, pointed out that such an act would bring government operations to a halt, and had the seals removed.

It should not seem surprising that no comprehensive economic development program was ever officially initiated by the Rhee government. A hurriedly drafted three-year economic development proposal was offered by the Ministry of Reconstruction in 1957, but it was not even approved by the Rhee cabinet until its meeting of April 15, 1960. A student uprising

[10] Kim Un-t'ae, *Hanguk chŏngch'i non* (On Korean politics) (Seoul: Pakyongsa, 1982), p. 304.
[11] "Hanguk kyŏngje pansegi" (A half century of the Korean economy), *Hankook Ilbo* (August 24, 1991): p. 6.

that commenced on April 19 subsequently ousted the Rhee regime, rendering the proposal moot. The main thrust of Rhee's "economic policy" appeared to have been to graphically highlight Korea's dire need of foreign economic and military assistance to maximize foreign aid.[12] He also emphasized import substitution for what little manufacturing there was in South Korea.

Well into the 1950s, Korea continued to be dependent on American aid, as it had been throughout the Korean War. Thanks to American and other generous aid and the extremely parsimonious spending pattern of the Rhee government, however, Korea was poor but virtually debt free as she entered the 1960s. In sum, for twelve years Korea under Rhee was "an almost totally nonfunctional society" economically.[13] Not surprisingly, Korea's per capita income was estimated at about $81 in 1959, the year before Rhee was ousted, a negligible improvement over $67 in 1953, at the end of the war. Further, inflation spiraled during the period. The average Korean barely subsisted, while the president was preoccupied with prolonging his tenure in office. The aging and increasingly cantankerous autocrat did precious little to advance the national economy or to better the lives of the people, from whom he was well insulated.

Even before the infant republic had been formally inaugurated, forceful challenges to its very existence were mounting. These challenges included hit-and-run attacks on South Korean authorities by pro-Communist guerrillas and bloody uprisings by a desperately impoverished citizenry and peasants, some of whom were undoubtedly affiliated with the South Korean Labor Party, the Communist branch in South Korea. North Korea dispatched armed and trained guerrillas who trekked down the rugged T'aebaek Mountain ranges, which form the spine of the rabbit-shaped peninsula. Local rebels often joined forces with Communist partisans in these mountains. South Korean police and the constabulary had to engage in exhausting subjugation campaigns against largely Communist-inspired rebels. In these extermination campaigns against those who would destroy the infant republic the civil liberties so elegantly enumerated in the constitution were often forgotten.

One of the worst rebellions against the authorities in South Korea began in the largest offshore island, Cheju, on April 3, 1948, when Communist guerrillas from an extinct volcanic mountain there attacked police stations and government offices. The guerrillas were eagerly supported by villagers on the island, particularly those who were dissatisfied with

---

[12] American military and economic grants amounted to about $12 billion total from 1945 to 1965. George E. Ogle, *South Korea: Dissent within the Economic Miracle* (London: Zea Books, 1990), p. 17.

[13] Jon Huer, *Marching Orders: The Role of the Military in South Korea's "Economic Miracle," 1961–1971* (New York: Greenwood Press, 1989), p. 12.

the American military government and local Korean authorities, as well as with the move to establish a separate South Korean government through the general election, then scheduled for May 10, 1948. To what extent the South Korean Labor Party manipulated local resentment of the Cheju islanders remains uncertain. However, the rebellions were ferocious, and the South Korean police and constabulary forces attacked the rebels and villagers mercilessly. Before the rebellion ended a year later it was believed to have claimed some 60,000 lives, or about one-fifth of the island population.[14]

The Cheju Rebellion also occasioned a large-scale mutiny in the Korean constabulary only a month after the establishment of the republic. On the night of October 19, 1948, the Fourteenth Regiment of the constabulary, which was being dispatched to Cheju Island to subjugate the rebels there, mutinied in the port city of Yŏsu on the southwestern tip of Korea. Some three thousand mutineers killed twenty officers, including three battalion commanders. In four hours the rebel troops attacked poorly armed police stations and defenseless local government offices, won over a large segment of the civilian population by urging revenge against the oppressive local police, and declared Yŏsu a "liberated area." Spreading rumors that all Korea had fallen to the rebels, the insurgents marched on October 20 to capture the nearby town of Sunch'ŏn. Here, however, troops loyal to the South Korean government checked the advance by October 27 and dealt summary punishments to both the mutineer and local rebels.[15] It was during the Yŏsu-Sunch'ŏn Incident that Park Chung Hee was arrested, interrogated, and sentenced to death by court-martial. Later he collaborated with the government by exposing Communist-cell members in the constabulary and thus saved his own life. Predictably, these bloody rebellions and extreme right-wing reactions were a great impetus to the open suppression of the civil liberties enumerated in the South Korean constitution. The political and cultural environments became suspicious, intolerant, and oppressive.

It was in this atmosphere that the National Security Law was hurriedly introduced to the National Assembly. The law was promulgated

---

[14] John Merrill, "The Cheju-do Rebellion," *Journal of Korean Studies* (1980).

[15] Citing former Soviet Colonel General Terenty F. Shtykov's recent *Memoirs*, Yi Ki-bong asserts that the Yŏsu-Sunch'ŏn *rebellion* was ordered by the Communist authorities in North Korea and the Soviet Union, possibly by Stalin himself. Shtykov was the chief Soviet delegate to the U.S.–Soviet Joint Commission, which had failed in 1947 to find mutually acceptable solutions to unify Korea and instead turned to the establishment of the two "separate" governments by 1948. Yi Ki-bong, "Pukhan chŏmnyŏng soryngun sunowe hoego: Yŏ-sun kunbanran sakŏn Stalin chisi yŏtta" (Recollections of a Soviet Occupation Army Chief in North Korea: Stalin Ordered the Army Mutinies in Yŏ-sun), *Sin Dong-A* (July 1995): pp. 380–94. Yi also wrote that General Shtykov established a guerrilla warfare command in the north in 1947.

on December 1, 1948, and passed by the brand new legislature less than two months after the Yŏsu-Sunch'ŏn mutiny. This law, with many amendments, is still in force today, half a century later. Article 1 of the law bluntly stated that the law's purpose was to ensure "the national security and interests" by protecting "the State" from the "enemy" of the state.[16] Article 5 defines the "enemy" as "any association, groups or organizations" that conspire against the state, and provided draconian punishments for such enemies. The law itself recognized that it was closely "related to the rights and freedoms of the people guaranteed by the Constitution," It was evident that the law could be used against political opponents of the South Korean government as, for example, Article 22 stipulated: "Any person who publicly defames constitutional organs . . . by distributing documents, sound recordings, drawings or pictures . . . under the instructions from the associations, groups or organizations . . . shall be punished with penal servitude for not exceeding ten years."[17] Thus, any adverse communication regarding any organ or person named in the constitution could be punishable for up to ten years. Initially the law was applied against members of the South Korean Labor Party.[18] Subsequently, however, the law was often applied largely for the purpose of South Korean regime maintenance by curbing press freedom, political activities by religious organizations, labor unions, and anti-American behaviors, among others.[19]

The Korean War and the Rhee Autocracy

Meanwhile, the occupation forces of both the Soviet Union and the United States had withdrawn from North and South Korea, and the emerging North Korean leader Kim Il Sung had begun preparing for what he and others apparently believed would be a successful blitzkrieg to unify the peninsula under Communism. Recent archival research in Moscow by a number of scholars and those records released by the Russian government after the collapse of the Soviet Union clearly indicate that Kim repeatedly sought and ultimately received approval from both

[16] Secretariat, House of Representatives, Republic of Korea, "The National Security Law," (December 1, 1948): p. 1.

[17] Ibid., p. 8.

[18] Pak Won-sun, Kukka poanbŏp yŏngu (The Study of the National Security Law), vol. 2. (Seoul: Yoksa bip'yongsa, 1992), pp. 15–16.

[19] A most exhaustive study of the applications of the National Security Law in different categories of activities by the Korean regimes, from the First Republic to the Sixth Republic, is found in Volumes 2 and 3 of Pak Won-sun, Kukka poanbŏp yŏngu.

Parts of Seoul were reduced to a huge junkyard of debris during the Korean War, 1950–53. (The U.S. National Archives)

Joseph Stalin and Mao Zedong to launch the war against the south.[20] These findings establish that the assertion that "the military action by North Korea on June 25 was a defensive response to provocations by the South, is simply false."[21] The Korean War, which erupted with a full-scale invasion by the northern forces all across the thirty-eighth parallel on June 25, 1950, less than two years after the inauguration of the Rhee government, was a total war for the Koreans, who lost an estimated million lives among civilians alone and suffered damages estimated at three billion dollars. The battle line in the war swept across the 150-mile-wide peninsula four times in the midsection of the country, and the South Korean government turned into one of the worst authoritarian wartime governments.

By the time a truce was signed in July 1953 Rhee had become an undisputed autocrat. Some of his potential rivals who had not been eliminated earlier by militant "rightist" terrorists were taken to the north by the retreating Communist army, which occupied some 95 percent of South Ko-

[20] "From the Russian Archives: New Findings on the Korean War," translation and commentary by Kathryn Weathersby, *Cold War International History Bulletin*, Woodrow Wilson International Center for Scholars (Fall 1993): p. 14.

[21] Ibid. For divergent views see Bruce Cumings, *The Origins of the Korean War*, 2 vols. (Princeton, NJ: Princeton University Press, 1981 and 1990), and John Merrill, *Korea: Peninsula Origins of the War* (Newark, DE: University of Delaware Press, 1989).

Hapless refugees in a snow-covered field fleeing from the second communist army forged through central Korea in January 1951. (The U.S. National Archives)

rea at one point, everywhere but a tiny pocket including the wartime capital of Pusan at the southeastern tip of the peninsula. In Pusan, which was placed under martial law, Rhee had rammed a constitutional amendment through the besieged National Assembly surrounded by the military police on July 7, 1952. The amendment was to have the president elected by direct vote of the people. It had little to do with enhancing the political rights of the people, but everything to do with Rhee's obsession to be reelected. A vast majority of the people who had to struggle for their daily survival in wartime Korea had had no opportunity to learn about Rhee's often despotic behaviors. In fact, many people still held Rhee in awe as the "father of the nation," but National Assembly members who watched Rhee at close range had become increasingly hostile to him.

The constitutional amendment of 1952 set a precedent of manipulating the constitution for the political expediency of a ruler. While Rhee's role as the stern symbol of South Korea in the darkest hours of the Korean War should not be underestimated, Rhee crassly took advantage of the crisis of the Communist aggression to make himself an unchallengeable autocrat. A year after the termination of the war, when South Korea was just reemerging from the rubble of the three years of destruction, Rhee had another constitutional amendment adopted by the pliable legislature, on November 29, 1954; this one would repeal the constitutional prohibition against a third four-year presidential term in the case of the first president, Rhee himself. With these constitutional amendments, Rhee, then seventy-nine, hoped to become a constitutional autocrat-for-life. Toward the end of his regime, Rhee and his government of obsequious ministers resembled an old dynastic court of a king and his *yangban* officials. As Rhee became absolutely powerful, his regime turned into a corrupt and arrogant clique that remained aloof from the people, whose lives had hardly improved during Rhee's twelve-year rule.

The "Righteous Student Uprising" (1960) and the Second Republic

It is worth noting that the traditional obsession with education of the young, probably attributable to the Confucian emphasis on learning, was reflected in the constitution, which provided: "All citizens shall have the right to receive an equal education correspondent to their abilities . . . compulsory education shall be free." The Education Law had already been legislated and promulgated in 1949, and a compulsory education system was inaugurated for the primary level in the very first years of the republic. The education of the young continued even during the Korean War in makeshift barracks and sometimes outdoor classes. Educational opportunities were also rapidly expanded at higher levels, driven by the people's traditional and sustained interest in education. In due time these drives were to have a far-reaching impact on both political development and economic growth.

Meanwhile, if it was astonishing that Rhee at eighty-five was running in 1960 for another four-year term, it was not surprising that the ruling clique around Rhee was determined to ensure his victory in a direct popular election that had to be held in accordance with the "democratic" constitution. Those who had vested interests in the political and economic order in the First Republic were determined to ensure that his younger vice presidential running mate, Yi Ki-bung, would succeed Rhee, should Rhee die during the term. Instead of seeking a "democratic" mandate through a fair election held on March 15, 1960, the rigging of that election was ensured throughout South Korea. Specific instructions were sent out by the Home Ministry to police chiefs throughout the nation stipulating the exact plurality by which the Rhee–Yi team was to be "elected." When votes were "counted," it was announced that the team won a lopsided victory. Many people were overcome by a feeling of bewilderment and resentment but felt powerless to challenge the formidable Rhee regime.

Few persons outside the small port city of Masan knew that a riot had broken out on election day. Indeed, the public there had become convinced that the election was being brazenly stolen by the ruling clique. The people of Masan felt suffocating fury but were helpless against the reinforced police force. When, on April 11, 1960, a fisherman discovered the body of nineteen-year-old high school student Kim Chu-yŏl with a tear-gas shell imbedded in one eye, however, all Masan suddenly went out of control. The people's anger finally reached an exploding point. The resulting Masan riot triggered a rapid succession of massive student demonstrations in Seoul and other major cities beginning on April 16. Owing to the people's abiding interest in education, there were some 903,000 middle school, high school, and college students in 1960; that figure had been approximately 128,000 in 1945. Nearly a million students could potentially demonstrate against the Rhee government; demonstrating students were soon joined by their professors, a dignified and respected group who seldom participated in anything like street demonstrations. Some angry citizenry also joined the demonstrators.

On April 19 more than three thousand Seoul students surged to the road leading to the presidential mansion. The police initially fired tear-gas shells, and when the angry students pressed forward crushing barricades, the police fired into the crowds. By midday more than 100,000 indigenous persons, including numerous citizens who joined the demonstrating students, were battling the police. Demoralized and outnumbered, many policemen took off their uniforms and went into hiding. Others fired into the demonstrators, and hoodlums mobilized by proadministration groups isolated and brutally beat young students. Across the city there were 125 dead and more than a thousand wounded. This came to be called the "Righteous Uprising of April 19" or the "4.19 Student Uprising."

Characteristically, President Rhee declared martial law once again and heavily armed soldiers were brought into Seoul blaming "devilish hands of the Communists" for disturbances throughout South Korea. President Rhee had just taken stern military measures when he found his position frontally challenged from an unexpected source. On the afternoon of April 19, U.S. Secretary of State Christian A. Herter called in the Korean ambassador to deliver a message that: "this Government believes that the demonstrations in Korea are a reflection of public dissatisfaction over the conduct of the recent elections and repressive measures *unsuited to a free democracy*"[22] (emphasis added). American officials in Korea remained

---

[22] U.S. Department of State, Historical Office, *American Foreign Policy: Current Documents 1960* (Washington, DC: Government Printing Office, 1964), p. 680.

silent in public. Many observers believed, however, that the Americans there also played a quiet but decisive role in furthering the cause of the antiadministration demonstrators. The United Nations command in Korea, led by U.S. General Carter B. Magruder, had tactical control of the Korean Army. Korean soldiers mobilized for martial law duty showed no signs of shooting the demonstrators. Some young students climbed atop tanks stationed in Seoul, and the students and soldiers engaged in friendly conversations. In fact, the army seemed to maintain a strict "neutrality" between the Rhee administration and the demonstrators. At a moment when the very life of the Rhee regime trembled in the balance, its coercive force suddenly evaporated.

Street demonstrations continued. As smiling soldiers mingled with students and their supporters in Seoul, demonstrations spread to all major cities in South Korea. After a series of tense conferences in the presidential mansion, where students' incessant antigovernment howls could be heard, Rhee finally resigned on the evening of April 26; Rhee's defense minister and the martial law commander had told Rhee that further bloodshed could be avoided if he did so. Rhee, who constitutionally commanded the fourth largest standing army in the world, was ousted when the internal "righteous uprising" attracted external moral support—this time from the United States—for "free democracy" in Korea. Rhee left Korea for Hawaii and later died there as a lonely exile.

It is noteworthy that these series of upheavals of 1960 developed into what might be called a "populist" attack on a regime that was expected to be "democratic" but turned despotic. The events began as student demonstrations in the remote southeastern city of Masan, initially with the limited political objective of petitioning to President Rhee for the resignation of his vice president-elect. It was reminiscent, in some respects, of another "populist" uprising of 1894, the Kabo *Tonghak* uprising, which began with the modest goal of petitioning the king to clear the name of the martyred founder of *Tonghak* but quickly spread. The ideological groundings were different, however: the first was religious and the second had essentially a "democratic" justification. However, to the extent that *Tonghak* could be taken as a protodemocratic teaching, the differences might be less significant. In both instances, when the authorities responded ruthlessly and oppressively the anger of the people affected exploded and swept away a long-entrenched regime. In any case, the concept of a "righteous uprising" was reaffirmed and took deeper root in the political awareness of the Korean people. A contemporary precedent of a "righteous uprising" was established.

The Second Republic. The Second Republic was the direct outcome of the almost unexpectedly sudden fall of the First Republic. Because the presidential system of government was partly due to the insistence of Syng-

(From left to right) The Rhees and the Yis. Yi Kang-sŏk, the older son of Vice President and Mrs.Yi Ki-bung, Mrs. Francesca Rhee, President Syngman Rhee, Vice President Yi, Park Maria (Mrs.Yi), and Yi Kang-uk, the younger son of the Yis. Yi Kang-sŏk was the adopted son of the Rhees, and the Yis, including Kang-sŏk, committed group suicide at a cottage on the presidential compound as the Student Uprising of April 1960 forced President Rhee out of office. (Joong-ang photograph)

man Rhee, those who were engaged in the reinstitution of a new government turned to a responsible cabinet system. It was the system that had initially been considered seriously by the drafters of the original constitution in 1947–1948 until they were persuaded otherwise by Rhee. In 1960 Yu Chin-o, then president of Korea University, stated that it was the common feeling among the people that we should escape from the hell of a presidential system and adopt a democratic parliamentary system of government.

The 1948 constitution was drastically amended on June 15, 1960. Unlike the constitution of the First Republic, which was heavily American influenced, the constitution of the Second Republic was written by Korean lawmakers who intended to adopt a "democratic" system that would not succumb to presidential domination. The amended constitution provided for an elaborate parliamentary system of government. The ceremonial head of the government would be a president elected by a two-thirds majority of the legislature (Article 53). The National Assembly became a bicameral body, whereas it had been a unicameral in the First Republic. The president would name a prime minister, who would be confirmed by a simple majority vote of the lower house, the House of Representatives (Article 69). The prime minister was the chief executive (Article 70) and would head the State Affairs Council (cabinet); the cabinet was collectively responsible to the lower house (Article 70).

The 1960 constitution significantly expanded the democratic rights of the people.[23] Amended Article 13 flatly declared that "the people's press and publications freedom and the freedom of assembly and associations shall not be restricted." Gone was the escape clause "except as provided by law." Similar protections of the people's rights were also found in a number of articles of the amended constitution. There was no doubt about the "democratic"intent of the Korean legislators, who became the heirs to the Righteous Student Uprising.

A national election was held on July 29, 1960, to constitute a new National Assembly in which the Democratic Party, the main opposition party against the Rhee autocracy, occupied 175 seats out of 233 in the lower house. The Democratic Party also occupied thirty-one of fifty-eight seats in the House of Councilors. After five months of an interim government, Chang Myŏn (John M. Chang) was elected prime minister on August 19. However, the members of the ruling Democratic Party, who had struggled together against Rhee, were almost evenly split into two warring factions when the governing authority was suddenly handed to the opposition party. This political division gave birth to the New Democratic Party, which was distinct from the Democratic Party—a phenomenon reminiscent of factional struggles among Confucian scholar–officials of yore. This fact in a cabinet system of government meant political gridlock regarding practically every issue while accumulated problems in South Korea demanded effective government that was capable of urgently addressing socioeconomic problems.

Premier Chang, a devout Catholic layman, was different from Rhee, though Chang also hailed from one of the most distinguished families in Korea.[24] Chang (1899–1966) studied at the Agricultural and Forestry School in Suwon, a public vocational school under Japanese control, before studying education and religion at Manhattan College in New York from 1920 to 1925. Later reflecting on this period, he wrote:

From this time, I studied and experienced freedom and democracy, and cultivated a practice of speaking and acting as directed by a religiously formed conscience. I believed that the effective and direct path of con-

---

[23] Oh, *Korea: Democracy on Trial,* pp. 72–82.

[24] An indication is that the Chang family was featured in a full-page story in *Chosŏn Ilbo* (1 April 1995, p. 19). The daily newspaper did a feature series on "distinguished families" of Korea.

President Yun Po-sŏn (left) and Prime Minister Chang Myŏn (John M. Chang) of the Second Republic, 1960–61. (The Korean Information Office)

tributing to the future of our nation under Japanese imperialism was through the education of the people, and realized that uplifting our national virtue should be rooted on religious faith.[25]

Returning to Korea via Rome Chang taught at the Tongsŏng Commercial School for seventeen years and subsequently served as its principal. Above all, he was an exemplary Catholic to his students and to others.[26] His political career began with the liberation of Korea from Japanese rule. He served as the first Korean ambassador to the United States and as prime minister under Rhee, but by 1956 he ran as the vice presidential candidate of the opposition Democratic Party. When the opposition presidential candidate died of a heart attack just before the May 1956 election,

[25] Han Ch'ang-u et al., eds. *Hanalŭi mili chukchi ankkonŭn: Chang Myŏn paksa hwoegorok* (Unless a Grain of Barley Dies: Recollections of Dr. Chang Myon) (Seoul: Catholic Press, 1967), pp. 27–28.

[26] Song Wŏn-yŏng, *Chae-i konghwakuk: Chang Myŏn ch'ongni kongbo bisŏkwan Song Wŏn-yŏng ŭi chongch'i ch'aehŏm* (The Second Republic: Political Experience of Wŏn-yŏng Song, Premier Chang's press secretary) (Seoul: Saemto, 1990), pp. 58–73.

Chang was elected vice president representing the opposition party—a strange lineup that was allowed under election laws at the time. It was a most uncomfortable position to occupy under the cantankerous and vengeful Rhee, who loathed the vice president and his representation of opposition to the Rhee administration.

Where Rhee was caesaristic but decisive, Chang was gentler and deliberate. An avalanche of accumulated problems that his government inherited in 1960 demanded urgent daily solutions, but the soft-spoken premier had to be responsible to a rancorously divided National Assembly. While most people expected quick solutions to myriad problems, many of which were attributable to the haughty and corrupt Rhee regime, the Chang government was quickly approaching paralysis. The most impatient in this situation were the newly empowered students, who continued to demonstrate, some 2,000 times with roughly 900,000 participants during the one-year period after the demise of the Rhee regime, demanding urgent actions by the Chang regime on many fronts.[27] An explosive issue faced by "the government by demonstrations" was a demand for ex post facto "revolutionary legislation" to punish ousted Rhee administration officials. On October 11, 1960, scores of students wounded during the April uprising physically occupied the rostrum of the National Assembly, which subsequently agreed to pass a special law to punish anyone who committed unlawful acts in connection with the May 15 elections of the president and the vice president, and also to suspend the citizenship of anyone who committed grave antidemocratic acts.[28] This special law was adopted in clear violation of the legal principle prohibiting ex post facto legislation as an addendum to the extensive constitutional amendments of 1960.

The economy. The Korean economy was desperately underdeveloped when the Second Republic was established. The per capita gross national product in 1960 was only $79, then one of the lowest in the world. Immediately after the inauguration of the Chang cabinet the secretariat of the State Affairs Council (cabinet) commissioned eight Korean universities to conduct a carefully structured survey to ascertain what the people most urgently requested of the government. In December 1960 the survey teams of these universities asked some three thousand South Koreans about "their most urgent requests to the government." The top eight responses were as follows:[29]

[27] Stephen Bradner, "Korea: Experiment and Instability," *Japan Quarterly* 8, no. 4 (1961): p. 414.

[28] Kim Ch'ol-su, *Hanguk honpŏpsa*, p. 559.

[29] *Dong-A Ilbo*, 28 December 1960.

Relief measures for the unemployed	20.8%
Price stabilization	17.9%
Adjustment of price of farm products	13.8%
Liquidation of usurious loans to farmers and fisherman	11.6%
Crime control and maintenance of order	3.9%
Equitable taxation	3.1%
Support of medium and small businesses	2.0%
Solution of housing problems	1.0%

Thus more than 70 percent of the responses named the solution to economic problems as their "most urgent" request to the new government. Clearly it was not political concerns such as enhancing democratic rights that the people were concerned with. The Chang government, keenly responsive to public sentiment, promptly began focusing its attention on economic woes.[30] To reallocate its meager financial resources the Chang government attempted to reduce the size of the Korean military, some seven years after the end of the Korean War. However, this attempt encountered immediate and fierce resistance not only from the Korean military but also from the United States, which was concerned about regional military balance. The United States was then providing some 40 percent of the Korean defense budget. The idea of downsizing the military was therefore quietly dropped.

Barely three months after his cabinet began to function—in an utterly chaotic political arena following the unexpectedly swift collapse of the Rhee regime—in December 1960 Premier Chang himself proudly unveiled the very first formally announced plan in modern Korean history for economic development. The plan was drafted by the Council for Economic Development and was followed by additional details announced by the council in February 1961. This "Five-Year Plan for National Development" had the relatively modest goal of undertaking such public-works projects as land development, reforestation, and road and dam construction. It was publicly admitted that the plan was modeled after the New Deal projects of the United States, and that economic assistance to be boosted by the Kennedy administration in support of a "democratic" government in Korea would largely finance the plan's implementation. The projects were to be hurriedly commenced in the spring of 1961. What was swiftly executed instead in May was a military coup. Just as the First Republic had died a sudden death approximately a year earlier, the Chang cabinet of the Second Republic quickly evaporated some eight months after its inauguration, thus marking the end of the first two republics headed by duly elected civilians.

[30] Han Sŭng-ju, *Chae-i konghwakuk kwa hanguk ŭi minjujuŭi* (The Second Republic and Democracy in Korea) (Seoul: Chongno sŏjŏk, 1983), pp. 105–26.

✸

The First Military Coup and Economic Growth, 1961–1979

For more than thirty-two years, from 1961 to 1993, South Korea was ruled by military-dominated governments. From May 1961 to December 1963 the military directly ruled the country through a military junta that was grandiosely called the Supreme Council for National Reconstruction (SCNR). It was headed by Major General Park Chung Hee. Park executed the first successful military coup d'état in contemporary Korea on May 16, 1961, which ushered in an extended period of military domination of Korea. Significantly, it was during Park's rule that rapid economic growth was triggered and changed Korea from a largely agrarian society into an industrial nation. When Park's rule came to an abrupt end in 1979, Lieutenant General Chun Doo Whan then seized power; he was succeeded in 1988 by retired Lieutenant General Roh Tae Woo. In many ways Park left a defining mark on Korean politics and economy, and he deserves particular attention here.

"A Son of a *Tonghak* Rebel"

Park's origins could not have been more different than those of either the well-born and well-educated President Syngman Rhee of the First Republic or Premier Chang Myŏn of the Second Republic. Unlike the two chief executives before him, who were born near the end of the nineteenth century, Park was born in 1917. He was the eighth child of an impoverished farmer who joined the *Tonghak* peasant rebels. Park's father was in his twenties when he "participated in the *Tonghak* revolution" and was arrested but "pardoned immediately before he was to be executed."[1] The desperate circumstances of Park's birth in a tiny, mud-walled, thatch-roofed house are reflected in the story that his mother, upon learning that she was pregnant for the eighth time, reportedly drank a large quantity of soy sauce and repeatedly jumped from a large soy sauce pot in an unsuccessful attempt to abort him.[2]

Park's life up to the outbreak of the Korean War was a continuous struggle to survive. Park had to walk to his grammar school, some three miles, often unprotected from the drenching rain or knee-deep snow. He then went to an austere normal school in Taegu that gave him inexpensive vocational training to teach at grammar schools. He was evidently uninspired by the normal school teaching, ranking seventy-third in his class of seventy-three in his fourth year. Confidential comments on his "attitudes" in his school records include such notes as "depressed," "muttering complaints," "lacking in honesty," and "appears to be from a poverty-stricken background." However, he excelled in Japanese-style fencing and gymnastics. Park managed to enter the Military Academy of Manchukuo, the puppet state of imperialist Japan.

While a sizeable number of his compatriots were struggling against Japan in Manchuria, China, the Soviet Union, and the United States, to regain Korean independence, training at the Academy was a path for Park to become a member of the officer corps of the Japanese imperial army. Upon his graduation from the military academy in Tokyo in 1944 Park was assigned to the Japanese army in Manchuria (the Kwantung army) in the final stage of the Pacific War. A year later, after Japan surrendered, his dream of building a career in the Japanese military was shattered. He quietly returned to his native home a defrocked Japanese army lieutenant, penniless and jobless, unprepared for anything other than teaching at a rural common school where he might not have been welcomed by nationalist-oriented teachers. It was fairly predictable that Park would join the newly established Korean constabulary, as did most of his contemporaries with similar military backgrounds. Thus in September 1946 he resumed the military career that he had begun at about the age of 23.[3]

Park rose steadily in a rapidly expanding army in the divided peninsula until October 1948, when he was arrested and sentenced to death for associating with Communist insurrectionists of the Yŏsu-Sunchŏn Rebellion. His constabulary unit was being dispatched to Cheju Island, where

---

[1] Pak Chŏng-hui (Park Chung Hee), "Naŭi sonyŏn sichŏl" p. 512.

[2] Kim Chin-bae, "Yŏkdae det'ongnyŏng chongsin bunsŏk" (A Psycho-Analysis of Successive Presidents), *Wŏlgan Kyŏnghyang* (February 1989): pp. 314–15.

[3] Paek Nam-ju, ed., *Hyŏngmyŏng chidoja Pak Chŏng-hi non* (On Park Chung Hee, the Revolutionary Leader) (Seoul: Inmulkaesa, 1961), pp. 39–42. Chŏng Mok-ku, *Chŏnki Pak Chŏng-hŭi* (A Park Chong Hee Biography) (Seoul: Kyoyuk pyŏngnonsa, 1966), Chap. 1.

large-scale rebellions were occurring against the American occupation and the South Korean government that was then being established. The Rhee government had launched a determined campaign of liquidation of subversive elements in the South Korean military forces, and Park saved his own life only by cooperating with government investigators. Park allegedly gave a long list of like-minded officers and enlisted men, who were then taken out to fields and shot. This incident spoke volumes about the self-centered survival instinct and shamelessly ruthless aspects of the man, but it also cost him his army commission once again (he had also lost it at the end of the Pacific War). Park did not have any other employable skills, and was retained as a civilian employee of army intelligence. He was reinstated in the officer corps after the outbreak of the Korean War, which witnessed the collapse of a substantial part of the South Korean army in the face of a well-prepared invasion by a much superior North Korean military.

The first coup d'état. By the end of the devastating Korean War, in 1953, Park had advanced to the rank of brigadier general. However, several years after the war, when he was still a two-star general, his military career in peacetime Korea was once again threatened, this time with involuntary early retirement. Well-connected and unscrupulous generals managed to survive and become affluent, but Park was uncorruptable and his family's livelihood depended on his meager army salary. In a four-year span from 1957 to 1961, he was given no less than nine trifling assignments, an unmistakable message that he was slated for forced early retirement if he did not take the initiative and resign. At the time of his successful military coup in 1961 he was only 44. By then he had acquired a wide variety of practical experience in managing large and varied operations and a keen awareness of economic concerns. He was also clearly a pragmatist without humanitarian or political scruples but with well-honed survival skills.

Park reportedly had begun plotting a military coup in the early 1950s during the Korean War, when President Rhee was growing autocratic. Park led an austere life, unlike many other young generals, who ostentatiously enjoyed the privileges of rank. He also cultivated a wide-ranging network of anti-status quo, reform-, and coup-minded young officers. After years of plotting, Park succeeded in mobilizing a relatively small force of army and marine units that struck swiftly and forcefully at Seoul, the heart of the Second Republic. Premier Chang naively trusted his army chief of staff, General Chang Do-yŏng, who controlled what was then the fourth-largest standing army in the world, to defend his constitutionally installed government. But the only force that was actually brought to bear on the access bridge to Seoul was a small detachment of lightly armed military policemen. The coup in the predawn hours of May 16, 1961, was a success. Park mobilized the coup units without the approval or the knowledge of the United Nations Command (UNC) in Korea. The U.S. commander who then headed the UNC had had "command authority" over the Korean military since July 15, 1950, when President Rhee had hurriedly transferred "command authority over all (Korean) land, sea, and air forces"[4] to him in the critical early period in the Korean War. The American command authority in South Korea thus had been breached during the coup, though the Korean military depended almost completely on the United States for its weapons and equipment.

Justification by Economic Growth

General Park's ideas about politics and the economy may be gleaned from a few brief but revealing tracts hastily published under his name shortly after the coup. In *Chidojado* (The Leader's Way), the general who had just executed a military coup against the democratically constituted government of the Second Republic proclaimed his "belief in democracy"[5] in a brief section of seventeen lines. He claimed that he led the coup to "overthrow the anti-democratic system" of the Second Republic, which, according to many unbiased observers, was most democratically oriented. After all, it had been the direct outcome of the student uprising against the Rhee regime. Park declared that he led what he called "the military revolution" to lay down the foundation for a "true, free democracy in Korea—certainly not for the establishment of a new dictatorship and totalitarianism."

Uri minjok ŭi nagalkil (The Path for our Nation) is an important exposition of General Park's political ideas. The term "administrative democracy" was coined in this tract and became a political buzzword during the Park regime. That publication revealed that Park's thoughts about the economy were far more coherent, populist, and egalitarian than were Rhee's. Park emphasized that without "economic equality," political democracy is no more than an "abstract, useless concept."[6]

In a strikingly revealing statement, Park then declared in *Kukka wa hyŏngmyŏng kwa na* (The Country, the Revolution, and I) that most Asian countries, including Korea, "have to resort to undemocratic and *extraordi-*

[4] James I. Matray, ed., *Historical Dictionary of the Korean War* (New York: Greenwood Press, 1991), pp. 444–45. This transfer of "command authority" should not be confused with the Taejon Agreement, which dealt mostly with the status and rights of the U.S. armed forces in Korea.

[5] Seoul: Kukka chaekŏn ch'oego hoegui, 1961, p. 24.

[6] Seoul: Tonga ch'ulpansa, 1961, pp. 107–8.

nary measures in order to improve the living conditions of the masses. . . . one cannot deny that people are more frightened of poverty and hunger than totalitarianism. . . . The purpose of this revolution is to reconstruct the nation and establish a self-sustaining economy, and its essential purpose is to restore to all the people the political and economic systems which had become the possession of a few privileged classes."[7]

In a society with a deeply rooted Confucian tradition that held legitimacy to be essential for a government to work, Park was keenly aware that his successful military coup did not create legitimacy for the military junta. Further, in traditional Korea military officials had been seen as inferior to the civilian group of the *yangban*. However, with his impoverished origins and experiences as an incorruptible army officer, Park was far more sensitive than Rhee or Chang to the desperate economic deprivation of the common people in the appallingly underdeveloped Korean economy. The per capita annual income in 1961 in South Korea, which remained largely agrarian, was $82. Under these circumstances the coup had to be quickly justified to the people, who had become increasingly political as they were exposed to general elections between 1948 and 1961. Though the first president of the republic was elected by the National Assembly, the presidential elections in 1952, 1956, and 1960 were by direct popular vote, and voter participation was 88 percent, 94 percent, and 97 percent, respectively, for the three presidential elections.[8] Elections for National Assembly members were held in 1948, 1950, 1954, 1958, and 1960, and voter participation in them was also high.

On January 1, 1962, barely six months after the military takeover, General Park, in his capacity as chairman of the Supreme Council for National Reconstruction, announced with great fanfare the "First Five-Year Economic Development Plan, 1962–1966." Park evidently decided to risk his own future and that of what he called "military revolution" on this bold and comprehensive economic initiative in the hope of justifying his military coup and legitimizing his regime. He quickly committed the full weight of his power and that of his military junta in support of the unprecedented economic plan, which became his "marching order."[9] It was audacious politics of justification and legitimization by economic growth.

It was indicative of this soldier's intelligence orientation that Park first created the Korean Central Intelligence Agency (KCIA) on June 10, 1961, shortly before he launched the Economic Planning Board (EPB) on July 21, barely two months after the coup. The KCIA was far more than just an

[7] Seoul: Hyangmunsa, 1963, trans. Leon Sinder, pp. 105–7.

[8] *Korea Annual 1994* (Seoul: Yonhap News Agency, 1994), pp. 100–101.

[9] John Huer, *Marching Orders: The Role of the Military in South Korea's "Economic Miracle," 1961–1971* (New York: Greenwood Press, 1989), pp. 150–63.

intelligence-gathering organization. It quickly became an extremely powerful and pervasive force of coercion and control for the Park regime, not only in the political arena but also in the economic sector, even including labor control. The EPB was designed to be Park's central headquarters to coordinate economic development. The EPB quickly replaced the old Ministry of Reconstruction, which had amounted to little more than a unit administering U.S. aid, and absorbed the Budget Bureau of the Ministry of Finance. Later the EPB also absorbed the Statistics Bureau of the Ministry of Home Affairs. The central Bank of Korea was also brought under EPB control, as were privately owned commercial banks, whose stocks had been confiscated by the military junta. Further, the EPB minister was upgraded to the key position of deputy prime minister to head all economy-related ministers. Thus the EPB was made a highly centralized and powerful body, second only to the office of the president.

Thus was created a command center for rapid economic growth. Park was at the top, directly commanding the twin engines of the KCIA and the EPB. All of South Korea was soon mobilized by the powerful and determined military regime that energetically coopted groups of economists, scientists, engineers, managers, entrepreneurs, and others who could embrace the concrete goals of rapid economic growth. It was not difficult to mobilize the common people, who still led subsistence-level lives—some one-third of them were under- or unemployed in the early 1960s—to follow Park's "marching orders" promising them jobs and liberation from poverty.

Many uncompromising intellectuals, like the "principled literati" of yore who refused to obey despotic monarchs, often at the cost of their own lives, clung to a belief that "democracy" in South Korea should not be sacrificed on the altar of uncertain economic growth championed by an illegitimate military junta. Many of these intellectuals were dealt with brutally by the KCIA. Most of them did not literally lose their lives, but their "principled" stances cost them their livelihoods as they became "released professors" or "fired journalists" or "antirevolutionary elements." Their voices persisted throughout the era and grew increasingly desperate and louder toward the end of the period as the military-dominated authoritarian regime became increasingly dictatorial.

Economic development plans. The hurriedly drawn first five-year economic development plan was followed up by more carefully crafted economic development plans: the second, 1967–1971; the third, 1972–1976; the fourth, 1977–1981; the fifth, 1982–1986; and the revised sixth, 1988–1991. Each was built on the accomplishments of the previous plans. Until his assassination in 1979, Park himself wrote a succinct introduction to each plan as an indication of his personal commitment to economic growth. Such an action by a chief executive—be it a monarch, a president, or a prime minister—was unprecedented in Korean history. This political commitment was quickly matched with concrete executive actions, as Park proceeded methodically to create the machinery needed to achieve his economic goals. Park's choices of vice premier and minister of the EPB revealed his single-minded commitment to economic growth as he appointed tough-minded professionals to the posts. A prime example of such an appointment was that of Chang Ki Young, a self-made vice governor of the Bank of Korea, whose formal academic credentials ended with graduation from Sŏnlim Commercial High School. Park's commitment was also evident in his appointments of economy-related ministers. Unlike Rhee, who appointed political sycophants to all cabinet posts, Park appointed to such posts as Industry, Finance, and Agriculture people with specialized professional knowledge or experience in economic fields. It is worth noting that Park appointed no one from a military background to an economy-related post, though there were many from the military in more politically sensitive cabinet posts such as Defense, Home Affairs, and Legal Affairs. Thus Park bifurcated his government into economy-related and political–administrative areas while insulating and protecting the economic positions from the vicissitudes of Korean politics.

Early in the Park government the term "administrative democracy" was given a peculiar but concrete meaning with a massive "purge" of complacent bureaucrats who were replaced by former military personnel. Immediately after Park's inauguration approximately 36,000 employees, roughly 10 percent of the government bureaucracy then, were replaced. The infusion into the bureaucracy of disciplined, young, and eager workers who had been discharged from the military and were thus jobless, had an unsettling but energizing impact on the entire administrative operation.

Another major departure from the practices of the Rhee administration was the significant boost to governmental institutions related directly to the economy. Given the sagging economy, which was dependent on foreign aid, the Rhee administration had constantly overemphasized frugality to the point that the government was nearly nonfunctional in many economy-related areas. For instance, in 1959, a year before the Rhee regime was overthrown, there were some forty-one government bureaus and divisions dedicated to wide-ranging economy-related functions, from agricultural and industrial development to import and export promotion. By 1967, however, the number of these functional units had increased to 295, reflecting in part the increased volume of activity in these areas. Coupled with the centralization of government powers under Park, the strengthening of the bureaucracy began to create a military-dominated "bureaucratic authoritarianism" in South Korea. Manifestations of the changes included the increase in government employees from approximately 240,000 in 1960 to about 670,000 by 1986.

The Park government also initiated a huge and successful effort at upgrading Koreans' scientific, technological, and other professional knowledge and skills. For instance, the Korean Institute for Science and Technology (KIST) was established in 1968, not only to enhance advanced scientific and technological knowledge but also to encourage the dissemination of advanced industrial technology. Subsequently, the Korean Advanced Institute of Science and Technology (KAIST) was founded in a campuslike setting as a teaching institution. The government then actively engaged in recruiting Western-educated, mostly American-trained scientists, paying them competitive salaries and subsequently providing them with modern living quarters as well. A number of similar institutions such as the Korea Development Institute (KDI), which also recruited numerous economics Ph.D.s, again mostly American educated, were introduced and joined the institutional "brain trust" behind the "intensified" economic growth in South Korea.

An economic take-off. South Korea became a beehive of activity shortly after the announcement of the ambitious five-year plan, which gave an unaccustomed surge of hope to Koreans that their country's economic life would soon improve. It was in this milieu that the military, the only group that clandestinely organized a well-financed political party while all civilians were barred from any political activities, suddenly called for presidential elections on October 15, 1963. The constitution had once again been revised on December 26, 1962, to make the presidency stronger than ever before, overshadowing the cabinet and the legislative and judicial branches. Immediately before the election Park retired from active military status and became a "civilian" presidential candidate supported by a new political party that was throbbing with youthful energy.

Predictably, Park was the winner over Yun Po-sŏn, the ceremonial president of the Second Republic, but by a paper-thin margin, 42.6 percent to 41.2 percent. Thus began the military-dominated Third Republic with an elected president, albeit a minority president. The Park government regained legitimacy, but on a very narrow base. The need to enlarge that base through rapid economic growth was clear. Park's "marching orders" in the form of successive five-year economic plans issued forth, and South Korea was transformed into a mobilized workplace. A regimented, "Confucian," and paternalistic "Korea, Inc." was born. Slowly and then noticeably—some say miraculously—the Korean economy "took off"[10] by the

---

[10] W. W. Rostow, *The Stages of Economic Growth*, 3d ed. (Cambridge, UK: Cambridge University Press, 1990), pp. 5–17.

Former Major General Park Chung Hee, as he narrowly defeated Yun Po-sŏn, former President of the short-lived Second Republic in the presidential election of October 15, 1963. (The U.S. National Archives)

mid-1960s, thanks in part to favorable external conditions, including a wide-open American market, and gathered momentum that lasted into the 1970s. Per capita GNP skyrocketed from $82 in 1961, the year of the coup, to $1,644 in 1979, when Park was shot to death.

The main policy features and stages of the Park government's direct involvement in pushing rapid economic growth could be summed up as follows[11]:

Active governmental involvement in the economic sphere from the beginning;

Heavy emphasis on externally oriented growth from about the Second Five-Year Plan period (1967–1971);

Concentration on heavy and chemical industries in the Third Plan period (1972–1976);

[11] John Kie-chiang Oh, *The Dilemma of Democratic Politics with Economic Development in Korea* (Seoul: Korea Development Institute, 1990), pp. 8–38.

During the Third Republic headed by President Park, the Korean economy expanded rapidly under a policy of export-led growth. The Gold Star company was an early leader in Korea's electronics industry, which experienced conspicuous growth in international and domestic markets. (The Korean Information Center)

Emphasis on high-tech development from the Fourth Plan period (1977–1981); and

Legal and political support for cost efficiency, including low wages.

President Park was fiercely determined to achieve economic plan goals and to take full political credit for that achievement. As the Korean economy began taking off, in the mid-1960s, Park and his extensive public relations machine made every effort to highlight Park's heroic role in it. Wearing the requisite white gloves or hard hat, he occupied center stage in innumerable and well-staged ribbon cuttings and openings of new bridges, highways, and other public works projects. However, if Park and his ardent supporters, including KCIA, which was heavily involved in domestic political manipulations, expected a landslide victory in the 1967 presidential election, they were mistaken. Yun Po-sŏn, the figurehead president of the Second Republic whom Park's troops had violently overthrown, managed to garner some 40.9 percent of the popular votes cast, against 51.4 percent for Park, who had all the advantages of an incumbent and used them to the maximum degree. Park's victory margin was slightly more than one million votes out of more than eleven million total votes cast. There were four other "civilian" candidates who, together, received nearly one million votes. Speculations persisted whether the KCIA stealthily encouraged and financed the candidacy of these civilians to divide voters, who still questioned the legitimacy of the Park regime despite the tangible economic benefits they enjoyed.

The *Yusin* (Revitalization Reform) and Dictatorship

Having held power for some ten years, Park's obsession with the presidency was still boundless when he won his second four-year presidential term in 1967 at age fifty. About half the electorate supported him, thanks to his government's economic successes; he continued to be lionized by his blindly loyal and totally subservient lieutenants. While maintaining a presidential public image, Park was an absolute military dictator to these subordinates, who always addressed him as "Your Excellency" and jumped at his slightest command, day or night. The chief of the presidential secretariat, the head of the presidential bodyguards, the director of the KCIA, and a small number of special assistants personally anointed by Park formed an absolute and extraconstitutional power center in Korea. As the middle-aged Park could not imagine anything better for himself than the powerful presidency, his underlings' positions, prestige, and wealth in turn depended on Park's presidency. Together they convinced themselves that Park was the only leader in Korea who could sustain economic growth and also maintain national security thanks to his military experience. Pro-Park members of the National Assembly were pressured to initiate moves to eliminate the constitutional limitation on the presidency to two terms by August 1969, just as Rhee and his supporters had done in November 1954, only to be ousted from office by the massive student uprising of April 1960.

Having removed the term limitation on the presidency, Park was more determined than ever to overwhelm his civilian opposition in the 1971 election by whatever means necessary. All the coercive or persuasive powers of the KCIA, then headed by the most notorious and brutal director, Kim Hyŏng-uk, and the nationwide network of "anti-Communist" or other progovernment and neighborhood organizations were to be totally mobilized in support of the Park candidacy down to the lowest level. By 1971 all military commanders were loyal Park supporters, as were police chiefs across South Korea. Park's campaign war chest was limitless, as he was known to have collected astronomical amounts of slush funds from large industrial and business conglomerates that could benefit directly from political favors, including defense and public work contracts, low-interest loans, and import–export and other licenses.

Kim Dae-jung candidacy. Against this formidable incumbent, Kim Dae-jung, then forty-six, emerged as the opposition candidate of the New Democratic Party. He had been one of the two most persistent and courageous proponents of democracy in Korea (the other being Kim Young Sam), excoriating military-dominated authoritarianism since the coup led by Park. As Park's dictatorial patterns even as an elected president became increasingly visible and unbearable, Kim Dae-jung's anti-Park and antidictatorship rhetoric escalated and consequently attracted a more "progressive" or "radical" following than Kim Young Sam, who remained relatively moderate. Soon Kim Dae-jung's detractors accused him of "pro-Communist leanings"—a fatal flaw in a post-Korean War South Korean politician. For this reason, it was widely believed that Park preferred to run against Kim Dae-jung, who could be depicted by Park's powerful propaganda apparatus as pro-Communist in the divided peninsula.

Park ran an extremely well-financed campaign, boasting of economic attainments under his rule and highlighting uncertain international environments, while warning against voting for a man with "uncertain ideological leanings." Three minor candidates also ran, but with no hope of winning the race, merely dividing anti-Park votes. Again it was speculated that some of these minor candidates were encouraged and financed by the KCIA. When the votes were tallied, Park had won 53.2 percent and Kim 45.3 percent, with a winning margin for Park of some 947,000 votes of about twelve million total votes cast. The margin was narrower than that in the 1967 contest with the aging Yun, who had lost by some 1.2 million votes. In his victory Park was incensed, and the power elite around him alarmed. It was evident that there was a large and stubborn group of voters opposed to military-dominated authoritarianism despite the vaunted economic growth.

Park himself initiated a series of moves to ensure that he would never again face a popular election to remain president. He apparently decided to use the sense of uncertainty in South Korea regarding national security for domestic political purposes. International developments that contributed to the sense of uneasiness in Korea included the 1969 Nixon Doctrine, which essentially advocated an Asia-for-Asians policy, and particularly the notification a year later that a U.S. combat division, a third of the American troop strength there, would be withdrawn by 1971. This came at a time when news from Vietnam was unnerving many Koreans.

Suddenly martial law was declared throughout the country on October 17, 1972. The National Assembly was dissolved. Political parties were banned. All colleges and universities—the bastions of opposition to arbitrary and undemocratic measures—were closed. Park stated that these moves were necessary to eliminate the conditions fostering "disorder and inefficiency . . . and to develop the free democratic institutions best suited for Korea."[12] A drastically amended constitutional draft was endorsed by an emergency cabinet meeting, making it possible for Park to prolong his presidency indefinitely through an indirect presidential election by the newly created National Conference for Unification (NCFU), to be chaired by Park himself. The conference was to consist of 2,359 "non-partisan deputies" from small districts that could be readily controlled by the ruling groups. Moreover, the president was empowered to nominate one-third of the National Assembly members for election by the NCFU, and also to dissolve the Assembly whenever he deemed it necessary. The new constitution was approved by a national referendum conducted on November 21, while the country was under martial law, and was promulgated as the so-called *yusin* (revitalizing reform) constitution before martial law was lifted on December 13, 1972. Many called these events the second, "bloodless" coup executed by Park.

Even though Park was properly elected by popular vote until 1971, his presidency had been praetorian and caesaristic and his tenure after the imposition of the *yusin* rule in 1972 became increasingly more tyrannical and vengeful. One incident illustrates this point. From all accounts, Park hated with a passion his vocal civilian opponent, Kim Dae-jung. Park had defeated Kim in the 1971 presidential contest by an unimpressive margin, leading him to fear that he might lose a future election and the presidency. But the paranoia of the tyrannical regime did not stop with the drastic political–institutional changes of the "revitalizing reform." Kim Dae-jung, by 1971 a sworn nemesis of Park, was kidnapped August 8, 1973 from a Tokyo hotel by KCIA agents, who planned to dispose of Kim somewhere between Japan and Korea. It turned out later that the Japanese police had learned about the abduction shortly after the ambush in the hotel, and the American CIA was notified. The American ambassador in Seoul, Phillip Habib, rushed to the Korean presidential mansion and bluntly told Park Chung Hee that the United States government wanted Kim back alive. Five days after the kidnapping, a bruised and drugged Kim was abandoned on the street near his Seoul home.

A Nation Transformed and the Middle Class

It was undeniable that Park had turned into a crass military dictator; it was also indisputable that in large measure he personally had led the economic growth in South Korea. Once he had secured his power base after the suc-

---

12 *Tong-A Ilbo*, 18 October 1972, p. 1.

cessful coup he had become a hands-on economy president. Following the adoption of a policy of an export-led growth from the second five-year plan period, 1967 to 1971, Park personally presided over monthly export promotion meetings. At these meetings Park heard reports and suggestions from business leaders and provided instantaneous solutions to problems attributable to bureaucratic red tape and made decisions on resources allocations to promote exports. Park also awarded prizes at widely publicized and frequent ceremonies to leaders of major enterprises that achieved or exceeded export goals, and these leaders—obviously moved by such presidential recognition, which would have been unthinkable under President Rhee—in turn delivered spirited exhortations to workers to produce and export more. Even while working the longest hours in Asia and receiving low wages, many of these workers were also caught up in the late 1960s and early 1970s in the pervasive mood of proudly accomplishing economic "miracles" for the first time in Korean history.

When South Korea was politically stabilized, managing successive presidential elections in 1963, 1967, and 1971 and showing signs of economic vitality, aswarm with low-paid but disciplined and productive workers and inexperienced but eager entrepreneurs, foreign capital began to flow into Korea. While the United States was gradually phasing out economic aid to Korea, Japan became the first major provider of an aid and loan package after the signing of the Japan-Korea Normalization Treaty in 1965. Such an agreement would have been unimaginable under President Rhee, who hated the Japanese passionately. As the government was extremely solicitous to foreign investors, legislating tax breaks for foreign investors and strike-free environments at enterprises with foreign capital investments, foreign investments began to trickle in at first, and soon became a veritable flood.

Park's presidential successor, General Chun Doo Hwan, was equally determined to succeed economically, even at the heavy cost of democratic rights of the people, particularly the workers and intellectuals. These former generals gave the nation its orders and most Koreans followed them for a quarter of a century, until the prolonged stresses of the headlong economic expansion under strict political regimentation became onerous and until many Koreans—particularly the workers—began to question whether the fruits of the spectacular growth were being distributed equitably. Meanwhile, it is an indisputable fact that the country realized unprecedented economic growth, as highlighted in part by the data in Table 1 on page 62.[13]

---

[13] It might be argued that the table could be divided into a number of parts, e.g., periods under presidents Park, Chun, Roh, Kim, and so on. However, the data are in a single table to show the larger picture and also that the economy appeared, to a large extent, to have acquired its own momentum during the period covered in the table.

Table 1. Selected economic indicators

Year	GNP (current prices) (in billions of won)	Per capita GNP (US$)	Export (in millions of $)	Economic growth rate (%)
1953	48.2	67	39.6	
1954	66.9	70	24.2	5.1
1955	116.1	65	18.0	4.5
1956	152.4	66	24.6	−1.4
1957	198.8	74	22.2	7.6
1958	207.2	80	16.5	5.5
1959	221.0	81	19.9	3.8
1960	246.7	79	32.8	1.1
1961	296.8	82	50.9	5.6
1962	348.6	87	54.8	2.2
1963	488.0	100	86.8	9.1
1964	696.8	103	119.1	9.6
1965	805.9	105	175.1	5.8
1966	1032.9	125	250.3	12.7
1967	1245.1	142	320.2	6.6
1968	1575.7	169	455.4	11.3
1969	2030.1	210	622.5	13.8
1970	2776.9	243	835.2	7.6
1971	3406.9	288	1067.6	9.1
1972	4177.5	318	1624.1	5.3
1973	5355.5	395	3225.0	14.0
1974	7564.5	540	4460.4	8.5
1975	10064.6	590	5081.0	6.8
1976	13818.2	797	7715.3	13.4
1977	17728.6	1008	10046.5	10.7
1978	23936.8	1392	12710.6	11.0
1979	30741.1	1640	15055.5	7.0
1980	36749.7	1589	17504.9	−4.8
1981	45528.1	1719	21253.8	5.9
1982	52182.3	1773	21853.4	7.2
1983	61722.3	1914	24445.1	12.6
1984	70083.9	2044	29244.9	9.3
1985	78088.4	2194	30283.1	7.0
1986	90543.0	2503	34714.5	12.9
1987	105629.8	3098	47280.0	12.8
1988	123579.2	4040	60696.4	12.2
1989	141794.4	4994	62377.2	6.7
1990	171488.1	5569	65015.7	9.0
1991	206681.2	6518	71870.1	9.1
1992	229938.5	6749	76631.5	5.0
1993	265517.9	7466	82235.9	5.9
1994	303772.6	8467	96013.2	8.4
1995	348284.3	10037	125058.0	8.7
1996	354854.1	10548	129715.1	6.9

Source: Compiled from Bank of Korea, *Kyŏngje t'ongge nyŏnbo* (Annual Economic Statistics) and Economic Planning Board, *Major Statistics of Korean Economy,* various volumes. (Numerous other indicators, such as import amounts, unemployment, exchange rates, and the like are also available in the sources cited.)

While it has been well established that the country paid extremely high political and human costs as Park and Chun resorted to extremely "undemocratic and extraordinary measures," it is undeniable that per capita GNP grew from less than $100 when the military coup was executed in 1961 to more than $10,000 by 1995. The Korean economy had grown remarkably, often at double-digit rates. In the process, the whole economic structure of the country underwent far-reaching transformations, as shown by the data in Table 2.

In 1961 Park wrote in his preface to the first five-year plan that "a majority of the working people" of South Korea were still engaged in agriculture. Approximately thirty years later, less than one-tenth were in "agriculture, forestry, and fishery," and the country had a primarily manufacturing economy with a burgeoning service sector. This transformation, with its heavy emphasis on growth through import and export, was accomplished while the "strong developmental state," headed by former generals who had made economic growth a primary basis for their legitimacy, played pivotal roles in planning, priority setting, resource allocation, protection, and assistance. A noteworthy but unsurprising fact from an annual examination of the foregoing data is that political disturbances and transformations had almost immediate and significant, albeit brief, economic repercussions. For instance, the economic growth rate was 3.8 percent in 1959 toward the end of the Rhee regime but dipped to 1.1 percent in 1960 when the student uprising toppled the government, only to rebound to 5.6 percent in 1961. The disruptions of the military coup in 1961 were reflected in a low 2.2 percent rate in 1962, only to rise to 9.1 percent by 1963. A sharp fluctuation came when Park was assassinated in 1979, also the year of the second oil shock, when the growth rate stood at 7.0 percent compared with 11.0

Table 2. Korea's economic structure

	1970	1980	1990
Agriculture, forestry, and fishery	26.0%	14.9%	8.7%
Manufacturing	21.2	29.7	29.2
Wholesale and retail trade, restaurants and hotels	15.7	12.7	12.9
Finance, insurance, real estate and business service	8.2	11.0	14.9
Transport, storage and communication	6.7	7.6	14.9
Electricity, gas and water	1.5	2.0	2.2
Mining and quarrying	1.3	1.3	0.6

Source: Economic Planning Board, *Major Statistics of Korean Economy 1996*, pp. 216–17.

In the early 1970s, the Korean economy expanded into heavy and chemical industries, including steel manufacturing and shipbuilding. The Hyundai Motor company was a leader in the mass production of automobiles for both foreign and domestic markets. (The Korean Information Center)

percent for the year before. It plummeted to -4.8 percent in the wake of Park's death and subsequent political turmoil, in the midst of the oil shock, to recover to 5.9 percent in 1981. The "democratic" transformation of 1987–1988 also immediately and significantly affected the growth rate, at 12.2 percent in 1988, sinking to 6.7 percent in 1989 and rising to 9.0 percent in 1990. It is thus apparent that the Korean economy has been almost immediately and visibly sensitive, in the short run, to political engineering and vicissitudes. Short-term effects of the Korean economy on politics were not as clear, as economic growth from the Third through Fifth Republics—from 1963 under Park through 1987 under Chun—failed to directly affect overall political orientation.

Another observable fact, from a different perspective, is that the Korean economy had been acquiring a momentum of its own in terms of medium- and long-term growth until very recently. Despite relatively short-term fluctuations occasioned by political turmoil, the economy adjusted itself to changing politics each time within a few years and resumed its growth until the late 1980s. The sheer volume of the economy had been expanding rapidly and tremendously, making some of the *chaebŏl* (conglomerates) world class, diversified, sophisticated, wealthy, and powerful. Many of them became more autonomous than when they had been struggling to take off and were tightly controlled and directed by the government. Consequently, the government–business relationship became symbiotic in the late 1980s.[14] It is still continuing to evolve as indicated by continual policy debates in the early 1990s over many pertinent issues including that of growth versus stability and equity.

Byproducts of the growth-first policy. After a generation of government-directed economic expansion, certain byproducts of forced growth had become increasingly more evident. Offshoots of the headlong "growth-first" policy included the imbalance among economic sectors, particularly between heavy and light industries; the inequitable distribution of wealth, which created an abysmal gap between rich and poor; the heightened tension between numerous workers and their employers, leading to frequent and acrimonious labor disputes; and lagging social welfare measures, particularly in housing and health care. Less tangible but equally important byproducts of the material growth-at-any-cost policy include rampant materialism, corruption, moral decay, and crime.

Because the government chose—often arbitrarily—the target sectors and industries for rapid growth, allocated capital and resources to these targeted industries, channelled policy-directed loans and credits, and favored large conglomerates to attain planned growth efficiently and rapidly, these decisions created a pronounced imbalance among industrial sectors. The imbalance became most evident after the "Pronouncement for Development of Heavy and Chemical Industries" was issued by Park in January 1973, largely in the name of self-reliant national defense. Mammoth *chaebŏl* emerged and overshadowed medium and small businesses, creating another kind of lopsided imbalance. Ten of twenty-seven private concerns in developing countries that made the Fortune 500 list in 1982, for instance, were Korean *chaebŏl*.[15]

The economic gap between employers and the working poor also grew. Because the export-directed Korean growth relied on state-sanctioned cheap labor that was barred from strikes in numerous industries with foreign investments, factory workers received extremely low wages, lower than those earned in Singapore or Taiwan—until very recently—let alone Japan. According to the Christian Research Institute on Social Issues in Korea, some 11 percent of single male workers, and about 59 percent of

---

[14] Eun Mee Kim, "From Dominance to Symbiosis: State and *Chaebŏl* in Korea," *Pacific Focus*, no. 2 (1998): pp. 105–21.

[15] Jene K. Kwon, *Korean Economic Development* (New York: Greenwood Press, 1990), p. 36.

single female workers earned less than what the Institute viewed as the minimum living wage in urban centers in 1984. The Gini coefficient index, which shows the degree of concentration of income, also indicated similar maldistribution, according to 1989 data published by the Economic Planning Board. Further, Korean workers labored an average of 54.7 hours a week in 1986, much longer than in Japan, Taiwan, or Singapore. At the same time, many of these workers could not afford adequate housing, which remained a major problem area in any consideration of social equity or fairness in a country where the population was still increasing at an annual rate of 0.97 percent in 1990, a drop from 1.99 percent in 1971. Health care was another Achilles' heel in Korean development. The rate of persons per available hospital beds, an indicator of health-care availability, was 215 according to Economic Planning Board data in 1990. This was much worse than the rates of 76 in Japan and 171 in the United States, but lower than the rate of 232 in Taiwan.

Emergence and growth of the middle class. Despite these imbalances and inequities, or in part thanks to them during the transitional periods, economic growth was sustained under another general-turned-president, Chun Doo Whan. While growth continued for a prolonged period, the nation was transforming gradually and on many levels. First, thanks to the traditional Korean eagerness for education, a large number of South Koreans were educated beyond the compulsory level. The number of middle and high school enrollees, for instance, jumped from about 802,000 in 1960 to 4,169,000 in 1980—a fivefold increase in twenty years. College-level enrollment also skyrocketed, from approximately 101,000 in 1960 to 602,000 in 1980, only to surpass the one million mark less than a decade later—an astounding tenfold explosion in thirty years. These figures were truly record shattering in Korean history, as well as in comparison with other nations.

Meanwhile, thanks to the combined effects of sustained economic, educational, and sociopolitical changes there emerged a phenomenon with significant long-term political implications. A large majority of Koreans began, from about the mid-1970s toward the end of the Park period, to identify themselves probably for the first time as members of the middle class.[16] The phenomenon continued to grow through the Chun period, despite the oppressive political practices of that regime. Historically, in many societies an educated middle class, unlike the uneducated impoverished classes, tends to have a sense of economic and political vested interest in the affairs

[16] A discussion of the middle class could come in the next chapter in conjunction with the "civil society" question. I decided, however, to study middle class issues here in connection with an examination of economic growth.

of society and sometimes discernibly liberal political values. A large-scale survey conducted by the respected daily paper *Dong-A Ilbo* in April 1987, at the end of the Chun period, reported that 76.7 percent of those interviewed defined themselves as members of the middle or lower-middle classes: 38.4 percent of the middle class and 38.3 percent of the lower-middle class.[17] Another comprehensive study conducted by the Social Science Research Center of Seoul National University in cooperation with a mass-circulation daily, *Hankook Ilbo*, in May 1987 reported that some 68 percent of 1,043 respondents identified themselves as members of the middle class.[18] Still another national opinion survey, "Social Class as Perceived by Respondents (1988)," released by the Economic Planning Board in 1989, indicated that 60.6 percent of respondents perceived themselves as members of the middle class; 21.7 percent as members of the upper-middle class; and 38.9 percent as members of the lower-middle class.

These percentages do vary somewhat, but it is remarkable that a large majority—about two-thirds according to two authoritative surveys—of South Koreans at the end of the Chun regime subjectively believed that they belonged to the middle class. How was the term, "middle class," defined? Objectively, as distinguished from the subjective feeling of belonging, according to the Economic Planning Board, a member of the middle class should meet the following criteria:

1. Family income is at least 2.5 times that of the legally defined minimum living cost;
2. Owns and lives in a separate house or an apartment or rents a house or an apartment on a long-term basis with a sizeable deposit to be refunded on vacating the property;
3. Is employed on a full-time basis or owns his or her business; and
4. Received high school or higher education.[19]

Obviously this definition leaves many questions unanswered, such as what constitutes family income in a society in which average family size was 4.3 people in the late 1980s. There was often more than one wage earner in a family and some, particularly female, workers earned less than living wages. Did such female workers themselves qualify as mem-

---

[17] *Dong-A Ilbo*, 4 April 1987. Cited in Wonmo Dong, "The Democratization of South Korea: What Role Does the Middle Class Play?" (Unpublished paper presented at the annual meeting of the Association for Asian Studies, Washington, D.C., March 17–19, 1989), pp. 10–11.

[18] Seoul National University, Social Science Research Center, *Hanguk ŭi chungsan ch'ŭng* (The middle stratum of Korea) (Seoul: Hanguk Ilbosa, 1987), p. 27. An additional 16 percent responded that they were leading a "reasonably well-off life."

[19] *Social Indicators in Korea* (Seoul: Economic Planning Board, 1988), p. 289.

bers of the middle class? The other criteria also begged clarification. For instance, could owning a house and renting an apartment be treated equally? Could a person with a high school diploma really qualify as a member of the middle class? Could the concept of "middle class" in Korea stand close scrutiny?

Evidently the term had been used quite loosely. For instance, the Economic Planning Board announced on January 25, 1989, that some 61 percent of the population had qualified in 1988 as middle-class citizens on the basis of income, education, property, and living standard. Only about two months earlier, on November 22, 1988, the same board had announced that 35 percent of the population was estimated to have belonged to the middle class in 1980. Even when one took into account that the Economic Planning Board was the key agency of the government that had been flaunting the benefits of economic growth to the citizenry, it was surprising that the size of the middle class was said to have nearly doubled in a mere eight years. This was but one incident of how loosely the "middle-class" figures were bandied about in Korea. However, even tough-minded scholars and organizations critical of the government's claims admitted that the size of the middle class had indeed expanded significantly. For instance, Professor Han Sang-jin of Seoul National University applied stricter "objective" criteria, including that of "the family income exceeding 75 percent of the government-reported average family income," and concluded that about 48 percent of the Korean population belonged to the middle class in terms of both subjective self-identification and objective criteria.[20] In recent years a veritable flood of literature on the growing middle class has appeared; Professor Han's percentage was near the low end. Certain other studies by organizations that have been habitually antagonistic toward the government and its claims of economic advancement gave even lower figures.

Nevertheless, as one had informal talks about the middle class with South Koreans who had no reason to exaggerate their socioeconomic attainment, it quickly became clear that many of them believed they were living "far better than ever before"; some flatly stated that they never dreamed they would be so well off. They stated that they belonged "at least to the middle class" economically, not only in terms of the traditional three basic needs of adequate clothing, food, and housing but also in such amenities as air conditioners, which they still use sparingly because the cost of electricity remains high, and even Korean-made private cars, which clog roads throughout the country. These were indeed spectacular improvements over what little they had during the austere days of the Rhee period, particularly the war-devastated 1950s. When compared with

[20] Pak Hyong-jun, "*Chungsan ch'ungron ŭl tasi saenggak handa*" (Rethinking about the Middle Class Thesis), *Wŏlgan Chungang* (August 1988): pp. 592–93.

those periods, in fact, most South Koreans felt positively rich materially.

Assessing the political values of the middle class was a far more difficult task than gauging some measurable economic indicators. A series of careful studies conducted by several social scientists and well-respected daily papers reported that the Korean middle class, like similar classes in other societies, understandably placed the highest premium on economic and political stability. This class also favored the gradual democratization of Korean politics; many members of the middle class in fact named democratization as their motive for political participation, such as attendance at political rallies and voting, according to various surveys conducted in 1987. Among them, an authoritative survey conducted by the Social Science Research Center of the Seoul National University deserves special attention here. According to the preface to *Hanguk ŭi chungsan ch'ŭng* (The Middle Stratum in Korea),[21] an important survey by the Center was conducted with the financial assistance of *Hankook Ilbo*, which claims the largest circulation among Korean newspapers. It was noteworthy that the survey was actually conducted in December 1986, the last year of the oppressively dictatorial Chun regime and several months before the "democratization declaration" by Roh Tae Woo, on June 29, 1987. A representative sample of 1,043 people in various parts of the country was designated; the survey was based not only on very detailed questionnaires but also on interviews by qualified interviewers chosen by a balanced team of university professors in different parts of South Korea. This survey found that some 68 percent of respondents identified themselves as members of the middle class. Some interesting findings included that these percentages of respondents nationally, from four different regions, agreed with the following propositions[22]:

96%   The constitution should guarantee the people's right to rebel against an undemocratic government.

87%   It is desirable to enhance human rights even at the cost of slowing the economic growth rate.

85%   The middle class has contributed to the development of the country.

83%   It is preferable to slow down the rate of economic growth for the sake of social stability and balance.

75%   The middle class is the central force for democratization.

72%   While the words of the middle class members are critical (of autocratic politics), their deeds fail to follow their words.

70%   Democratization increases the possibility of national reunification.

63%   My political influence is limited.

18%   Freedom of the press is guaranteed in Korea.

[21] Seoul National University, *Hanguk ŭi chungsan ch'ŭng*, p. 3.
[22] Ibid., pp. 74–245.

Interpreting responses to sixty-one propositions, including the above, Professors Han Wan-sang, Kwon T'ae-hwan, and Hong Tu-sung concluded that a hefty majority of the middle class showed "an ardent desire for democratization."[23] They pointed out that a large majority agreed with the "University Professors' Declarations" urging democratization of Korean politics, and that 73 percent supported the "Middle and High School Teachers' Declarations for Democratization of Education." The survey was taken in 1986, when the military dictator Chun was still in firm control of the country's politics while finishing his sixth year as president, which made the political content of the responses all the more remarkable. It is clear that the educated middle class gradually acquired a liberal political orientation even while presidents Park and Chun ruled the country as virtual dictators. Although the middle class grew rapidly thanks to the remarkable economic growth triggered and sustained by military dictators, it simultaneously became antidictatorial. The middle class as a whole was poised in 1986 to play an active role with its "deeds" in support of the democratization of Korean politics even at the cost of slowing the economic growth rate.

This inclination toward middle-class activism was a significant new phenomenon, as the class for nearly two decades had tended to be passive—sometimes conservative—in the sense that it valued its economic well-being and a political order that protected and enhanced its economic vested interests. This was probably why the growing middle class often watched, as bystanders, the numerous worker and student demonstrations against greedy entrepreneurs and oppressive regimes. Perhaps incidents of desperate workers' self-immolation, cases of strike busting, some torture incidents, and the abuse of the police forces such as the "Y. H. incident" in which the police brutalized female workers were isolated events to which the middle class could not respond. However, when the excessive use of power by arrogant conglomerates and by the government which always backed business and consequent massive turbulence threatened the stable economic order as a whole, the vested economic interest of the middle class was also threatened. This became the time for middle-class activism.

The politicized middle class. To learn the nature and the extent of middle-class participation in antigovernment moves it is useful to see what occasioned such events in the spring and summer of 1987. Two especially odious and tragic incidents occurring within six months of each other demonstrably incensed not only young students but also older members

23 Ibid., pp. 16–17.

of the middle class. The first was the widely reported "incident of sexual assault by police interrogators" of July 1986. Kwŏn Yŏng-suk, a former Seoul National University student, was allegedly hired as a factory worker after underreporting her educational credentials. It had been known that well-educated and militant reformers, many of them from middle-class backgrounds, were drastically falsifying their education levels in their applications for employment as factory workers—for example, a college graduate would purport to be a high school dropout—and, when hired, were engaged in the agitation and organization of less educated and generally passive female coworkers. Kwŏn was one such worker, and was arrested by the police. According to Kwŏn, while undergoing interrogation she was sexually assaulted by the police. Unlike other female workers who chose not to publicize sexual assaults in a society that often attaches a stigma to female victims, Kwŏn decided to expose the police violence. The public outcry was instantaneous in a country in which there had been long-simmering resentment of police arrogance and brutality.

Another shocking incident was the death by torture in January 1987 of Pak Chong-ch'ŏl, a student activist at Seoul National University, an elite institution with many students from middle-class backgrounds. Pak died while being interrogated by the police regarding his political connections. The incident was reported and although the authorities admitted the death, they initially attempted to portray it as an accident. When a medical examiner contradicted the authorities, at some risk to his own safety and career, outraged students demonstrated on the streets, but were largely contained by riot police. However, tensions continued to build as the government became increasingly more arrogant and as businesses under the one-sided protection of the government became patently greedy and exploitative. Student demonstrators were soon joined by large numbers of workers. Significantly, this time the citizenry clearly sympathized with the demonstrators. Some brought water to thirsty demonstrators and even joined the demonstrations.

Another major event that exposed the ruthless character of the authoritarian regime and the plight of some workers was the storming by riot police of the Seoul headquarters of the opposition National Democratic Party (NDP), led by Kim Young Sam, on August 9, 1979. Shortly before that date, the owner of the Y. H. Tading Company, a garment manufacturer and one of numerous textile and apparel producers who constituted an important segment in the export-oriented economic boom in the 1970s, fled to the United States with his company's liquid assets. Many garment workers in Korea then worked under sweatshop conditions. Female workers protested the unconscionable abandonment and demonstrated in the plants. True to its probusiness patterns, the government sent in the police and 200, mostly teenage workers were beaten mercilessly.[24] Desperate for a sympathetic hearing, some 190 workers fled to the headquarters of the opposition National Democratic Party and staged a hunger strike. In the middle of the night on the third day of the sit-in, 1,000 riot policemen stormed opposition party headquarters, beat the female workers with truncheons, and threw them bodily into waiting police vans. One worker was killed, and about 100 people, including members of the opposition party who were in the building, were wounded. Even for the haughty Park regime, the international media coverage of the so-called "Y. H. incident" should have been foreseeable, but the attacks were ordered nevertheless.

Kim Young Sam, the NDP leader whose headquarters had been stormed by the police, bitterly attacked the Park government for losing touch with the working people and for the bankruptcy of Park's moral authority to govern, and demanded that Park resign. Park's fury in return was unleashed in a hitherto unprecedented parliamentary move. While the police blocked opposition legislators from entering the National Assembly chamber, the pro-government assemblymen slavishly voted on October 4, 1979, to punish Kim by stripping him of his Assembly seat. As a result, on October 13, an event that the Park regime probably did not foresee occurred. All sixty-nine opposition assemblymen resigned their seats—an unprecedented event in the history of the Korean legislature. Political paralysis resulted. The floor of the National Assembly was the only arena in which criticisms of the Park government could be voiced. Now even that outlet was blocked.

The remaining arenas of opposition were university campuses and the streets. Protesting students who had hitherto been largely content to vent their frustrations by shouting slogans on their campuses now poured into the streets. The demonstrations spread to the southern port city of Pusan, the legislative district Kim Young Sam represented. Student riots began on October 15, two days after the mass resignation of the opposition legislators, and were initially contained by riot police to campuses. Suddenly some 1,000 students emerged at night in downtown Pusan and marched down the streets chanting antigovernment slogans and demanding that Park resign. What most outraged the Park regime was that a large number of presumably middle-class citizens spontaneously joined the demonstrating students, and together they battled with the riot police into the night, attacking police boxes and government buildings with rocks and firebombs. Rioting continued the following night, when scores of additional police boxes and vehicles were burned by at least 5,000 students and innumerable citizens.

True to form, the Park government declared martial law in Pusan early on October 18. Rioting then erupted in the nearby city of Masan, where police stations and other government buildings were assaulted by howling students and citizens. No sooner had the government clamped a "gar-

[24] Ogle, *South Korea*, p. 92.

rison decree" on Masan in an attempt to contain antigovernment violence in the Pusan–Masan area than the unrest spread to Seoul, Taegu, and Ch'ŏngju in central Korea. The situation was reminiscent of the eve of the mammoth student uprising of 1960 that had toppled the Rhee regime.

The assassination of Park. It was under these circumstances that Park called a dinner meeting on October 26 in a cozy dining room in the KCIA annex in the compound of the presidential mansion. The dinner was hosted by Kim Jae Kyu, KCIA director, and attended by Park and his chief bodyguard and confidant, Ch'a Chi-ch'ŏl, and the head of the presidential secretariat, Kim Ke-wŏn. At that time in Korea, when government institutions and laws meant very little, these were arguably the four most powerful men. As was often the case, attractive females—that evening a model and a singer—were seated on both sides of the president.

Ch'a was an extremely boorish former soldier who had been at General Park's side when he executed the 1961 coup. Park had not only appointed this man chief of the powerful presidential security guards in 1974, but also was increasingly dependent on him for political advice; it was believed that Park was acting on his advice when the nighttime attack on the opposition party headquarters was ordered. It was inconceivable that an onslaught by one thousand helmeted police could be launched against the opposition party building without explicit authorization by Park himself—an incident that spoke volumes about the mindset of the president and his probable thoughts on rioting students and citizenry even as he dined. Kim Jae Kyu and Kim Ke-wŏn were hardly soft-spoken doves. Kim Jae Kyu had been Park's classmate at the Korean officers' candidate school, a former lieutenant general who was handpicked by Park to head the KCIA. Seemingly mild-mannered Kim Ke-wŏn, too, was a four-state general, and also an exdirector of the KCIA—a sure sign that he was trusted implicitly by Park. However, it was widely believed that in the late 1970s Park was listening more to the likes of Ch'a than the two Kims.

When the dinner began, Ch'a lambasted Kim Jae Kyu for his failure to foresee the Pusan–Masan situation and being "soft" on demonstrators. Ch'a then reportedly demanded that tanks be dispatched to the Pusan–Masan areas to mow down demonstrators. In a stunning move, the KCIA director suddenly shot Ch'a and then Park at point-blank range, killing them both. As prearranged, KCIA men outside the dining room shot and killed four presidential guards and wounded and disabled a fifth before they could respond. This, then, was the bloody end of the man who had led the 1961 military coup. His ambition to be a life-term president was shattered seven years after imposition of the *yusin* rule, ending the Fourth Republic. It was not the demonstrators who killed Park, but his handpicked security chief, who was at the apex of the power structure, completely separate from all other institutions and the people.

✷

CHAPTER 4

The Usurpation of Power and the Demand for Democratization, 1979–1987

After President Park was killed amidst fierce and sustained antigovernment demonstrations, Ch'oe Kyu Ha, a career diplomat and bureaucrat, became acting president of the transitional government. Ch'oe was Park's prime minister at the time the first assassination of the chief executive in contemporary Korea occurred. The nation was in profound shock, and an emergency cabinet meeting of the transitional government declared martial law over most of the country, excluding Cheju Island, and appointed the army chief of staff, General Chŏng Sung Hwa, martial law commander.

Even under martial law, however, there arose a strong expectation and long pent-up demand that the country would be freed from the grip of harsh authoritarianism and would reestablish a "democratic" government, as had been envisioned by the original constitution in 1948. For the first time since the imposition of *yusin* rule in 1972, public opinion surveys were taken, in December 1979. These surveys indicated that a vast majority of the people, some 73 percent of those interviewed, clearly favored far-ranging political reforms and "democratization" of the government. Concretely, respondents favored a direct popular election of the president, whose powers should be curtailed; enhanced authorities for the legislature and the judiciary to check presidents who become overly powerful; and a system of local autonomy—all to be accomplished within six to nine months.[1]

[1] *Tong-A Ilbo*, 1979, December 25, 3 and 7 January 1980.

In a special announcement on November 10, 1979, Acting President Ch'oe declared that the constitution would be amended "to promote democracy" and that a new election would be held under the amended constitution. "Emergency decrees" that had been issued by the Park regime, mostly so it could stay in power, were revoked, and the civil rights of Park's rivals, including former president Yun Po-sŏn and ex-presidential candidate Kim Dae-jung, were restored. Also restored by February 1980 were the civil rights of several hundred professors who had been fired from their posts for opposing the Park regime or for not collaborating with it in controlling antidictatorship students, religious leaders whose rights had been stripped for the same reasons, journalists who had been critical of the military dictatorship, and students who had been arrested for demonstrating against Park. These events created the euphoria that was known as the "Seoul spring."[2] Kim Young Sam, then head of the National Democratic Party, called for a complete dismantling of the *yusin* system decreed by the Park regime and a thorough democratic reform of the government. The National Coalition for Democracy and Unification, formed by Kim Dae-jung and other opposition leaders, also demanded rapid democratization of political processes and the government and bitterly criticized Ch'oe for attempting to work under the old *yusin* system.

The "12.12 Coup." All these actions, however, turned out to be mere shadow boxing. The real seizure of power—largely behind the scenes and under cover of darkness had already occurred when a couplike seizure of power occurred within the military, the locus of naked power in Korea, on December 12, 1979. The "12.12 coup" was led by Major General Chun Doo Hwan.[3] Chun headed the Defense Security Command, one of the interlocking intelligence structures Park, in his increasing paranoia, had established to protect himself and his administration. It was a supreme irony that Park was killed by his handpicked KCIA director, the nerve center of these structures, and that the Defense Security Command, another of the interlocking organizations, was then given the task of conducting the official inquiry into the assassination. Following some "intensive investigations" on December 7 General Chun quietly called General Roh Tae Woo, commander of the Ninth Army Division, to Seoul and told him that army chief of staff and martial law commander Chŏng, their military superior, would be arrested and charged with complicity in the assassination of Park Chung Hee.[4] After

---

[2] Kim Sam-ung, ed., *Sŏulŭi pom minju sŏnŏn* (The Democratic Declarations during the Seoul Spring) (Seoul: Ilwŏl sŏgak, 1987), pp. 14–56.

[3] Ch'oe Po-sik, "Che-o konghwakuk chŏnya: 12.12 p'yŏn" (The Eve of the Fifth Republic: The 12.12 Phase), *Wŏlgan Chŏson* (May 1996): pp. 497–631.

[4] *Silrok: Ch'ŏngwadae* (Veritable Records: The Blue House), ibid., p. 175. *Hankook Ilbo*, 24 August 1994, p. 8.

nightfall on December 12, several thousand troops from units commanded by officers belonging to an extensive secret network within the army over-powered the armed guards at the official residence of General Chŏng, ar-rested him, and quickly occupied the Defense Ministry and Army head-quarters. Chŏng was formally charged with complicity with Kim Jae Kyu in the assassination of Park. Kim was subsequently executed.

The *Hanahwoe* (One Association)

The successful 12.12 coup by General Chun, who subsequently estab-lished the Fifth Republic, as well as major events in the Sixth Republic un-der General Roh, cannot be adequately explained without a brief exami-nation of an extraordinary subterranean network within the Korean army. In retrospect, if Park's most significant accomplishment was economic de-velopment, one of his most pernicious evils was the privatization of mili-tary–political controls, with Park at the epicenter. The first military coup of 1961, personally led by Park, was spearheaded by a coterie of the eighth graduating class of the Korean Officer Candidates School. Specifi-cally, a group of lieutenant colonels was linked to General Park through Park's nephew-in-law, Lieutenant Colonel Kim Jong Pil, an intelligence officer. When Park's military coup succeeded in 1961, it was Kim Jong Pil who quickly organized and became the first director of the KCIA, one of the very first organizations launched by Park's military junta, ostensibly for national security but in fact for internal political surveillance and con-trol in the maintenance of the military regime. The KCIA was created on June 10, 1961, less than a month after the May 16 coup and just before the next most important institution, the Economic Planning Board, was launched. The powerful KCIA was a public institution, though its opera-tion and budget remained hidden.

Toward the end of 1961 a completely private organization within the army, the *Ch'ilsŏngwoe* (Seven Star Association), was organized. Captain Chun Doo Hwan, a very early and fanatical supporter of Park's coup, headed this secret organization. By March 1, 1964, the organization had changed its name to the *Hanahwoe* (One Association).[5] In the beginning, the *Hanahwoe* was composed of a small clique of the first graduating class from the regular four-year Korean Military Academy (or the eleventh class from the inception of the military academy). Captain Roh Tae Woo, Chun's military academy classmate, was one of the founding members of the secret association. The other charter members included eight captains,

[5] Wŏlgan Chosŏnbu, *Pirok: Hangukŭi Daet'ongnyŏng* (Hidden Records: Presidents of Ko-rea) (Seoul: Chosŏn Ilbosa, 1993), pp. 296–97.

Kim Bok-dong, Chŏng Ho-yŏng, Ch'oe Song-taek, Kwŏn Ik-hyŏn, Son Yong-kil, No Chong-ki, Pak Kap-ryong, and Nam Chung-su.

Thus began clandestine but regular meetings of the *Hanahwoe* at the Seoul home of Chun Doo Hwan.[6] Roh Tae Woo was always present as Chun's righthand man. This association, with Chun's and Roh's class-mates from the military academy as the nucleus, secretly and systemati-cally recruited ambitious and bright army officers, mostly from the Yŏng-nam (the Kyŏngsang provinces) area, where Park, Chun, and Roh had been born. The organization cautiously expanded by recruiting carefully screened cohorts from each graduating class of the military academy, down to the twenty-third class (counting the Chun and Roh class as the eleventh). In an army that had not fought a war since 1953 but had wit-nessed the quick and seemingly easy capture of the government by Park, the association gradually became an ambitious secret army within the army. Members swore absolute allegiance to one another above all else, and also that anyone betraying the group's secrecy and allegiance would be meted out "subhuman treatments." In lieu of any explicit mission statement, given the secret nature of the group, the association became a mutual promotion group with underlying political ambitions. The mem-bers shared politically sensitive intelligence, as well as information on promotions and assignments, and gradually controlled numerous key posts at many working levels of the army.

The private group was energized when Chun became chief of the Per-sonnel Section of the KCIA and moved to protect secret association mem-bers from criticism and unfavorable performance evaluations. Further-more, Chun actively played the role of middle man between the highest-ranking officers and *Hanahwoe* members. Chun, who had served as an aide-de-camp to Park when he was head of the military junta, con-vinced Park that he was his most trustworthy follower. Park was con-stantly on guard against the possibility of a military takeover that would oust *him*, having unleashed just such a force himself. Even Kim Jong Pil, his loyal nephew-in-law and director of the KCIA, his closest confidant in planning and executing the 1961 coup, did not escape his paranoia. When Kim appeared to be on his way to becoming too powerful, Park estab-lished the Capital Garrison Headquarters largely to defend himself and his regime, and eased Kim out of the KCIA directorship. Park sought to create a more private and personally dependable defense network within the army. Therefore, it should not be surprising that Park soon became the ultimate patron of the *Hanahwoe* through a few trusted army generals, in-cluding General Yun Pil-yong, capital garrison commander, who served

6 Song Ui-sŏp, "Dakyumentari Hanahwoe" (Documentary: The One Association), *Chugan Hanguk,* 1 June 1993, p. 29.

as the invisible "godfather" of the *Hanahwoe*. Yun, too, was later disgraced when Park was led to believe that his garrison commander harbored political ambitions.

Those in the *Hanahwoe* in fact had two distinct chains of command: the regular military command and the *Hanahwoe* chain—a pattern somewhat comparable to the dual chains that a government official who was also a member of the Communist Party had in some countries. The *Hanahwoe* chain acquired increasingly more vital significance to the members, and it remained to be seen which command would reign supreme if the regular military command conflicted with the secret society's directives. Chun, the prime mover of the *Hanahwoe*, had begun his manipulations almost immediately after the 1961 coup by engineering an appointment for Roh as intelligence officer of the counterintelligence unit of the KCIA. The bond between Chun and Roh became inseparable as both rose steadily in army rank. Roh succeeded Chun five times in a series of key posts—an amazing fact that is not explainable without the *Hanahwoe* connection. Meanwhile, hundreds of secret society members thrust their tentacles up and down the military, always promoting one another's advancement in the army and quickly snatching up the best assignments for *Hanahwoe* members.

By 1979, when a power vacuum was suddenly created with Park's assassination, the *Hanahwoe* was powerful enough to play the central role in the brutal seizure of power by Chun Doo Hwan. Falsely alleging that General Chŏng Sung Hwa, army chief of staff and commander of martial law, had conspired with Park's assassin, officers belonging to the *Hanahwoe* ordered their armed units to a surprise attack on the martial law commander's official residence on the evening of December 12 and arrested their superior. Chun's stern dictate to all members of the organization was to follow his orders only, disobeying all orders from the regular chain of command. Chun and the *Hanahwoe* cabals then tricked and lied to those unit commanders who did obey the regular military chain of command and thus prevented the mobilization of troops to thwart the seizure of power by Chun. Several "loyalist" unit commanders were invited to a well-inebriated dinner party at a Seoul restaurant immobilizing those present and their units for a few crucial hours of military operations to seize power.

The 1979 coup and the Combined Forces Command. Under cover of darkness, the coup troops then forcibly occupied the Army headquarters and the Ministry of National Defense, both of which were confused and in disarray. In addition to Roh Tae Woo, commander of the Ninth Division, the leaders of the 12.12 coup included Brigadier General Paek Un-taek, commander of the Seventy-first Security Division; Major General Pak Chun-byŏng, commander of the Twentieth Division; Colonel Chang Se-dong, commander of the Thirtieth Guard Unit of the Capital Garrison Command; Colonel Hŏ Hwa-pyŏng, chief secretary of the security command; and many others.[7] It took some 7,500 troops to accomplish the coup within the military. Compare that to the 1,400 soldiers needed by Park Chung Hee in 1961 to overthrow the Chang Myŏn government, which constitutionally commanded what was then the fourth largest standing army in the world. A key actor in the 12.12 blitzkrieg, second only to Chun Doo Hwan, was none other than Roh Tae Woo, commander of the Ninth Army Division, then strategically stationed near Seoul. At the telephoned request of his *Hanahwoe* chief Chun, Roh promptly dispatched the crack Twenty-ninth Regiment of his division with tanks and armored personnel carriers, which quickly occupied the capitol building, among other places. Their menacing presence was immediately felt in the heart of the government district of Seoul. Clearly these troop movements were made against the regular Korean army command, which made some clumsy attempts at thwarting the well-coordinated and determined putsch led by Chun.

The Korean units involved in the 12.12 coup were moved without requisite notification to the commander of the American–Korean Combined Forces Command (CFC). When the CFC was created in 1978 to replace the United Nations Command (UNC), the mission of defending South Korea against external aggression was transferred from the UNC, which had existed since the Korean War, to the CFC. According to the "terms of reference" for the CFC, dated July 27, 1978, the commander in chief was to "exercise operational control (OPCON) over all forces assigned or attached to the command in the prosecution of assigned missions," but both the United States and the Republic of Korea retained "the national right of command, including the right to remove units from the CFC OPCON upon notification."[8] The CFC commander was an American general; the deputy commander was a Korean general.

When Major General Chun Doo Hwan executed a seizure of power on December 12, 1979, Korean military units, including elements of the Ninth Army Division commanded by Major General Roh Tae Woo, who was guarding the most critical area between Seoul and the military demarcation zone, were suddenly moved to Seoul without notification to the CFC. Naturally the CFC commander, General John A. Wickham, was incensed. This bitter displeasure was immediately communicated to Chun. With notable dispatch, Washington also delivered a "strong warn-

---

[7] *Hankook Ilbo*, 2 December 1995, p. 5; *Choson Ilbo*, 22 April 1996, p. 6.

[8] United States Information Service (USIS), "Backgrounder: United States Government Statement on the Events in Kwangju, Republic of Korea, in May 1980" (Seoul: Press Office, USIS, June 19, 1989): p. 5. Much of the agreement dealing with military operations remains classified.

ing" addressed to Chun for violating the CFC's operational control. A State Department warning was sent to Chun on December 14—less than two full days after his December 12 putsch—by U.S. Ambassador William H. Gleysteen. Chun ruthlessly pushed the consolidation of his dictatorial power against increasingly massive and fierce demonstrations by Korean students and opposition political leaders demanding a restoration of "democracy" even while the country was under partial martial law. However, when Chun made himself director of the powerful KCIA on April 14, 1980, the seizure of power by the self-proclaimed "new military" he headed was all but complete.

Frustrated, General Wickham attempted in vain to resign from his post in Korea. While Wickham was visiting in the United States from May 14 to 18 to "discuss the Korean situation" with his superiors, the "new military" authorities quietly notified the CFC on May 16 of their intent to remove the Twentieth Division, which had riot-control training from CFC OPCON. The CFC deputy commander, General Baek Sŏk Chu, quickly acknowledged the release notification.

The Kwangju Massacre (1980) and the Politics of Deception

Where these units would be used became clear as full martial law was declared on May 18, including on Cheju Island, and opposition leaders including Kim Dae-jung and Kim Jong Pil were arrested and Kim Young Sam was placed under house arrest. Once again colleges and universities were ordered closed and the National Assembly was suspended by the "new military" authorities. It was under these circumstances that students from some fifty-five universities and colleges together with citizens in many urban centers in mid-May staged, once again, massive street demonstrations against the so-called "new military" regime. The demonstrators decried the soldiers' trampling on promises of "democratic reforms" of the Seoul Spring.[9] Numerous opposition political and opinion leaders, including former president Yun Po-sŏn and "134 literati" issued public statements excoriating the antidemocratic moves of the "new military."

The most fierce and sustained street demonstrations took place May 18 in Kwangju, the capital of South Chŏlla Province, historically a bastion of popular protest against unjust and oppressive authorities. The May events in Kwangju were once again a manifestation of the recurring pattern of accumulated indignation of the "righteous" people erupting against extreme injustice and oppression. This pattern dated back at least

---

[9] Kim Sam-ung, *Sŏulŭi pom minju sŏnŏn*, pp. 174–271.

to the *Tonghak* uprisings, many of which occurred in the Chŏlla Provinces in the late nineteenth century, and was manifested again in, among others, the 1919 March First Independence Movement against Japan, the Kwangju Student Movement of 1929 against Japanese colonialism, and the "righteous" student uprisings that overthrew the Rhee regime in 1960. Kwangju was also the stronghold of unwavering supporters of Kim Dae-jung, the most unswerving nemesis of dictatorship and a favorite son of the Chŏlla Province. With the imposition of military dictatorship by Park Chung Hee, particularly after the so-called *yusin* (revitalizing reform) decree in 1971, there occurred an almost unbroken series of violent resistance movements against the military dictatorship in many urban centers of South Korea. Kwangju was often a visible leader in these protests.

This "tradition" was continued in mid-May in Kwangju, home to some 730,000 residents in 1980. The Chŏlla Provinces had produced a fair number of prominent political and government leaders in the first decade of the republican government. Kim Sŏng-su, a highly respected educator and founder of the Korea Democratic Party in 1946 and briefly vice president under Rhee, for example, hailed from a Chŏlla Province. However, the area had clearly been discriminated against economically ever since the advent of the military-led rule headed by Park Chung Hee, from the Kyŏngsang region, which benefited economically by the introduction of numerous industrial projects. The fact that Kim Dae-jung, the most fierce opponent of the military dictatorship, was from the South Chŏlla Province only contributed to the military regime's anti-Chŏlla politics. Concretely, Park demonstrably kept Chŏlla people from high-level government or military positions, a practice that was continued under his successor, Chun.[10]

The educational center of a once well-to-do agrarian province, in Kwangju there were thirty-eight high schools, nine junior colleges, a teachers' college, two other colleges, and two universities, in total enrolling some 110,000 high school or higher-level students in 1979.[11] Students at Chŏnnam and Chosŏn universities, as well as those at the Kwangju Teachers' College, continued fierce antimilitary demonstrations on the streets near these schools, even after students in other cities ceased demonstrating in the face of the declaration of full martial law by the "new military."

The massacre. As troops attempted to disperse the students, paratroopers with fixed bayonets relentlessly pursued fleeing students into shops to which they fled and through back alleys into private homes and beat

---

[10] Sung Chul Yang, *The North and South Korean Political Systems* (Denver: Westview Press, 1994), p. 540.

[11] Chŏng Sang-yong, et al., *Kwangju minju hangjeng* (The People's Struggle for Democracy in Kwangju) (Seoul: Tolbege, 1990), p. 150.

them mercilessly with their riot-control clubs and rifle butts. Many students were left profusely bleeding or hauled away in military vehicles. The incensed citizens who witnessed this barbaric behavior poured into the streets to join the demonstrating students in response. On May 19 student demonstrations in Kwangju thus turned into a massive student–worker–citizen uprising. In solidarity, hundreds of buses and taxis formed the longest caravans Kwangju had ever seen; their drivers seemed to be attempting to demoralize the troops with their cacophony of blaring horns.[12]

When the howling waves of 100,000 students and supportive citizenry surrounded the provincial government building and packed Kŭmkang Street on May 21 the paratroopers opened fire at the demonstrators. Instantly there were bleeding bodies curled up on the pavement. Infuriated students, aided by bus and taxi drivers, fanned out to raid armories in Kwangju and several other towns in the province. Now armed, students occupied the provincial government building and declared Kwangju a city liberated from the military dictatorship of Chun Doo Whan. This was an unprecedented event even in historically volatile Kwangju.[13] Undoubtedly this was the most alarming frontal challenge to the so-called "new military" under Chun, who was determined to reestablish order and capture the presidency as quickly as possible. Kwangju had not been part of Chun's careful scenario in his capture of power. In time powerful brigades from the Special Warfare Command, the Seventh Paratroop Brigade, the Thirty-first Division based in Kwangju, elements of the Twentieth Division that had been removed on May 16 from CFC OPCON, and other reinforcement units completely surrounded Kwangju. While relentlessly continuing to tighten the encirclement, these unit commanders feigned efforts at negotiating with the Kwangju citizen leaders.

Chun Doo Hwan's wrath and impatience with Kwangju were made clear to General Chŏng Ho-yŏng, Chun's *Hanahwoe* cohort and special warfare commander, who personally directed military operations in Kwangju. In the predawn hours of May 27 units spearheaded by tanks and armored personnel carriers—and, some say, helicopters—indiscriminately unleashed their brutal and overwhelming power against Kwangju "democracy fighters." By all accounts, the Korean military engaged in a most barbaric carnage of Kwangju citizenry.[14] By the government's own

---

[12] Song Sŏn-te and Kim Pyŏng-u, interview by author, Kwangju, 19 June 1996.

[13] Chong Sang-yong, et al., pp. 215–16.

[14] *Kwangju Maeil* Chŏngsa 5.18 t'ukbyŏl ch'ŭichepan (The Special Reporting Team of the *Kwangju Maeil* (daily) for a Correct History of May 18), *Chŏngsa 5.18* (The Correct History of May 18) (Seoul: Sahwoe pyŏngnon, 1995), pp. 144–404. 5.18 Kwangju minjung hangjeng yujokhwoe, (The Survivors' Association of the May 18 Kwangju People's Struggle for Democracy) ed., *Kwangju minju hangjeng pimangnok* (A Memorandum on the Kwangju Peoples' Struggle for Democracy) (Kwangju: Mip'ung, 1995), pp. 53–123.

count, more than two hundred people were killed and thousands were wounded or arrested. Most think actual casualties were much higher.[15] Most of the identified dead were buried in a bleak and crowded cemetery on the hillside of Mangwŏl-dong, Kwangju.[16]

In many respects the Kwangju incident was the culmination of a long series of violent demonstrations by the people demanding the recognition of their basic democratic rights. The bloody incident occurred in Kwangju in part because the city had become a boiling point of long-simmering resentments of the military-led authoritarian rule that discriminated against the Chŏlla region, which, of course, had produced Kim Dae-jung. Kwangju erupted when a military usurper, Chun, was about to impose his iron rule over South Korea. Kwangju alone rose up while other cities became quiet upon the declaration of a full martial law. The Kwangju events represented the bloodiest massacre openly perpetrated as a full-scale military operation, coordinated for over a week, involving nearly 20,000 troops[17] against the South Korean citizenry and students by the South Korean military in peacetime Korea.

Thus the Chun regime began stained from the outset with the blood of the Kwangju citizenry. The Martial Law Command characteristically charged Kim Dae-jung, nemesis of military dictators, and twenty-three Kim supporters with conspiracy to violently overthrow the government. Kim—who, according to many detached observers, had struggled for decades to realize democratic politics—was characterized as a dangerous revolutionary "sympathetic to the Communist northern puppets" and a conspirator who "engineered the Kwangju turmoil," according to a military tribunal that summarily sentenced him to death.

The manipulations. What ensued were a series of astounding confusions and resentments occasioned by statements by American and South Korean officials and Machiavellian manipulations and outright deceptions orchestrated by the "new military." In an interview with a Korean National Assemblyman, U.S. Ambassador Gleysteen allegedly stated that the United States had "approved" the movement of the Twentieth Divi-

---

[15] Rev. Arnold Peterson, an American missionary who was in Kwangju during the uprising, wrote a diary-style account of the "Kwangju Democratic Uprising." He said that the death toll stood at 832, according to what he heard from "a Korean intelligence source." Peterson also insisted he witnessed military helicopters firing at the people indiscriminately. *Korea Herald*, 12 March 1995, p. 6.

[16] This author visited the cemetary, 20 June 1996. A new, spacious "hallowed ground" was consecrated in May 1997 at a nearby spot to rebury the remains of the "democracy fighters" in a properly dignified setting. Kim Young Sam's scheduled visit early in his presidency to the Mangwŏl-dong cemetery was blocked by angry Kwangju citizens, who recalled that Kim came to power by collaborating with Roh Tae Woo, Chun Doo Whan's handpicked successor.

[17] Chŏng Sang-yong, et al., *Kwanju minju hangjeng*, p. 218.

sion used to suppress the Kwangju rioters brutally, whereas the fact that the Twentieth Division had been removed from the CFC OPCON through a simple process of "notification" days before the incidents in Kwangju. Similarly, a U.S. Department of Defense spokesman stated on May 23, 1980, that the United States had agreed to release the troops from the OP-CON of the CFC.

Despite displeasure with Chun's new military, the highest U.S. authorities in Korea and the Carter administration were undoubtedly more concerned about immediate security matters than about the Korean people's democratic rights, though the latter concern was repeatedly expressed by Gleysteen in his private communications with Chun Doo Whan who neglected to report that to the Korean people. The Carter administration was concerned that the 1980 whole-scale demonstrations against the Chun authorities might lead to a situation similar to that in Iran. There the Shah had been forced to leave the country following violent and massive demonstrations despite a declaration of martial law, thus leading to the establishment in early 1979 of the Ayatollah Khomeini regime, which was decidedly anti-American. Ambassador Gleysteen reported to Washington that "at least 150,000 people (of Kwangju) [were] involved" in the anti-Chun regime demonstrations.[18] Though this figure might have been slightly exaggerated beyond the Korean estimate of 100,000, the danger of the Kwangju demonstrations' dislodging a de facto military regime in Seoul, and thereby creating a political and possibly a military vacuum, presumably appeared real to Washington. While moving the aircraft carrier *Coral Sea* toward Korean waters on May 23, the Carter administration, still smarting from the Iranian episode, quietly opted for relative stability and continuity under the "new military."[19] Alternatives were severely limited, once the Chun takeover was a fait accompli. Gleysteen told the Korean foreign minister that the U.S. government would recognize the Chun regime's efforts at restoring order in Kwangju and in preventing demonstrations in other areas, adding that the U.S. stance should not be made public, lest it create an impression that the United States was colluding with martial law authorities, which would in turn stir anti-American sentiment.[20]

[18] Tim Shorrock, "U.S. Knew of South Korean Crackdown," *Journal of Commerce*, 5 March 1996, p. 1A. Sharrock obtained declassified U.S. State Department and Defense Intelligence Agency documents under the Freedom of Information Act. The White House meeting on May 22 to discuss the Korean situation involved, among others, Secretary of State Edmund Muskie, Deputy Secretary of State Warren Christopher, Assistant Secretary of State for East Asian and Pacific Affairs Richard Holbrooke, National Security Advisor Zbigniew Brzesinski, and Secretary of Defense Harold Brown.

[19] Pak Sŏng-wŏn, "Miguk, sin kunbue kkulyŏ danyŏtta" (The United States was led around by the New Military), *Sin Dong-A* (May 1996): pp. 110–28.

[20] Ibid.

Subsequently, however, government-controlled radio in Kwangju broadcast that the United States had "approved" the dispatch of the troops to Kwangju, and that continued to be the gist of news stories appearing in the Korean media for weeks under martial law. When the United States made a public announcement on May 22 urging all parties involved to exercise maximum restraint and undertake a dialogue in search of a peaceful settlement in Kwangju, the Korean media did not report it. Although the Voice of America (VOA) broadcast it, VOA listenership among Koreans was limited, and the Korean media under martial law remained silent.

Shortly after the bloody Kwangju incident, General Chun himself told a meeting of Korean publishers and editors that the United States had been informed in advance of his December 12 seizure of power, his appointment as director of the KCIA, and the declaration of full martial law preceding the Kwangju massacre. The U.S. embassy declared that Chun's statement "simply was not true and Chun knew it."[21] The Associated Press reported the embassy's denial, but again it was not carried in the Korean press. Startled, Ambassador Gleysteen's press secretary visited with each of the publishers and editors who had met with Chun to correct the "disinformation," but yet again the Korean media under martial law did not print it.

What the Korean media highlighted instead were remarks attributed to General Wickham by a Korean reporter to the effect that the Korean people were like "lemmings" who should be led by a strong leader—by implication at the time, Chun. The fact was that John Wickham utterly detested Chun because Chun had surprised the American CFC commander by using Korean troops in executing a military coup in December 1979. Gleysteen was also credited with making the choice remark that demonstrating students, presumably including those in Kwangju who had been mowed down by Korean troops, were "spoiled brats."[22] Slogans of demonstrating students became "decidedly anti-American for the first time."[23] To make matters worse, even a highest-level communication was distorted by the Korean authorities. Jimmy Carter wrote to Chun Doo Hwan upon the latter's "election" as president by a rubber-stamp "electoral college" on August 27, 1980, and, while reconfirming the U.S. security commitment to Korea, stated that the political liberalization must take place in Korea and democracy should be quickly restored—points also made to Chun by Ambassador Gleysteen. However, the Korean

21 USIS, "Backgrounder," p. 24.

22 Donald N. Clark, "Bitter Friendship: Understanding Anti-Americanism in South Korea," in Korea Briefing, 1991, ed. Donald N. Clark (Boulder, CO: Westview Press), pp. 147–67.

23 Ogle, South Korea, p. 91.

media headlined a different picture: "Carter: Personal Message to President Chun Expresses Support for Korea's New Government" (*Dong-A Ilbo*) and "Security Commitment to Korea: The Major U.S. Policy" (*Joong-ang Ilbo*).[24]

To those who were growing increasingly embittered by what they perceived to be American support for the new regime, whose members' hands were "dripping with the blood of Kwangju students and citizens," the mot disturbing event was President Chun's high-profile visit with the newly inaugurated President Reagan at the White House on February 2, 1981, as Reagan's second foreign visitor.[25] Chun's triumphant visit to several American cities and with Reagan on the fifth day of his stay in the United States was carefully made into a huge media event in Korea, apparently to boost the aura of Chun's legitimacy. Few in Korea noted at the time the connection between this visit and the end of martial law on January 24 and the commutation of Kim Dae-jung's death sentence just two days before Chun had received the invitation to meet with Reagan.[26]

Actually, high-level efforts at saving Kim Dae-jung's life had been made in the summer of 1980 during what turned out to be the last months of the Carter administration. It was made known to American authorities by early fall 1980 that General Chun was anxious to be invited to Washington "not only to signify full regularization of U.S.–Korean relations but to give an aura of legitimacy to his new government."[27] As a quid pro quo for a Reagan invitation, Chun promised to commute Kim Dae-jung's death sentence, according to two former American ambassadors.[28] Ironically, General Chŏng Ho-yŏng, the special warfare commander some called the "butcher of Kwangju" for personally directing the massacre, was Chun's special envoy to Washington. Chŏng promised that Kim's life would be spared if Chun were to be invited by Reagan.[29] This trade-off remained discreetly under wraps at the time. Not surprisingly Kim Dae-jung's supporters were among the most outspoken critics of Chun's visit, which was publicized in Korea for weeks.

[24] Ibid., p. 25.

[25] Following Reagan's first foreign visitor on January 28, 1981, Prime Minister Edward Seaga of Jamaica.

[26] *New York Times*, 2 February 1981, p. A8.

[27] William H. Gleysteen, Jr., "Korea: A Special Target of American Concern," in *The Diplomacy of Human Rights*, ed. David D. Newsom (Lanham, MD: University Press of America, 1986), p. 98. Gleysteen was American ambassador to Korea from June 1978 to June 1981. The "new military" engaged in an all-out effort to arrange an official visit and even sent a special envoy to Washington, General Chŏng Ho-yŏng, Chun's confidant and commander of the special warfare command, which had played a key role in the Kwangju massacre. *Hankook Ilbo*, 7 February 1996, p. 8.

[28] Gleysteen, *Korea*, and James R. Lilley, in an interview with *Wŏlgan Chosŭn*, July 1988, p. 57. Lilley headed the American Embassy from November 1986 to January 1989.

[29] *Hankook Ilbo*, 7 February 1996, p. 8.

By most accounts the Fifth Republic, headed by Chun, was undoubtedly the most nakedly authoritarian regime on the whole in contemporary Korea. Chun himself was more consistently and brazenly heavy handed than his predecessor, Park Chung Hee, who at least showed some sensitivity to popular demand and the people's economic needs. Park was popularly elected until the *yusin* of 1972, when the presidential election system by direct vote was replaced by a system of election by a huge electoral college that could be readily manipulated by the ruling party. Also, Park could justifiably point to the spectacular economic growth in South Korea during his tenure. During that time the per capita GNP skyrocketed from $100 in 1963, when Park assumed the presidency, to $1,640 in 1979, when he was assassinated.

While the economy essentially maintained that growth rate during the Chun regime, which kept inflation under tight control, notoriously authoritarian and politically insensitive measures—hallmarks of a dictatorship—became common occurrences. For instance, the Legislative Council for National Security, an arbitrary creature of the "new military" that suspended the National Assembly, decreed the Press Law on December 26, 1980. That law in effect abolished press freedom by suddenly "merging" out of existence some two-thirds of the news media and leaving roughly the same proportion of journalists jobless.[30] Adoption on December 30, 1980, of "basic labor laws," including the Labor Union Law and the Labor Dispute Settlement Law, drastically curtailed workers' rights. When the workers went on strike to demand their fair share of the prosperous economy, the police put a stop to it. The government and its coercive forces regularly sided with business, particularly those enterprises in which foreigners invested heavily. Americans constituted the second largest and most visible group of investors, second only to the Japanese, who often hid behind Korean partners.

Antiauthoritarian politics as anti-Americanism. Antigovernment student and worker demonstrations increasingly became anticapitalist, antiforeign, and predictably anti-American. Almost in direct proportion to the intensifying dictatorial pressures of the Chun regime, the rhetoric of protestors became more and more desperate and radical. The degree of student and worker desperation in the early and mid-1980s was gruesomely demonstrated by some seventy incidents of self-immolation including some who jumped to their deaths from high buildings.[31] This mode of desperate

[30] Kim Tong-sŏn, "Palsimnyŏn ŏnron t'ong paehap naemak" (Inside the Mergers and Abolition of the Media in 1980), *Sin Dong-A* (September 1987): pp. 576–91.

[31] Kim Chong-ch'an, "Palsip nyŏndae pun-t'usin chasalcha dŭl" (Those Who Self-immolated or Jumped to Death in the 80s), *Sin Dong-A* (November 1987): pp. 385–403.

protest had not been unknown in Korea, but the scope now was unprecedented. "Down with the Chun Dictatorship!" and "Yankee Go Home!" became the twin battle cries, particularly after the Kwangju massacre. Clandestine "conscientization movements" were launched on college campuses, now imbuing activists with a neo-Marxist ideology calling for the complete restructuring of domestic society and denouncing the United States for dividing the Korean peninsula in the first place and then supporting dictatorial military governments, especially the Chun regime.

The radical student movement now began to coalesce around the *minjung* (roughly, the people) ideology, an eclectic blend of nationalism, Marxism, left-Catholic liberation theology, antidependency economic views, antiwar and antinuclear slogans, national reunification demands, and a Western European-style peace movement. The *minjung* ideology rested on two central tenets. It asserted, first, the Korea's problems stemmed from the "original sin" of the division of the country by the United States in August 1945, seldom recalling how the United States had in fact liberated Korea from the Japanese or why the United States proposed the thirty-eighth parallel as a temporary demarcation line to accept the surrender of Japanese troops. The ideology held that the division led to Korea's political, economic, military, and cultural "dependence" on the United States.

The second major tenet, flowing from that dependency, was that the successive United States–backed regimes that had ruled Korea since the founding of the republic were against the people (*minjung*), the nation (*minjok*), and democracy (*minju*).[32] Certainly not all young people and students believed in these ideas, but some 62 percent of eligible voters in Korea were between the ages of 20 and 39, and university students constituted some 2.7 percent of the total population of South Korea in the mid-1980s, compared with 2.0 percent in the United States, and 1.5 percent in Germany, where more vocational training is emphasized. Thus the *minjung* ideology resonated among a large number of students and the younger generation in Korea.

While students and other demonstrators battled against military dictatorship in Korea, the radicals among them in the 1980s made the United States *the* enemy, the villain behind the hated military regimes and the barrier to democracy and national reunification. Soon these students were forming alliances with alienated workers. This was the time when many radical students, disguising and underreporting their educational backgrounds, became factory workers to organize other workers. The spring of 1986 was a peak time in the radicalization of student activism and the rise of virulent anti-Americanism.

[32] Wonmo Dong, "University Students in South Korean Politics: Patterns of Radicalization in the 1980s," *Journal of International Affairs* 40, no. 2 (1987): pp. 233–55.

Predictably, the Chun regime became increasingly apprehensive about these radical student movements and progressively more oppressive, introducing a "Campus Stabilization Act" that was aimed at suppressing student movements. Equally predictably, the students became even more desperate and violent. A vicious action–reaction cycle set in. In the heat of such an escalating cycle, violence against American targets likewise escalated. The Chun regime did little to discourage anti-American expressions so long as they deflected and dissipated some antiregime fervor. For anti-American demonstrators, the United States was remote and could not punish them in any case, whereas the dreaded punitive arms of the Chun regime were proximate and swift. It was in this volatile atmosphere that the death of Seoul National University student Pak Chong-ch'ŏl at the hands of the police was revealed in January 1987. Pak died during an "interrogation" intended to reveal the whereabouts of fugitive Pak Chong-ŭn, the reported mastermind of a 1985 USIS library takeover. Massive demonstrations in 1987 with convulsively far-reaching consequences had their origins in an anti-American action that had taken place two years earlier. This revelation of police brutality incensed and galvanized students and the civil groups alike against the Chun regime, as had the discovery in April 1960 of the body of high school student Kim Chu-yŏl, a tear-gas shell embedded in one eye, did against the Rhee government.

"Civil Society" and Explosive Demands for Democratization

While the colossal political, military, and economic events in Korea were occupying the attention of many, there was growing simultaneously with the emergence of the sizeable middle class a significant social force. Just as the *Hanahwoe* network remained underground for nearly two decades, the growth of this social force was almost imperceptible at its beginning. The imposition in 1972 of the *yusin* system by Park provided the spark that led to a loose alliance among opposition political organizations, religious groups, intellectuals, students, workers, and—after the 1973 kidnapping of Kim Dae-jung by the KCIA—human rights advocates. These groups were fairly isolated and autonomous in their own spheres until the loose alliance among them began to form a nationwide campaign, the "One Million Signature Campaign for Constitutional Change," in December 1973. Catholic churches, headed by Stephen Cardinal Kim, who had acquired a respected national stature as a religious leader who had not been coopted by authoritarian regimes, held dozens of "prayer meetings for the nation" in 1974. The Myŏngdong Cathedral, atop a hill in central Seoul, where Cardinal Kim resided, had long been a recognized sanctuary for antidictatorship dissidents—students, workers, and strikers. Even martial law troops and riot police would not violate the sanctuary of the cathedral. Young Catholic priests formed the National Catholic Priests' Corps for Realization of Justice (NCPCRJ) in September 1974. Such groups as the Christian Youth Council for the Defense of Democracy, the Catholic Labor Youth, the Urban Industrial Mission, and the Korean Christian Academy also joined the antidictatorship alliance.[33]

Evidently Christians constituted an important group in the energized, autonomous, voluntary, and self-supporting "civil society" bound by shared values. The number of Christians in South Korea had been increasing rapidly, perhaps more so than in any other country at that time. In 1945 their numbers were only about 300,000 in the entire peninsula, but by 1974 that figure had exploded to about 4.3 million—3.5 million Protestants and 800,000 Catholics, roughly 13 percent of the total South Korean population.[34] Many Christians were better educated than the average Korean and many belonged to the politically conscious middle class, which was responsive to the catchwords, "the restoration of democracy." They also had organizations and networks that could be reinforced at least every Sunday.

The anti-*yusin* coalition, in which Christians played a significant role, issued the "Democratic Peoples' Charter" in 1975, the "Democratic Declaration to Save the Nation" in 1976, and the "March First Democratic Declaration" in 1978. These declarations failed to impress the dictatorial Park regime, but did encourage an increasing number of citizens to join the ever-growing number of voluntary citizens' organizations, enlarging and energizing civil society. Groups that had been hitherto indifferent to political problems, including professionals, white-collar workers, technicians, factory managers, independent businesspeople, and even low-ranking public bureaucrats, identified themselves with the goals of political democratization. Those were the goals advocated by the newly formed New Korean Democratic Party (NKDP), which became the largest opposition bloc in the National Assembly following the February 1985 elections. The NKDP was composed of the followers of the two best-known opposition leaders, Kim Dae-jung and Kim Young Sam, both Christians who had championed democratic reforms. A "grand alliance of civil society and political society against Chun's authoritarian regime was finally formed."[35]

Shortly after the shocking torture death by the police in January 1987 of Pak Chong-ch'ŏl, a Seoul National University student, a survey by Seoul

[33] Kim Sunhyuk, "Civil Society in South Korea: From Grand Democracy Movements to Petty Interest Groups?" *Journal of Northeast Asian Studies* (Summer 1996): p. 89.

[34] Nam Koon Woo, p. 74. The rapid increase has continued and many believe that more than 25 percent of the total population are now Christians.

[35] Kim Sunhyuk, *Civil Society in South Korea*, p. 91.

National University in May 1987 reported that 85.7 percent of the middle class wanted to protect human rights even at the cost of economic growth.[36] Massive demonstrations were sustained in response in many urban centers in the spring of 1987 against the brutally autocratic Chun regime. The demonstrators demanded "democratization" and "reform" of Korean politics and government, partly through sweeping constitutional amendments, because the 1972 *yusin* constitution with its "electoral college system" of indirectly electing the president had become the handmaiden of Park and Chun. For months, while the street demonstrators continued to battle the riot police, Chun himself appeared amenable to the constitutional amendment idea. On April 13, 1987, however, he set off a political bombshell. Chun announced that he was reversing his public pledge to amend the constitution to allow a direct, popular election to choose his successor. It became abundantly clear that Chun and his henchmen were determined to prolong a military-dominated regime by denying the people the right to elect the next president. Both the people's resentment and opposition politicians' despair were reaching a boiling point.

Chun invited some thirty top lieutenants of the ruling Democratic Justice Party to the presidential mansion on June 2 and revealed his decision to anoint Roh Tae Woo his successor, to be elected by the electoral college Chun controlled. The invited guests dutifully applauded the decision while a tearful Roh thanked his chief.[37] The ruling party held its party convention on June 10 and a remarkable 99 percent of the 7,309 party delegates rubber-stamped the Roh candidacy for an indirect election to the presidency. On that very day what has subsequently been called the "6.10 Struggle" began, led by a wide coalition of opposition and civil society groups collectively calling themselves the "People's Movement to Win a Democratic Constitution." The coalition demanded a constitutional amendment to allow a direct presidential election and a series of democratic reforms.

The people's march. Mammoth and often violent antigovernment demonstrations exploded almost simultaneously in Seoul and some twenty other cities and quickly spread in subsequent days to a total of thirty-seven urban centers. There had been innumerable demonstrations in South Korea since the establishment of the First Republic, but the scale and nature of demonstrations in the summer of 1987 were unprecedented. Initially, the protestors were young students and workers, as usual. But what was sur-

---

[36] *Hankook Ilbo*, 9 June 1987, cited in Kim, p. 91.
[37] Yi Pyŏng-do, "Hidae ŭi kongjak: 6.29 sŏnŏn" (The Extraordinary Manipulation: The 6.29 Declaration), *Chukan Hanguk*, 23 August 1993, pp. 2–3.

prising to both Korean and international journalists alike was that older and much better-dressed people were also participating in these street demonstrations. Furthermore, the numbers of these latter demonstrators increased daily. Having hurriedly interviewed many of these older demonstrators, the journalists reported an important new phenomenon: many demonstrators were "middle class" members. In the past the middle class had kept its distance from the street clashes as long as the economy remained stable and their economic well-being was not threatened, but this time they evidently decided to throw their usual caution to the winds and join the antiregime struggle.

In 1987, when these changes were occurring, all economic indicators were exceptionally strong. The nation's economy was growing at an astounding rate of 12.8 percent, a record high since 1977. Per capita income was high for Korea, at $3,098, compared with $2,503 in 1986. Major factors behind the high growth in this period were the so-called "three lows"— the low price of crude oil, the low value of the U.S. dollar against the Japanese yen, and low international interest rates. South Korea was exporting some $47 billion worth of goods, compared with $35 billion the year before, and investments in fixed production facilities were correspondingly high. Evidently, it was no for economic reasons that the middle class was actively and in large numbers participating in these demonstrations. Its members, too, were now demanding political reforms, summed up as "democratization," a term that had motivated numerous opposition leaders and students but apparently had little concrete meaning to the larger public and middle class until 1987, when an arrogant and ruthless dictator was simply no longer acceptable.[38]

With the ranks of protestors thus swollen, daily clashes between stone-throwing demonstrators and riot police occurred incessantly, seemingly everywhere, and culminating in the "Great Peace March of the People" on June 26. Countless demonstrators literally packed the highways and byways around Seoul and most other urban centers that day. The demonstrations brought to mind the "people power" phenomenon in the Philippines a year before, when massive demonstrations swept Ferdinand Marcos out of office. For weeks South Korea was a tear gas–choked battleground where finely ground pepper gas residues could not completely be washed out for days following major clashes. The riot police were now outnumbered, exhausted, and often humiliated. It was speculated that the police were running out of tear gas canisters in June, but the "human waves" of demonstrators kept surging.

A crucial turning point came in mid-June, when a huge throng of students surrounded and isolated a detachment of sweat-soaked, bone-

[38] Cho, *The Dynamics of Korean Economic Development*, p. 52.

weary riot police in downtown Seoul. The students easily overpowered the police and took away their riot-control shields and clubs, padded riot-control uniforms, and tear gas canisters and set them on a bonfire on a busy thoroughfare while crowds in front of a department store cheered. Confident students, however, let the riot police go—unharmed but utterly humiliated and demoralized. It was a relatively small incident, but a news report had a huge psychological impact on the Chun regime and on the demonstrators. The Chun regime's defense against the Korean people was crumbling.

The desperate Chun regime now had to resort to the final defensive measure of mobilizing the military to crush the demonstrators. On June 19 Chun ordered some of his crack units to stand by to storm Seoul and deal with the demonstrators.[39] South Korea was on a precipice, facing an unprecedentedly bloody massacre of the people by its military—unleashed by the Chun regime, born on the heel of the Kwangju massacre—and the possibility of another coup toppling the regime and, in such an event, the likelihood of a civil war. However, Chun's own lieutenants, including his prime minister, recalled that the troops had not fired on the students demonstrating against the Rhee regime in 1960, and strongly counseled going the same route. Having seen the arrogant excesses of the Chun regime, some unit commanders were wary of Chun. Through a special envoy, Gaston Sigur, assistant secretary of State for East Asian and Pacific Affairs, the United States government sternly warned Chun on June 23 against the use of the Korean military for political purposes in the face of a potential danger from the north.[40] As in 1960, when students were demanding the ouster of an autocratic Rhee regime, the United States stood up against a dictator.

The surrender. It was under these circumstances that Roh Tae Woo, the ruling party's presidential candidate and Chun's anointed successor, disappeared from public view for several days. While in regular touch with Chun, Roh drafted a decidedly conciliatory declaration with the help of a handful of his closest confidantes. This was the famed June 29, 1987, "Declaration of Democratization and Reforms," which in essence accepted a direct presidential election system under a drastically amended and democratic constitution. This was a well-timed and politically adroit move that defused at the very last moment the explosive demands of the people and avoided a humiliating political defeat for himself, possibly

[39] Kim Song-ik, *Chon Tu-hwan yuksŏng chungŏn* (The Spoken Testimonies of Chun Doo Hwan) (Seoul: Chosŏn Ilbo-sa, 1992), p. 429.

[40] Kim Dong-hyŏn, "Yi Han-ki ch'ongni ka malhanŭn 6.29 chŏnya" (The Eve of June 29 According to Former Premier Yi Han-ki), *Wŏlgan Chosŏn* (October 1989): pp. 302–9.

even a huge bloodbath. Roh depicted the decision as a lonely and heroic move made to avert a political crisis and possible bloodshed:

> I have now come to a firm conviction about the future of our nation. I have anguished long and hard over the genuine mission of politicians at this historic time. . . . Today, I stand before history and the nation with an extraordinary determination to help build a great homeland.[41]

However, according to Chun's recording secretary, Kim Sŏng-ik, author of *Chŏn Du-hwan chŭngŏn* (The testimonies of Chun Doo Hwan), it was Chun who first decided to fake a surrender to the massive demand, for a direct presidential election could no longer be resisted in the face of tidal waves of angry demonstrators that threatened to crush anything standing in their paths. Chun described it:

> In view of the mounting demand for a direct presidential election, accepting such a demand would be the most popular move. I concluded that Candidate Roh should announce an acceptance of a direct election as his own decision. This single act should enable Roh to win over the two Kims. Thus I told Roh to accept the direct election system. Greatly surprised, Roh said it could not be done . . . the main reason being that he was not confident of a victory in an election contest against the Kims. . . . I told him that his acceptance of a direct election would make him a hero. I would guarantee his victory . . . by running the political organization for him and by giving him all the funds needed. Roh then asked for time.[42]

As the daily demonstrations grew and intensified, Roh, accompanied only by his chauffeur, visited with Chun at the presidential mansion. Without any staff present, only Chun's son taking notes, the two conferred for two hours, scrutinizing the final version of the statement. In view of the vociferous popular demands for democratic reforms, the scope of the draft declaration grew to become an eight-point statement. After making the dramatic statement on June 29, a grim-faced Roh left immediately for a well-publicized visit to the national cemetery to pay tribute to the war dead and national leaders buried there. Still keeping up the pretense, Roh stated "I intend to recommend" the democratization package he made public to President Chun,[43] and dramatically added that he would resign from all official posts and candidacies if Chun re-

---

[41] From Roh's introduction to the June 29 Declaration. Democratic Justice Party, *Prosperity*, 6 (July 1987), cited in Lee Manwoo, *The Odyssey of Korean Democracy: Korean Politics, 1987–1990* (New York: Praeger, 1990), p. 145.

[42] Yi Pyŏng-do, p. 3.

[43] James Cotton, ed., *Korea under Roh Tae-woo* (Canberra: Allen and Unwin, 1993), p. 317.

jected his recommendations. On June 30 Roh paid another visit to Chun at his presidential mansion—this time a well-publicized visit. In front of a battery of journalists Roh said to Chun: "Your Excellency, I am sorry." Roh was implying that he was surprising Chun with a political bomb-shell. On June 1 Chun "approved," presumably reluctantly, the Roh declaration through a special statement. The public staging of the political "surrender" was complete. The elaborate hoax lasted until the relationship between Chun and Roh cooled rapidly and then ruptured, a couple of years later.

If it was surprising to some that President Reagan received Chun very early in the former's presidency, it was even more surprising that Reagan received presidential candidate Roh Tae Woo at the White House in September 14, 1987, shortly before the December election in Korea. Vice President George Bush was also present. Roh was running against the two leading civilian candidates who had championed democracy in Korea for decades, Kim Young Sam and Kim Dae-jung, in the December 1987 presidential election. Everyone expected a close contest, and in view of the groundswell for democratizing and reform demands after a quarter century of military-dominated rule, it was hoped by many that a bona fide civilian candidate, instead of an exgeneral turned civilian, would win. The extent of election benefits Roh managed to extract from his visit with Reagan is, of course, debatable. However, it is undeniable that the Roh campaign played up the high-visibility visit with the American president and vice president, who were made to appear to be endorsing the Roh candidacy. Roh ended up winning the presidency by 36.6 percent of the popular vote; Kim Young Sam garnered 28.1 percent and Kim Dae Jung 27.1 percent. One wonders if the White House knew, as Chun and Roh did, that the two Kims would be unable to agree on a single opposition candidate and would thus divide the opposition vote. Simple mathematics showed that if one Kim ran and the other Kim supported him, they could have decisively defeated Roh. But that was not the case.

Fading anti-Americanism. With the advent of a directly elected Roh regime, many antidictatorship issues faded, although anti-Americanism as a manifestation of antidictatorship drives did not suddenly abate. Isolated attacks on American targets continued while the radical students demonstrated, demanding the arrest of former President Chun. However, there was no longer a South Korean government determined to characterize the Kwangju incident as a Communist-inspired revolutionary activity to overthrow the government. There was also a growing realization among the Korean people that an anti-American *minjung* ideology was largely a hodge podge of inconsistent, contradictory, anti-intellectual slogans. They were emotionally appealing when desperate students and workers under a brutally oppressive regime needed battle cries, but that appeal was diminishing under a duly elected government, and cooler heads began to prevail.

Furthermore, the nation was shocked by the report that a Korean Airlines (KAL) jetliner with 104 passengers and 11 crew members had vanished over Rangoon, Burma, in late November 1987. In mid-January 1988, the Agency for National Security Planning, the successor agency to the KCIA, announced that two special North Korean agents, allegedly acting on the instructions of Kim Jŏng-il, son and heir apparent to President Kim Il-sŏng, had planted a bomb that destroyed the KAL plane and everyone on it. Kim Hyŏn-hŭi, one of the two agents, made a televised confession on January 15, 1988, that she and another special agent had indeed placed the bomb in an effort to discourage participation by numerous countries in the 1988 Seoul Olympics. The security-first policies of the Korean and U.S. governments were resoundingly justified by North Korea.

What was also becoming clear was that by the end of the 1980s the United States was no longer represented in Korea by haughty, careless, and irascible ambassadors, generals, or spokespeople who would state incorrectly that the Americans "approved" the use of Korean troops in Kwangju, that the Koreans were "lemmings" who needed strong leaders, or that the demonstrating students were "spoiled brats." At the same time, the United States, as well as South Korea, was more conscious of the need to keep the peoples of both countries informed through timely announcements regarding important steps taken. This was a change from the time when the CFC arrangements were made in 1978 but it took more than eleven years until the U.S. Information Service issued its explanations, on June 19, 1989.

Thus a high tide of anti-Americanism subsided following the demise of the Chun dictatorship. However, a major source of anti-Americanism remained in the economic arena. Many South Koreans continued to feel "trade pressures" from the United States. Trade issues concerning, for example, rice and beef, in the late 1980s appeared to leave South Korean farmers largely blaming the United States, while government sources appeared to equivocate on these issues for political reasons. To avoid another round of anti-American displays, the South Korean government could have explained that some concessions had to be made by Korean government representatives in multilateral General Agreement on Tariffs and Trade (GATT) negotiations and that South Korea could not enjoy one-way benefits while depending on the world market for its export-oriented economy. Few South Koreans appeared to realize that in the 1980s South Korea exported some 30 percent of its products to the United States, while the United States typically sold about 3.5 percent of its total exports in South Korea. According to a survey in 1987, more than 40 percent of Korean college students understood that they would have to buy more foreign rice to continue to enjoy open markets abroad, certainly including the United States. Finally, most observers agreed that the extent of anti-Americanism even during the worst periods had been relatively mild after all. There remained even among shrill nationalists in South Korea in the 1980s a large and deep reservoir of goodwill toward the United States dating back to the Korean War, during which the United States played the key role in defending South Korea from aggression.

✪

CHAPTER 5

The Transition and Economic Problems, 1987–1992

In 1987 the most urgent interest of Chun and Roh was to have Roh succeed Chun as president. Chun was then finishing his constitutionally prescribed, nonrenewable, seven-year term and needed to have Roh elected, no matter how. Chun, then fifty-six years old, needed a sympathetic successor who would not prosecute him for his numerous illegal acts in seizing power before and after the Kwangju massacre and in ruling the country with an iron hand. Political reality then also included the widespread suspicion, which took many years to confirm, that Chun had been covertly receiving huge political donations, mostly from industrial conglomerates, just as his mentor and predecessor, Park Chung Hee, had done. In return, some conglomerates were known to be benefiting handsomely by being awarded large and lucrative contracts and loans; for example, for public projects. Having amassed a huge slush fund, Chun could confidently tell Roh that he would "give him all the funds needed"[1] and abundantly lubricate the ruling party to ensure his victory. Roh would be elected by whatever means necessary, including dividing anti-Roh votes predicted in support of civilian candidates who were expected to further genuine reforms and democratization.

The "Democratization and Reform Declaration"

The Roh declaration of June 29 mirrored political realities and needs in 1987, as shrewdly analyzed by Chun and Roh. As a reflection of Chun's and Roh's cynical awareness of the steps needed for them to survive and

---

[1] Yi Pyŏng-do "Hidae ŭi kongjak."

of the people's accumulated demands in 1987 for reforms and democratization, Roh's "democratization package" declaration deserves analysis.

Roh listed and commented on the following eight items in his lengthy declaration of June 29, 1987:

1. Direct Presidential Election System
   . . . the Constitution should be expeditiously amended . . . to adopt a direct presidential election system.
2. Revision of Presidential Election Law
   . . . to carry out elections democratically, it is necessary also to revise the Presidential Election Law so that freedom of candidacy and fair competition are guaranteed.
3. Amnesty and Restoration of Civil Rights for Dissidents
   I believe that Mr. Kim Dae-jung . . . should be amnestied and his civil rights restored. . . . All those who are being detained in connection with the political situation should also be set free.

The third item, appearing to enhance the rights of "democratic citizens," was a calculated ploy to divide and rule the "democratic" opposition by enabling and indeed challenging Kim Dae-jung by name to run for the presidency in 1987. Ever since the fiercely fought 1971 presidential elections, when Kim Dae-jung had garnered some 45 percent of the popular vote against Park Chung Hee's 53 percent, Kim had been public enemy number one of Park and his successors, Generals Chun and Roh. What was important in 1987 was that Kim, a most determined and "senior" fighter for democracy in Korea, would—only if he could—run for the presidency again. At the same time, Kim Young Sam was equally determined to become president, and in 1987 was both well known as a fighter for democracy and well poised as head of the Reunification Democratic Party. Chun and Roh knew that the two Kims by now were irreconcilably bitter political rivals and that one Kim would not yield to the other the presidential candidacy and form a pan-civilian opposition to Roh. Chun and Roh thus unleashed Kim Dae-jung into the political arena with the expectation that the Kims would resume their rivalry and thus divide the anti-Roh vote.

4. Strengthening All Basic Rights in the New Constitution
   . . . human dignity must be respected even more greatly and the basic rights of citizens should be promoted and protected to the maximum.

Simply put, Roh was proposing to restore constitutional rights that had been eradicated by the regimes headed by his predecessors, Park and Chun. Before the imposition of the so-called *yusin* constitution under Park, the constitution had included many provisions that guaranteed citizenship rights; Roh was proposing to return to such a pre-*yusin* constitutional pattern.

5. Promoting Freedom of the Press in New Press Law
. . . to promote the freedom of the press, the relevant system and practices must be drastically improved. The Basic Press Law, which may have been well meant but has nonetheless been criticized by most journalists, should promptly be either extensively revised or abolished.

Here again, Roh was simply proposing to abolish the draconian press law decreed by the Chun regime that effectively abolished freedom of the press.

6. Local Autonomy to Go Ahead as Scheduled
. . . freedom and self-regulation must be guaranteed to the maximum in all other sectors also . . . local councils should be elected and organized without any hitch. . . . Colleges and universities . . . must be made self-governing and educational autonomy in general must be expeditiously put into practice.

Local self-governance became a constitutional goal in 1948, although it was never effectively practiced. Even the constitutional principle of local autonomy was abandoned by Park "until the unification of the fatherland is accomplished," in some unforeseeable future. In his "democratization" package, Roh revived the local autonomy principle that Park had discarded. The regulation of most aspects of education at all levels by the central Ministry of Education had been a pervasive pattern from the beginning of the First Republic, and military dictators had tightened control measures over all campuses as antidictatorship student demonstrations escalated. Practically all the major campuses were effectively penetrated by intelligence agents of the government who dispensed liberal amounts of cash to willing, or even not-so-willing, faculty members or informants to prevent or break up student demonstrations. To defuse the deep resentment that had built up on most campuses, Roh proposed the promotion of educational autonomy to democratize education.

7. New Political Climate of Dialogue Essential for Democratic Growth
. . . a political climate conducive to dialogue and compromise must be created expeditiously, with healthy activities of political parties guaranteed.

For the democratic growth of the nation, Roh suddenly became the self-anointed champion of a free climate of dialogue that had been steadily eroding under the military dictatorship. This erosion accelerated with the successful military coup led by General Park in 1961—more specifically with the launching of the powerful KCIA almost immediately thereafter. In the name of "national security," but more often for the maintenance of military regimes, intelligence agents were perceived to be ubiquitous. Gradually, even "thought control" measures were institutionalized through the national security laws, press laws, campus stabilization laws, and the like for decades. In the summer of 1987 Roh was reacting to steadily mounting demands for an all-out political liberalization to eradicate decades of political oppression under his predecessors. Political parties had been feeble, fractious, and ephemeral creatures of political bosses.[2] Toward the end of the Rhee government it was said that South Korea had a "one-and-a-half" party system—the well-financed ruling party and anemic opposition party. At the outset of the military-dominated government under Park, however, all political parties were abruptly banned and opposition political figures were single-mindedly suppressed. Under these circumstances political parties were not much more than groups—some large, some small—following well-known political leaders. They were not issue-oriented and stable organizations of large groups of like-minded people consistently pursuing well-articulated political principles or interests. Roh now advocated that the state should "protect and nurture political parties, so long as they engage in solid activities." Though Roh still took a paternalistic stance, he was at the same time mirroring the widespread popular belief that political parties had to be nurtured and invigorated as "democratic organizations."

8. Bold Social Reforms to Build a Clean Society
  . . . bold social reforms must be carried out to build a clean and honest society. In order that all citizens can lead a secure and happy life, crime against life and property, such as hooliganism, robbery and theft, must be stamped out.

Again, as a reflection of the extremely serious popular concern at the time about rampant corruption, crime, moral decay, and insensitivity, Roh proposed building a "clean and honest society." Roh postured himself as a moral crusader who would lead the nation out of the morass. Of course, after his election as president Roh turned out to be the most greedy, corrupt, and unprincipled president in history, according to recent revelations of his solicitation and acceptance of unprecedentedly huge "political donations" from industrial conglomerates.

    [2] Yun Hyŏng-sŏp, "Hanguk chŏngch'i kwajŏng" (Political Processes in Korea), in Un-t'ae Kim et al., pp. 492–573.

Chronology of major crises, martial law, and constitutional amendments

Event	Martial law	Constitutional amendment
Riots in Cheju Island	10/17–12/31/48	
Revolts in Yŏsu		
and Sunchŏn	10/21–12/31/48	
Korean War	7/8/50–5/23/53	
		1st amendment 7/7/52 (Direct presidential election)
		2nd amendment 11/29/54 (Reelectable president)
Student uprising	4/19/60–6/7/60	
		3rd amendment 6/15/60 (Cabinet system)
		4th amendment 11/29/60 (Punish "antidemocratic acts")
Military coup	5/16/61–12/5/61	
		5th amendment 12/26/62 (Readopt presidential system)
		6th amendment 10/21/69 (Allow third presidential term)
"Revitalizing reform"	10/7–12/31/72	
		7th amendment 11/24/72 ("Revitalizing reform")
Riots in Pusan–Masan	10/19–10/26/79	
Park assassination		
and aftermath	10/27/79–5/17/80	
Kwangju uprising	5/17–10/17/80	
	10/1–1/24/81	
		8th amendment 10/27/80 (Fifth Republic)
		9th amendment 10/29/87 (Sixth Republic)

Through this well-written and widely publicized declaration, Roh appeared to perform single handedly the herculean task of breaking the gigantic political logjam that had been building up for at least a decade and a half, ever since November 1972 when Park Chung Hee imposed the *yusin* constitution. It was striking that the lengthy declaration mentioned nothing about Roh's economic policies, simply asserting that the country had "a trade surplus by stabilizing prices and improving our international competitiveness." Roh repeatedly emphasized that he was promoting "the liberal democratic system" in Korean politics. In any case, Roh's June 29 statement turned out to be a catharsis of 1987 that relieved the body politic of a monstrous political constriction.

Constitutional Amendments and the Peaceful Transfer of Power

By 1987 the constitution had been amended or rewritten, in part or in whole, eight times since its promulgation on July 17, 1948. This fact reflected the stormy Korean politics and also how the Koreans treated their constitution not as a fundamental law that should last but as a document that could be rewritten again and again to suit political changes.[3] By the summer of 1987 it was clear that the document needed to be extensively amended once again to usher in a new era of "democratization." The need was compelling because the series of amendments following the military coup of 1961, the so-called "revitalization reform" of 1972, and the second coup of 1979, had made the constitution a handmaiden of military dictators.

The constitution, extensively amended on October 29, 1987, has remained the fundamental law for South Korea. This was true not only during the Sixth Republic, headed by Roh Tae Woo, but also during the Seventh Republic, under Kim Young Sam, the first chief executive to take office without an amended constitution. Kim Dae-jung also assumed his presidency, in 1998, without a constitutional amendment, although another amendment to adopt a responsible cabinet system was part of an agreement between the Kim Dae-jung and Kim Jong Pil camps before they entered into a coalition before the 1997 presidential election.

Soon after Roh's June 29 "democratization" declaration, the National Assembly formed a special commission to amend the constitution that heard some 100 proposals made by the ruling and opposition parties. By October the National Assembly had adopted sweeping revisions to the constitution, which was ratified by a national referendum on October 27. A new basic law containing a preamble, 130 articles, and supplementary provisions was promulgated on October 29. This constitution of the Sixth Republic was the first South Korean basic law in forty years of turbulent constitutional history to be revised and adopted jointly by ruling and opposition party members in the Assembly.

The 1987 amendments. Clearly 1987 marked a new chapter in the constitutional history of Korea. The newly amended constitution retained ringing democratic aspirations in Article 1:

> The republic of Korea shall be a democratic republic. The sovereignty of the Republic of Korea shall reside in the people, and all state authority shall emanate from the people.

Recalling the dark days of military dictatorships, however, the amended constitution declared in Article 5, paragraph 2:

> The Armed Forces shall be charged with the sacred mission of national security and the defense of the land, and their political neutrality shall be observed.

[3] Yoon Dae-Kyu, *Law and Political Authority in South Korea* (Boulder, CO: Westview Press, 1990), pp. 96–108.

Persons in active military duty were now banned from occupying either the prime ministership or cabinet posts. As expected, the 1987 constitution visibly strengthened other "democratic" features of the document. Eliminated from the document were many of the familiar escape clauses attached in the past to the formal guarantees of rights that could be drastically compromised by subsequent legislation, such as "with the provisions of law," or "except as specified by law." In the 1948 constitution, for instance, most rights and freedoms "guaranteed" in the document could be taken away when the ruling elites decided it was necessary to do so "for the maintenance of public order or the welfare of the community." In contrast, Article 21, paragraph 2, of the 1987 document simply provided: "Licensing or censorship of speech and the press, and licensing of assembly and association shall not be allowed." Other examples are found in Article 12, paragraph 6: "All persons who are arrested or detained shall have the right to request the court to review the legality of the arrest or detention," and Article 33, paragraph 1: "To enhance working conditions, workers shall have the right to independent association, collective bargaining and collective action." There were no qualifiers attached to these provisions.

The most far-reaching changes, evidently aimed at restricting presidential authorities who had often become overpowering, were found in Chapter 3. In view of the lopsided imbalance of powers between the executive and the legislative branches ever since 1948, with the exception of the short-lived Second Republic, it was understandable that the 1987 document would attempt to correct the glaring imbalance. In addition to the normal legislative, budgetary, and ratification authorities, the 1987 constitution also conferred momentous powers on the National Assembly by stipulating:

> The National Assembly may inspect affairs of state or investigate specific matters of state affairs, and may demand the production of documents, the attendance of a witness and the statement of testimony or opinions necessary. . . .
>
> When requested by the National Assembly or its committees, the Prime Minister, members of the State Council or government delegates shall attend any meeting of the National Assembly and answer questions (Article 61)

Further, the National Assembly was given effective impeachment power against the president, the prime minister, members of the state council, heads of executive ministries, judges of the Constitution Court, other judges, members of the Central Election Management Committee, and other public officials designated by law. The impeachment power, seldom used in the past in the Korean republic, was made relatively easy to exercise against all officials named except the president. Officials other than the president could be impeached based on a proposal by one-third of the duly seated members of the Assembly and a concurrence of a majority of the members. The impeachment of the president could be proposed by one-third of the assembly members but needed a two-thirds vote. Furthermore, emergency decrees and measures by the president could be rescinded when he failed subsequently to obtain the consent of the National Assembly (Article 76). Martial law proclamations, so often abused by presidents in the past, had to be lifted when the National Assembly requested the termination of martial law with a simple majority vote (Article 77). Further still, the president had no power to dissolve the National Assembly.

The most important change embodied in the 1987 constitution was that the president was to be elected by universal, equal, direct, and secret ballot by the citizens for a single term of five years. The document stated that executive power is "vested in the Executive Branch headed by the president," who is also "the head of State" (Article 66). As usual, he is the commander-in-chief of the armed forces. The office of prime minister, a perennial feature of the Korean executive branch, was retained, although prime ministers lacked any significant authority under successive presidential systems of government. Of course, the sole exception was the Second Republic, which had a responsible cabinet system headed by a prime minister. The president would appoint the prime minister with the consent of the National Assembly. In the words of the constitution, but seldom in practice, cabinet members would be appointed by the president "on the recommendation of the prime minister" (Article 87). These appointments have been, in most cases, the prerogative of the president.

Judicial power is vested in the Supreme Court and in other courts. All judges are to hear cases "independently according to their conscience and in conformity with the constitution and law." However, the chief justice and other justices of the Supreme Court are appointed by the president with the consent of the National Assembly for a nonrenewable term of six years for the chief justice; the other justices had renewable six-year terms. Judges of other courts would be appointed by the chief justice with the consent of the Conference of the Supreme Court Justices for ten-year terms; they may be reappointed. There were no lifetime appointments, which tend to assure judicial independence.

Overall, with the extensive authorities allowed the National Assembly, including the power to inspect state affairs and interpellate executive branch members, and with the limitations imposed on presidential emergency powers and specifically on the martial law authorities, the presidency was relatively well delineated in the 1987 constitution. However, in the face of the long history of executive-dominated governments in Korea, how the constitutional provisions would unfold was to depend heavily on the strength of personality of the new president and on the composition of the newly elected National Assembly.

It was previously noted that the constitution, despite nine series of far-reaching amendments, has retained a chapter on the economy, just as it repeated its commitment to democracy. When the constitution was revised on October 29, 1987, to promote "democratic reforms" in Korea, the chapter on the economy took on new significance. The revised chapter declared: "The state may regulate and coordinate economic affairs in order to maintain the *balanced growth and stability* of the national economy, to ensure *proper distribution of income,* to prevent the domination of the market and the abuse of economic power and to *democratize the economy* through harmony among the economic agents." (Article 119; emphasis added)

The meaning of "the economic agents" was indicated when another clause in Article 119 reiterated "the freedom and creative initiative of enterprises and individuals in economic affairs." The government certainly had been an active agent, together with enterprises and individuals. Thus the economy was to be democratized through harmony among these three major agents. This chapter obviously contained several ambitious and sometimes inconsistent goals of the state in regulating and coordinating economic affairs such as maintaining balanced "growth" and "stability," ensuring "proper" distribution of income, and preventing the abuse of economic power. The inconsistencies and possible contradictions in the chapter obviously had to be worked out in the Sixth Republic and beyond.

Regarding agricultural land, Article 121 declared a "land-to-the-tillers principle" and categorically outlawed tenant farming. In view of the increasingly glaring gaps between regional economies, particularly between the *yŏngnam* region, namely the North and South Kyŏngsang Provinces and the *hŏnam* region, the North and South Chŏlla Provinces, Article 123 provided that "the State shall have the duty to foster regional economies to ensure the balanced development of all regions." This was evidently a constitutional response to the charges that Park, Chun, and Roh—all hailing from villages near Taegu in North Kyŏngsang Province—had favored economic developments in their native *yŏngnam* area and discriminated against the *hŏnam* region, the home base of their despised political enemy, Kim Dae-jung. Observers travelling through these regions readily noticed the stark differences in economic standards.

With a newly amended constitution, the 1987 presidential election was the first contest by direct popular vote in sixteen years, since Park Chung Hee had narrowly defeated his nemesis, Kim Dae-jung, in 1971, triggering the so-called 1972 "revitalizing reform," making Park in effect reelectable for life. The 1987 election was a critical contest in deciding whether Korea would have a bona fide civilian president or another retired general, one whose image was freshly etched on the minds of millions thanks to his June 29 "democratization declaration."

Roh Tae Woo. Korean voters now paid serious attention to Roh's background, which was remarkably similar to those of his classmate at the Korean Military Academy, Chun Doo Hwan, and their hero, Park Chung Hee. Unlike the leaders of the First and Second Republics, Syngman Rhee, Yun Po-sŏn, and Chang Myŏn, scions of "aristocratic" families, Park, Chun, and Roh hailed from peasant backgrounds. For the latter the common route to a respectable career and to power was the military establishment in Korea.

It was in a tiny farming hamlet in Kongsan County in a valley near present-day Taegu that Roh Tae Woo was born on December 4, 1932.[4] Roh was the older of two brothers raised by their mother, who had been widowed at age thirty, with financial help from his uncle, a manufacturer of stationery items such as pencils and carbon paper. Roh walked five miles each way through a mountain pass to graduate from the Kongsan primary school with a perfect attendance record. The financial circumstances and the caliber of pupils at Kongsan were indicated by the fact that only four of 150 graduates in 1944 went on to local middle schools. Roh entered the Taegu Engineering School, a vocational middle school, but three years later transferred to what is today the Kyŏngbuk Middle School. When the Korean War broke out he became a "student soldier (volunteer)," according to one biography, and soon enlisted in the Korean Army.[5] Thus began his military career at the age of eighteen.

While serving as a military policeman Roh read a notice that the first four-year military academy was accepting applications. What caught Roh's eye was that the military academy would provide a free college education in addition to military training—all at the government's expense. Roh acted quickly, and in January 1952 found himself a member of the first class of the regular military academy, then located in the peaceful southern port city of Chinhae. The Korean War ended in July 1953, and Roh was commissioned as a second lieutenant in October 1955, a member of the first graduating class of the regular military academy, the eleventh class of the academy from its inception.

Lieutenant Roh was assigned in due time to the Fifth Division, where he met Major General Park Chung Hee, then division commander. When

---

[4] Yi Kyŏng-nam, *No T'ae-u: yongki itnŭn pot'ong saram* (Roh Tae Woo: A Courageous Commoner) (Seoul: Ŭlyu munhwa-sa, 1987), pp. 66–67.

[5] Ibid., pp. 82–84.

Park led the 1961 military coup Roh was a captain serving as an ROTC officer at the school of education of Seoul National University. Along with his military academy classmates, including Captain Chun Doo Hwan, Roh rushed to the military academy, then located at T'aenung, near Seoul. Chun and Roh were among those who persuaded the academy cadets to demonstrate their support of Park's coup, and a march down the streets of Seoul by the cadets in their crisp uniforms followed. This demonstration, within days after the May 16 coup, boosted the morale of the coup leaders, who were not yet certain about the success of the military takeover, and also ended a supposed tradition of political neutrality among academy cadets.

As the coup meant, among other things, a whole-scale politicization of the Korean military, the politicization of Chun and Roh already became pronounced. In 1962 Roh became the head of the North Star Association, a private network among his military academy classmates, who also were becoming politically conscious. Chun was soon made a member of the special unit guarding Park, and Chun used this proximity to have his classmates from the *yŏngnam* region, including Roh, appointed to influential positions in the military junta. Following Park's inauguration as president of the Third Republic in December 1963, Roh rose steadily in the military, serving as commander of a Korean battalion in Vietnam, and commander of the Ninth Division when Park was assassinated on October 26, 1979. When the showdown between Chun and General Chŏng Sung Hwa took place on the night of December 12, it was Roh who quickly dispatched units from his division to secure army headquarters and the capitol, the literal and symbolic center of power.[6] Thus Roh played a crucial role in the 12.12 coup. The importance of Roh to Chun, who had been consolidating his power since the 1979 coup, was indicated by Roh's appointment on the day after that coup as head of the capital garrison command, the elite force at the disposal of the *Hanahwoe*-driven "new military" headed by Chun. Roh retired from the army in July 1981 as a four-star general at the age of forty-nine.

Roh was appointed political affairs (security and diplomacy) minister in the month of his retirement and put in charge of the high-profile task of getting the 1988 Olympics to come to Seoul. Diverting the people's attention to the Olympics and away from politics was a clever ploy by the Chun regime, which was widely perceived to have no legitimacy because Chun had seized power through the 12.12 coup and was elected president virtually unanimously by the so-called National Conference for Unification, the odious creature of the Park dictatorship. The conference had little to do with national unification but much to do with making Park a dic-

6 Ibid., pp. 141–43.

tator for life. As the conference met at a Seoul gymnasium on August 27, 1980, some cynics called Chun "the gymnasium president." President Ch'oe Kyu Hah, whose name was briefly linked to the "Seoul Spring," a resurgence of democracy on the morrow of Park's assassination, was formally ousted from the office of the president, which had been made into an empty shell under the "new military."

In the Chun cabinet a brand new ministry of athletics was created and Roh was appointed its first minister. As the interest in hosting for the first time in Korean history the international sports spectacular was heightened by the Chun regime, the mass media spotlight was redirected toward Roh. When the International Olympics Committee hesitated to bring the games to Seoul because it feared political instability on the Korean peninsula, Roh took a highly publicized trip to Switzerland to ask its members to reconsider. The Twenty-Fourth Olympiad was held in Seoul with great fanfare, and Koreans later took immense pride in having successfully hosted the international games. Roh was sure to take full credit for bringing it about.

President Chun was elected for his first full term by a newly formed electoral college on February 25, 1981. Under the amended constitution Chun was to fill a single seven-year term that would expire in early 1988. By early 1985 the political blueprint of the Chun–Roh team began to emerge. At that time the ruling Democratic Justice Party (DJP) set the goal of laying a foundation for its "second period of our rule," clearly signaling the intention to pass the power to a man handpicked by DJP President Chun. Step by step, the blueprint began to unfold.

In early February 1985 Roh was made an assemblyman through a national-constituency appointment by the ruling DJP, which also decided to elect its presidential candidate in a national party convention to be held in 1987. The DJP resolved on February 23 to name Roh party chairman, signaling his forthcoming designation as the party's presidential candidate, a shoo-in through the easily manipulable indirect election by the ruling party-dominated electoral college. The election of Roh as president was a foregone conclusion until the accumulated and suppressed energies of the coalition of opposition political groups and the civil society seeking reforms and democratization exploded cataclysmically in June 1987.

The direct election of Roh. In the direct presidential election held on December 16, 1987—the first such election in sixteen years—Roh won with a plurality vote because his rivals, Kim Young Sam and Kim Dae-jung, divided the opposition vote, just as Chun and Roh had calculated before issuing the June 29 declaration. Some 89.2 percent of 25,873,624 eligible voters participated in the election. The voting results are shown in Table 3 on page 110.[7]

[7] *Korea Annual 1988*, p. 77.

Table 3. The thirteenth presidential election: December 16, 1987

Roh Tae Woo, Democratic Justice Party	36.6%
Kim Young Sam, Reunification Democratic Party	28.0
Kim Dae-jung, Party for Peace and Democracy	27.0
Kim Jong Pil, New Democratic Republican Party	8.1
J. Y. Shin, Independent	0.2

It seems clear that Roh could not have won this important election had the three Kims—or at least the two Kims, Kim Young Sam and Kim Dae-jung—had the wisdom to unite against him. Numerous Korean notables pleaded with the two Kims to take just such an action under whatever compact they could reach—perhaps by taking turns running under the amended constitution, which stipulated nonrenewable five-year presidential terms. But instead both ran and both lost.

Roh's inauguration on February 25, 1988, marked the first peaceful transfer of presidential power in Korea since 1948. If a basic criterion of democracy is free and fair elections leading to peaceful changes of governments, albeit to a handpicked successor, the Koreans finally met this test in 1987. Recall that President Rhee, of the First Republic, was ousted from office through the student uprising of 1960; the Second Republic of Premier Chang was overthrown by the military coup led by Park in 1961; Park in turn was assassinated in 1979; and Chun had seized power through another coup in 1979. President Roh thus declared in his inaugural address:

> We gather . . . to proclaim a new beginning. . . . I assume the presidency forty years after a democratic government was first established in this country. . . . With the launching of the new Republic, we will sail steadfastly toward democracy. . . .
>
> The day when freedoms and human rights could be slighted in the name of economic growth and national security has ended. . . . The time has come to achieve a just and fair distribution of income so that every citizen can share the fruits of the growth.[8] (Emphasis added.)

To what extent Roh, the suddenly self-proclaimed "democrat," was convinced or even aware of the full meaning of what his well-educated and politically astute advisers and speechwriters undoubtedly wrote for him to say remained to be seen. The biggest question was whether Roh, who was used to issuing orders and being instantly obeyed, would have the temperament and the ability to manage a "democratic" government. His task was further complicated by the National Assembly elections held

---

[8] Cotton, *Korea under Roh Tae-woo*, pp. 322–24.

Table 4. The thirteenth National Assembly elections: April 26, 1988

Democratic Justice Party, Roh Tae Woo	125 seats
Party for Peace and Democracy, Kim Dae-jung	70
Republican Democratic Party, Kim Young Sam	59
New Democratic Republican Party, Kim Jong Pil	35
Independents and others	10

on April 26, 1988. That also produced an historic first in forty years of Korean politics, namely, the ruling party won a minority of seats, 125 of 299—fifteen seats short of a simple majority (Table 4).[9]

Opposition parties and independents, if united on certain issues, could now muster a healthy majority in the legislature, marking for the first time an era of what some pundits termed *yoso yadae* (roughly, a small ruling group, a larger opposition). As noted previously, the powers of the president were "weakened" in the constitution as amended in 1987, and now Roh, who had been elected by 36.6 percent of the votes, had to work with a legislature whose authorities were constitutionally "strengthened" in the same year. Thus with a sudden "democratization" following decades of military dictatorship, the pendulum had swung to an extreme and resulted in what would likely be a deadlock-prone government.

In a sense the Roh regime was reminiscent of the democratic but "weak" government of the Second Republic—Roh was a minority president and the National Assembly was divided among four parties, just as Chang Myŏn was a minority premier when the Assembly was deadlocked between the new and old factions of the Democratic Party. At least Premier Chang had been well educated and disciplined and knew politics. However, Roh, heading a "democratic" government, often appeared downright befuddled and lacked political or economic direction or expertise. The executive branch seemed to drift from crisis to crisis, while the newly emboldened legislative branch flexed its muscles seemingly with a vengeance—particularly in exercising its constitutional authority to inspect and audit the activities of the executive branch. This created interminable delays in enacting legislation sponsored by the executive branch or even in authorizing a national budget. The prices of checks and balances were suddenly exorbitant. However, most of the people, including the middle class, who had long resented the oppressive grip of authoritarian regimes, appeared to be tolerant of and even amused by an ineffectual executive's being pushed around by a spirited and sometimes audacious legislature, so long as their economic well-being was somehow not threatened and politics was conducted responsibly. However, thunderclouds soon gathered over the economic horizon.

[9] *Korea Annual 1989*, p. 142.

Mounting Economic Problems and the Three-Party Merger

Since 1962 five successive five-year plans had been termed "economic development" plans. The revised sixth five-year plan, for 1988–1992, was no entitled the "Economic and Social Development Plan." The 151-page plan acknowledged that "political democratization has brought with it a strong demand for economic democratization," in particular calling for an "equitable distribution of the fruits of economic growth." It was also openly admitted that the "growth-first" policy since the Park administration inevitably had resulted in huge gaps between different industrial sectors and various segments of society. The planners further acknowledged, with an unaccustomed candor, that Korea had reached a point at which the government must take appropriate steps to accommodate "demands from farmers, fishermen, low-income earners in urban areas, industrial workers, and other social groups if the nation is to attain cohesive and sustained economic development." It is worth noting that no mention was made of any private sector initiatives in meeting these needs.

The Roh presidency and the economy. Troubling questions immediately arose in many minds: even if President Roh were convinced of the need of a policy shift toward balance and equity, would he, an inexperienced minority president, be able to implement these policies? The Roh government was understandably cautious and hesitant, while urgent demands on the system became torrential in the "democratizing" period. Predictably, the most pressing problems arose in the economic sector, particularly in the form of bitter and frequent labor disputes and strikes in a period of exploding demands from the segment of the population that had been most suppressed and deprived for a generation.

The workers' increasingly vociferous demands for better wages and improved working conditions could no longer be contained. The number of unionized workers had swollen from 948,000 in 1980, the first year of the Fifth Republic, to 1,267,000 in 1987, its last year. Strikes occurred with increasing frequency and virulence, often resulting in sharp wage concessions by management, to the point at which in 1989 Korean aggregate wage levels were the second highest in Asia, below only Japan, according to the Labor Department. The wage increases were in many cases overdue and justified, but coupled with simultaneously declining labor productivity naturally undermined the competitive advantages internationally. According to data published by the president of the Korea Development Institute, a government organ, wage and productivity data were as in Table 5.

Table 5. Wages and productivity in manufacturing (average annual change, %)

	1983–1985	1986	1987	1988	1989
Nominal wage	10.1	9.2	11.6	19.6	25.1
Consumer price index	2.7	2.8	3.0	7.1	5.7
Real wage[a]	7.2	6.2	8.0	11.3	17.9
Labor productivity[b]	11.0	14.2	12.0	12.6	7.9
Unit labor cost ($)[c]	−6.4	−5.5	6.7	19.6	26.1

[a]Nominal wage divided by consumer price index
[b]Value added in manufacturing divided by those employed in manufacturing
[c]Unit labor cost in won currency divided by nominal exchange rate
Sources: Bank of Korea, *Monthly Bulletin*, various issues.

By the second year of the Roh regime, manufacturing wages were increasing by more than 25 percent annually, and the unit labor cost was soaring by 26 percent per year. At the same time there was a sharp decline in labor productivity of Korean workers, who were largely freed from harsh control measures of the past often including the involvement of the dreaded KCIA (whose name was changed to the Agency for National Security Planning Agency). Soon, entrepreneurs began loudly to profess the loss of their will or the ability to stay in manufacturing and to engage in intensified stock market and real estate speculations, which produced huge unearned profits for the rich and the powerful, who engaged in shameless *kwasobi* (excessive consumption), further exacerbating the rift between haves and have nots.

In the heyday of "democratic" press freedom there grew a heightened public awareness of the "abysmal gap between the rich and the poor" (*pinbu kyŏkch'a*), particularly in view of the conspicuous overconsumption by the nouveau riche. Because successful entrepreneurs and financiers were determined to defend their vested interests (*kidŭkkwŏn*) a confrontational, crisis atmosphere developed. Long accustomed to pervasive government involvement in solutions to problems large and small, the people again looked to the government to resolve the crisis. However, the government, now headed by a minority president, was no longer effective. The discontented, employers and employees, Right and Left alike, soon denounced the "democratizing" Roh regime as ineffective. Some went as far as calling the Roh government a "*no*" government, an anarchy.

The advent of this feeble government coincided with stiffening international economic competition partly due to the domestic wage-price jumps and productivity drops in 1989. The "double whammy" of political and economic crises suddenly loomed on the horizon. Some Korean opinion leaders began voicing concerns about the "Latin Americanization of Korea," meaning a crumbling economy after a quick flash of relative prosperity, coupled with political instability. The Korean economy, sensitive to political tremors, still seemed buoyant even at the beginning of 1989 but appeared pathetic toward the end of the same year. Ominous talks of "crisis" quickly reached a crescendo seemingly orchestrated by management and official sources, who were alarmed by bitter labor disputes attendant with wage hikes, which were highlighted in the mass media that were owned or heavily influenced by industrial conglomerates. In fact, however, the incidence of strikes dropped sharply, from 1,616 in 1989 to 322 in 1990. The pessimistic noises emanating from within were amplified by external media that observed, among other matters, that the Koreans had uncorked their champagne bottles too soon and that South Korea was, after all, a "worm" instead of an economic "minidragon." Some foreign investors were frightened away, and Korea's foreign-directed investment in the United States, China, and Southeast Asia rose sharply between 1987 and 1990. By 1990 Korean investments abroad were much higher than foreign investments in Korea, $1 billion and $800 million, respectively.[10]

The government economic management team, headed by Vice Premier Cho Soon, that confidently dedicated itself to a policy of balance and equity—policy lines eloquently pledged in Roh's inaugural address—was transformed by December 1989 to a "crisis management team," reportedly on instructions from Roh himself.[11] Unlike earlier vice premiers in charge of the economy who had enjoyed President Park's full support in pursuing the growth-first policy, Cho suddenly found that there was little presidential backing for the balance-and-equity policy, and he came under heavy attack by the powerful conglomerates. He needed unwavering political support from the president, who had solemnly declared the new policy less than two years earlier. Vice Premier Cho's team was replaced after only fifteen and a half months in office by Vice Premier Lee Sŭng-yun, who now advocated the old policy of growth and stability.

The calculating middle class. In this milieu, on a different level, the attitude of the middle class in support of reforms and democratization was not to last in the face of real or perceived threats to economic and political stability. A visible shift in the mood of the middle class came when the frequent worker strikes, accompanied by spiraling wage-price hikes, apparently threatened continued economic growth and stability, as well as international competitiveness. A feature article in *Dong-A Ilbo* highlighted that many Korean products were now seen as lacking quality while their prices rose sharply, due to the doubling of wages of manufacturing workers in three years.[12] Though the frequency of labor disputes continued to

[10] Korea Economic Institute of America, *Korea: Economic Update*, II, 2 (Summer 1991): pp. 1–3.
[11] *Dong-A Ilbo*, 14 December 1989, p. 1.
[12] *Dong-A Ilbo*, 19 March 1991, p. 14.

decline sharply in 1991, the theme of economic crisis so well orchestrated by big business and government was evidently accepted by members of the middle class. In sharp contrast to the 1987 political activism in support of democratization by many in the middle class, near the end of the dictatorial Chun regime, they were conspicuously silent in 1991.

At that time fierce student demonstrations erupted in many cities when a twenty-year-old college freshman, Kang Kyŏng-dae, died on April 25 after being beaten by plainclothes riot police. Unlike the high-handed management of a similar incident during the last months of the Chun regime, which had attempted to depict a death by torture as accidental, Roh was quick to dismiss his interior minister, who assumed responsibility for the police brutality. Reports on demonstrations protesting Kang's death in eighty-seven cities by an estimated 200,000 students and workers this time led by labor unions—the largest turnout since 1987—were balanced by stories on South Korean losses in international markets and inflationary pressures at home. Soon the mass media, both domestic and foreign, noted the conspicuous absence of the middle class and white-collar workers from the 1991 demonstrations; the *New York Times* went so far as to observe that "the middle classes appear fed up with unyielding attitudes"[13] of students and militant workers." Reportedly desperate for middle-class support, several students, doused with paint thinner, burned themselves to death in a desperate attempt at shocking the middle class into antigovernment action. Even then the middle class and white-collar workers remained unmoved.

Generally speaking, well educated and aware of democratic theories and practices in advanced countries, members of the middle class have theoretically supported political and economic reforms in Korea. It was widely agreed that such was the case in 1987, after nearly three decades of authoritarian rule. However, when democratization moves in the economic sector—specifically, the unbridled freedom to strike and consequent wage hikes seemed to threaten economic growth and stability, as well as social order—in 1991 the middle class seemed to switch its support to the conservative forces in government, political parties, and management. Thus the middle class became a quiet balancer between the ruling groups, which had almost always been conservative and authoritarian, and the forces that favored all-out democratization of Korean politics and economy.

Sometimes the middle class appeared to distinguish political "freedom" from economic "equality." During the "great democratic revolution" of 1987, the middle class clearly supported political freedom and

---

[13] *New York Times*, 9 May 1991, p. A3. Similarly, "South Korean Protests Lack Key Middle-Class Backing," was a headline in the *Washington Post*, 12 May 1991, pp. A22–24.

human rights. At the time it favored a liberalization of politics even at the cost of slowing economic growth, but when the democratization of 1987 unleashed a strong demand for economic equality, possibly at the expense of vested interests of the middle class, its members felt threatened and thus resisted measures promoting economic equality. The middle class held the paradoxical stance of favoring "reforms within stability,"[14] with an emphasis on stability at the beginning of the 1990s. This group apparently had serious second thoughts about reform for reform's sake without tangible benefits.

The three-party merger. An unprecedented and sweeping political realignment took place on January 22, 1990, when it was announced that Kim Young Sam's Reunification Democratic Party and Kim Jong Pil's New Democratic Republican Party would merge with Roh's ruling Democratic Justice Party. The hybrid organization, to be called the Democratic Liberal Party, would now control 217 of 299 seats in the National Assembly, a more than two-thirds majority, when the new "grand conservative coalition" was formally born by February 1990. There were no "progressive," left-leaning, or labor parties in the Assembly as a result of persistent anti-Communist campaigns by South Korean governments. Apparently the surprise merger had been engineered by three pragmatic politicians in a Machiavellian search of their political goals.

On Roh's part, this represented a breakthrough in freeing himself from the unbearable gridlock that the opposition-dominated National Assembly had imposed on his administration. Never mind that Roh was embracing a bitter political opponent, Kim Young Sam, who had excoriated Chun and Roh as ruthless military dictators, the worst enemies of democracy. Roh still would control the largest voting bloc in the newly merged party, 87 seats. For Kim Young Sam it was a calculated if unprincipled political maneuver to ingratiate the conservative ruling groups and eventually wrest control of the ruling party from within to capture the presidency. Ever burning with ambition to win the highest political prize, which he had coveted all his adult life, Kim Young Sam was entering into an "unholy alliance" with Roh, the very man he had bitterly castigated as a scheming military dictator. In fact, Kim had declared repeatedly that Roh should be punished for his "criminal role" in the December 12 incident as Roh moved a unit of the Ninth Division under his command to secure the capitol building in Seoul. Kim Young Sam justified his chameleonlike transformation as a "grave decision to save the nation" from governmental paralysis, but his real motivation was revealed by his

---

[14] "Chunggan ch'ung ŏdero kako itna" (Whither Goes the Middle Stratum)" (part of a feature series on the middle class), *Dong-A Ilbo*, 6 July 1991, p. 18.

(From left to right) Former opposition leader Kim Young Sam, President Roh Tae Woo, and another former opposition leader, Kim Jong Pil, as they announced on January 22, 1990, the merger of their three political parties. The merger gave birth to a "superconservative coalition," named the Democratic Liberal Party (DLP). Kim Young Sam managed to become the DLP presidential nominee in 1992 and was elected. Kim Jong Pil is now serving as the Prime Minister under President Kim Dae-jung. (The Korean Information Center)

statement that he had to "enter a tiger's lair to capture the tiger"—in his case the presidency. It was not surprising that many of his erstwhile supporters felt "betrayed" and seriously questioned his "character and his leadership as a fighter for democracy."[15] Forty-six members of the Reunification Democratic Party who followed Kim Young Sam and joined the merged party would make the decisive difference in the ruling party's fortune in the National Assembly.

Kim Jong Pil, the erstwhile righthand man of Park Chung Hee, played the key role in the secret merger negotiations. He won recognition as a member of the ruling triumvirate, as well as the prolongation of his and his party's political lives. His party had captured only thirty-five seats in the April 1988 assembly election, and his future and that of his party—standing alone—were precarious, at best. The most amazing fact was that members of the parties went along with the top-level personal decisions by Roh and the two Kims, all negotiated in great secrecy. Once again, the merger proved that Korean political parties were peculiarly personal cliques that formed, disappeared, or merged at the direction of key indi-

15 Lee Manwoo, *The Odyssey of Korean Democracy,* p. 134.

viduals, the "bosses." Whether the stabilized Roh government could exercise effectual political leadership remained the central question. With the advent of this bloated ruling party, another question arose in many minds: would this superparty, the product of a secret top-level political deal, become in time as arrogant and undemocratic as the similarly oversized Liberal Party had during the last years of the Rhee era?

The economy and the 1992 Assembly elections. A decisive answer to this question and the people's judgment of the designs of Roh and the two Kims were given in the March 24, 1992, election for the fourteenth National Assembly, roughly two years after the merger. Many former followers of Kim Young Sam felt "betrayed" by what they perceived as Kim's "unprincipled" political maneuvers in switching his longstanding position as an opposition leader. Further, the strange marriage of convenience produced "three parties under one roof" instead of a well-fused ruling party. Despite all-out public efforts to gloss over differences among the three parties, it became evident that right-wing followers of Chun and Roh did not spare behind-the-scenes efforts at isolating Kim Young Sam. A clear indication of such political in-fighting was the leak of a photocopy of a supposedly top-secret written agreement among Roh and the two Kims to the effect that the new party would promote another constitutional amendment to adopt a responsible cabinet system. Kim Young Sam had publicly opposed such a system, but the photocopy of the agreement clearly showed his signature. It was believed that the leak was made by Roh's confidants, who had access to the agreement, to embarrass Kim Young Sam.

What was most disturbing to the people was the economy, which was indeed weakening, growing only 4.7 percent in 1992, far below the government's expectation of 7 percent. This was the worst growth rate in decades. Powerful and rich conglomerates could absorb temporary setbacks, but numerous small and medium-sized businesses could not. A record number of promissory notes were dishonored in 1992, and 10,769 medium and small firms went bankrupt—leading to some widely reported suicides of these business owners. The number of unemployed workers rose sharply from 1991, and real estate prices, which had been skyrocketing in overpopulated South Korea, plummeted in 1992.

Under these political and economic circumstances the elections for the National Assembly took place on March 24, 1992. Though the polling was conducted calmly, turnout was one of the lowest in recent times; only about 70 percent of eligible voters came out for the first balloting for the legislature in four years. The government party, which claimed 215 seats in the 299-seat Assembly after the three-party merger, managed to elect only 149 of its members. This was one vote shy of a simple majority, recreating the phenomenon of four years earlier, when Roh's government party was the minority. The opposition Democratic Party, led by Kim Dae-jung, won ninety-seven seats, and the Unification People's Party, organized only two months before the election by the honorary chairman of the Hyundai Group, Chung Ju-yŏng, won thirty-one seats. Chung had bitterly criticized the Roh government's handling of the economy. Only by wooing some independently elected assemblymen could the government party muster a simple majority vote in the Assembly. Through an orderly and democratic election, the Korean voters forcefully "reshaped" the National Assembly and resoundingly repudiated the machinations of the three politicians.[16] Another index of voter discontent with those in power was that about one-fourth of the legislators were in the Assembly for the first time.

[16] *New York Times,* 27 March 1992, p. A3.

✪

CHAPTER 6

The "Civilian and Democratic" Government, 1992–1993

As Roh's single-term presidency was ending in 1992, there was no longer any question about duly electing—through a direct popular vote—another president. It was certain that Kim Dae-jung, a perennial candidate since 1971 and sworn nemesis of military authoritarianism, would again run. Still, no threat of another military intervention was made, no matter which civilian candidate won. The ruling Democratic Liberal Party held its party convention on May 19, 1992, and nominated Kim Young Sam, erstwhile head of an opposition party until the three-party merger of January 1990, as the government party candidate. It became clear that since the 1990 party merger, Kim Young Sam had successfully managed to secure at least the acquiescence of both President Roh and Kim Jong Pil as 95.7 percent of 6,882 ruling party delegates attended the convention and Kim received 66.3 percent of delegate votes. His rival, Yi Chong Chan, a 1960 graduate of the Korean Military Academy, received 33.3 percent of the vote despite his withdrawal as a candidate, indicating that there were more than 2,000 delegates within the ruling party who would not support Kim's candidacy for whatever reason.

Even as a jubilant Kim Young Sam accepted the nomination and vowed to "restore responsible politics," antiruling party and anti-Kim demonstrations erupted in twenty-two urban centers including Seoul, Pusan, and Kwangju. These demonstrations, organized by an "All-Nation Coalition for Democracy and National Unification," were spearheaded by thousands of students from leading universities in Seoul as well as in the Chŏlla Provinces. The coalition asserted that the ruling Democratic Liberal Party betrayed the democratically expressed wishes of the people in the 1987 presidential and the 1992 National Assembly elections, in which

Downtown Seoul today, where high-rise structures coexist with some remaining traditional buildings. (The Korean Information Center)

a minority president and a minority government in the Assembly were chosen. The coalition also denounced the ruling party, born of an "illicit union" of three parties, for nominating Kim Young Sam, who had, they said, betrayed many of his followers. However, the demonstrators were effectively scattered by more than 49,000 riot policemen ordered out en masse by the Roh government, which was determined to hold the party convention undisturbed.[1]

The First Civilian President in Thirty-Two Years

Candidate Kim Young Sam was named president of the ruling Democratic Liberal Party in September 1992, in a move by Roh evidently to give Kim all the advantages associated with being head of the government party. Kim Jong Pil succeeded Kim Young Sam as executive chairman of the ruling party. In an unprecedented and widely praised move, on October 8, 1992, Roh then named a politically "neutral cabinet" to administer

---

[1] *Hankook Ilbo*, 20 May 1992, pp. 1–2.

the country during the December presidential election. A respected senior scholar-administrator, Hyŏn Sung-jong, president of Hanlim University, was named the "neutral" prime minister. The lifelong educator and soft-spoken "last gentleman"[2] was seen as an ideal choice to head an apolitical administration for a brief period. Predictably, Kim Dae-jung, Kim Young Sam's longtime rival, was nominated formally by 60.2 percent of 2,348 delegates of the opposition Democratic Party on May 27. This nomination, too, was properly conducted within the major opposition party, which maintained order and decorum throughout the process.

Evidently indicating a growing disenchantment among business conglomerates with the government and/or the lineup for the presidential race that was emerging, a maverick candidate, multibillionaire and chairman emeritus of the Hyundai Group Chŏng Ju-yŏng hurriedly organized his own political party, the United People's Party, in early 1992 and proclaimed his presidential candidacy. This was the first time that a *chaebŏl* founder had personally entered a presidential race as a candidate, and it was evident that the Hyundai conglomerate's unlimited financial resources made this last-minute political debut possible. Also reflecting the growing friction between the government and the business world, Kim Woo Choong, chairman of the Daewoo Group, announced that he would run for president, but this announcement was quietly withdrawn. However, astute observers were quick to note that these moves by Chŏng and Kim reflected unmistakably changing state–business relations.[3]

In an unprecedented move the Korean military signaled for the first time in more than three decades its "neutral" stance in a series of lectures delivered at the National Defense Graduate School by the defense minister, the chairman of the joint chiefs, and the army chief of staff. These men emphasized that the military must concentrate its energies on its proper tasks of defending the country from external menaces.[4] This was in sharp contrast to the widely known practice of military commanders, from as early as the Rhee period, dutifully "delivering" votes from their entire units to ruling party candidates. These lectures could also be seen as the military's willingness to accept any legitimate winner, including Kim Dae-jung, who had been made out by the military leaders—particularly Park and Chun—to be "too leftist" and antimilitary to be acceptable as president.

The activated civil society and the 1992 presidential election. What had been utterly unprecedented were the activities of the civil society, notably the Citizens' Coalition for Fair Election, initiated by Son Pong-ho, a Seoul Na-

---

[2] *Hankook Ilbo*, 8 October 1992, p. 14.

[3] Eun Mee Kim, *Big Business, Strong State* (Albany, N.Y.: State University of New York Press, 1987), p. 200.

[4] *Hankook Ilbo*, 23 September 1992, p. 2.

tional University professor.[5] This was initially a loose coalition of citizen activists from fifty-six voluntary religious, women's, labor, and farmers' organizations; the number grew to include 250 organizations as others such as the influential Economic and Business Association and student organizations joined the movement. The coalition organized fifty local centers and some ten thousand citizen volunteers, in many cases college students, and established local watchdog groups to expose any corrupt or coercive practices in electioneering such as the distribution of gifts or money or the application of pressure by local officials, including the police. Son attributed the unprecedented interest in the movement to a heightened level of democratic political consciousness among the electorate. There had never existed such a large network of grass-roots citizens' volunteer coalitions in the entire history of republican Korea. In the past when activists—usually college students—protested against corrupt practices, they were often brutally attacked by hired thugs or, worse still, by "patriotic" youth group members or even the police. There were no reported incidents of such attacks on citizen volunteers in 1992. A foreign observer reported that "the South Korean people deserve most of the credit for bringing democracy to their country."[6]

Unlike in presidential elections held in the previous three decades, all three major presidential candidates in 1992—Kim Young Sam, Kim Dae-jung, and Chŏng Ju-yŏng—were bona fide civilians, with no military background or visible backing by the military. Chŏng, the Ross Perot of Korea, declared that the "politics by the two Kims," who had been active on the political scene without winning the presidency, should be terminated by his election. The true contest, however, was between Kim Young Sam and Kim Dae-jung, both onetime opposition leaders. The Kims campaigned vigorously and effectively, attracting huge crowds at mass rallies. The Korean news media estimated that three out of every four qualified voters attended at least one mass rally to hear either or both Kims.

The enthusiasm for a "democratic" election was palpable. Kim Dae-jung appeared more charismatic and eloquent than his rival and represented forces of the rapid democratic reforms and bold approaches to North–South reunification. Kim Young Sam, now representing a conservative supercoalition, was moderate in most policy matters, advocating a "reform amidst stability," with the emphasis on stability. Kim Young Sam proved an indefatigable campaigner. He had been a soccer champion in his high school days and a hiking enthusiast and daily jogger for decades. He campaigned just as energetically, taking full advantage of being the candidate of the abundantly financed ruling party. As the campaign pace

---

[5] *Hankook Ilbo*, 24 March 1992, p. 12.
[6] James Sterngold, in a special to the *New York Times*, 14 December 1992, pp. A1, A11.

quickened in the final stage, Kim Young Sam could afford to crisscross the country in helicopters according to well-laid plans to address more rallies. In contrast, the best Kim Dae-jung could do was to take commercial airline flights, which still do no reach most rural areas. Kim Young Sam clearly outcampaigned Kim Dae-jung and brought steady messages of "stability" to the people, who longed for just that after decades of turbulent politics.

When the ballots had been counted breathlessly, without the unsavory incidents that were all too common in the past, Kim Young Sam emerged the winner by a substantial margin, 41.4 percent to Kim Dae-jung's 33.4 percent. Chŏng Ju-yŏng, the last-minute entrant, received 16.1 percent of the vote. As in presidential elections since the 1971 contest between Park Chung Hee and Kim Dae-jung, it was clear that Kim Young Sam clearly benefited from deeply rooted regionalism among voters in the area of the populous southeastern province from which he hailed. Regionalism in reverse was also clearly operative, as Kim Young Sam received a negligible number of votes from the South Chŏlla Province. For instance, from Kwangju, the capital of South Chŏlla, Kim Young Sam won only 14,504 votes whereas Kim Dae-jung garnered 652,237 votes—some forty-five times more. Conversely, Kim Young Sam received 1,514,043 votes from his native South Kyŏngsang Province, which left 991,414 votes for Kim Dae-jung. Such lopsided voting cannot be explained without rampant regionalism that remained a serious political problem. Aside from the manifestations of deep-seated regionalism, however, the winning margin enjoyed by Kim Young Sam was considered large enough to be legitimate, and observers noted that Kim Young Sam received more widespread support from different social classes, educational backgrounds, age groups, and occupations than other candidates, indicating his popularity throughout the nation.[7]

Kim Dae-jung conceded defeat promptly and gracefully. In a healing concession speech unprecedented in Korean politics, Kim "humbly accept[ed] the people's judgment," adding that he firmly believed in Kim Young Sam's "ability to develop democracy in Korea and lay the groundwork for national reunification." Kim had previously lost two presidential bids, against Park Chung Hee in 1971 and Roh Tae Woo in 1987, and after the third defeat resigned his Assembly seat to "let history judge me and live a quiet life." Whether Kim, at age sixty-seven, had forever removed himself from the political arena remained to be seen, but he was believed to have won fresh respect from many with his graceful concession speech, which indicated a new level of maturity in Korean electoral

[7] Kil Soong-Hoom, "Political Reforms of Kim Young Sam Government," *Korea and World Affairs*, 17, no. 3 (Fall 1993): p. 420.

contests. Local media quoted a social worker as summing it up best: "This is a process of democracy, isn't it?" The peaceful transfer of power to a duly elected civilian president took place on February 25, 1993, the first time in thirty-two years.

Kim Young Sam. The first bona fide civilian president in thirty-two years, Kim Young Sam was born in 1927 into a well-to-do family that owned two aquaculture farms and several fishing vessels on the island of Kŏje, off Pusan. This only son was self-centered and mischievous.[8] Kim attended a four-year village school near his home and finished the last two years of his primary training at a regular grammar school some distance away from his home. In compliance with his grandfather's wish that he attend a well-established middle school, Kim was sent to a secondary school in Pusan—a major move for a pampered boy of Kŏje Island. While a student at what is today Kyŏngnam High School, he was an avid soccer player. This meant that he acquired an enduring habit of daily physical exercise but also that he had to spend long hours every day practicing soccer, leaving little time to engage in any systematic and wide-ranging reading. No biographies note that he was an outstanding student academically. However, one legend—said to be originated by a newspaper to indicate his audacious ambition—has it that he hung on the wall of his boarding-house room a handwritten declaration that he was to be "a future president of Korea."[9] This political ambition remained a driving force throughout his life.

In September 1948 Kim enrolled in the philosophy department of the College of Liberal Arts of Seoul National University, which then had just been reorganized as a comprehensive university and has since become the premier institution in Korea. Kim's minor field was political science. Admission to the philosophy department was easier than to the political science department, which attracted students with stronger academic credentials. The elective courses Kim took were mostly in political science, however. His academic record at Seoul National University was "average."[10]

A turning point in Kim's life came in his sophomore year, when he entered a prestigious oratory contest in Seoul. Kim won second prize, which was given out by Foreign Minister Chang T'aek-sang, well known for his high-profile service as the decidedly right-wing director of the

[8] O Il-hwan, *Daet'ongnyŏng kaŭi saramdŭl* (People on the Presidential Street) (Seoul: Myŏngjisa, 1992), pp. 170–72.

[9] Ibid., pp. 174–75.

[10] Son Se-il, ed., *Kim Dae-jung kwa Kim Young-sam* (Kim Dae-jung and Kim Young Sam) (Seoul: Ilwŏl Sŏgak, 1985), p. 290.

Metropolitan Police Bureau of Seoul, often a violent arena where leftists and right wingers battled. When Chang ran for a National Assembly seat in the second legislative election, held in May 1950, Kim became a campaign orator and contributed to Chang's successful bid. This cemented their relationship as patron and young protege. The campaign experience also aroused Kim's political ambition, and he began writing numerous letters to local notables in Kŏje Island so as to form an electoral base in his home district.

According to his official curriculum vitae,[11] Kim "joined the army during the Korean War . . . as a troop information and education specialist [and] worked as a writer of materials directed at North Korea." Evidently, the term "joined" is used in a very loose sense because he was neither an officer nor an enlisted man. Some eight months after he became what a biographer called a "student volunteer,"[12] Kim became a secretary to Chang T'aek-sang, by then vice chairman of the National Assembly. Thus, while the Korean War was raging and many of Kim's classmates were volunteering to serve actively in the South Korean military that was consuming innumerable young lives, Kim cleverly made his way to a safe center stage of the political arena under a powerful patron. Some characterize this as crass opportunism, but others see it as an early indication of his deft pragmatism.

In 1951 Kim married Son Myŏng-sun, daughter of a well-to-do manufacturer in Masan. By the time the third National Assembly election was held, in May 1954, a year after the end of the Korean War, Kim was just old enough to be eligible to run for the legislature. He predictably joined the ruling Liberal Party, and ran from Kŏje as a nominee of the powerful ruling party. Kim won a decisive victory and became an assemblyman at the age of twenty-six—an age record that has not yet been broken. Thus Kim began his career as an ambitious young man who adroitly took advantage of political opportunities with powerful patrons and with a ruling party led by President Rhee.

However, on November 17, 1954, when Rhee forced a constitutional amendment through the National Assembly to make himself eligible for a third term by the questionable means of rounding off a fraction of a vote, young Kim was incensed. Though he was a member of the Liberal Party and thus expected to support Rhee's brazen parliamentary manipulation, Kim cast a negative vote and bolted from the party along with eleven of its other members. He promptly began associating with leading opposition figures including Shin Ik-hi, Cho Byŏng-ok, Chang Myŏn, and Kwak

---

[11] Released by the Korean Information Office, Embassy of the Republic of Korea, Washington, D.C., November 15, 1994.

[12] O I-hwan, *Daet'ongnyŏng kaŭi Saramdŭl*, p. 176.

Sang-hun, and managed to become one of thirty-three charter members of the opposition Democratic Party. Thus began Kim's long career as an opposition politician.

Later Kim was elected to the National Assembly as an opposition party member from Pusan. He rose steadily in the opposition camp, serving as its floor leader five times. Noting that the opposition leaders who were attempting to unseat the autocratic septuagenarian Rhee were also authoritarian and old, Kim advocated that the new opposition standard bearer be in his forties.[13] In Korea, where age traditionally commands respect, this audacious suggestion raised many eyebrows. Presumably those in their forties would be less traditional, more liberal, and more flexible. By the early 1970s Kim was in his early forties. His political ambition was virtually transparent. In the 1971 presidential election, however, it was Kim Dae-jung, Kim Young Sam's intraopposition rival, also in his forties, who narrowly won the opposition party nomination, defeating Kim Young Sam. Presidential candidate Kim Dae-jung managed to garner 45.3 percent of the popular vote in his contest against President Park Chung Hee, who enjoyed the vast advantage of a powerful incumbency but received only 53.2 percent of the vote. Though Kim Young Sam publicly rejoiced in the opposition party nomination of a man in his forties, the personal rivalry between the two Kims intensified.

Also intensified were Kim Young Sam's criticisms of the increasingly dictatorial Park regime, particularly after it imposed on the nation in October 1972 the so-called "revitalizing reform," essentially to make Park reelectable for life. Kim missed no opportunity to excoriate the "dictatorial military regime," even with foreign media representatives. With a *New York Times* reporter he went a step further by advocating that instead of maintaining a supportive posture toward the Park regime, the United States should apply "public and direct pressure on Park" to "bring him under control."[14] The Park regime, eager for a counterattack, seized on the occasion and launched an intense media campaign, characterizing Kim as an American "flunky" calling for American intervention into domestic politics in Korea. Reportedly under direct orders from an incensed Park, ruling party members in the National Assembly voted unanimously on October 4, 1979, to "reprimand" Kim by stripping him of his assemblyman status. Kim was charged with "insulting the head of state" and "advocating foreign interference in domestic affairs."[15] The vote took place while the police blocked opposition legislators from entering the

---

[13] Son Se-il, *Kim Dae-jung kwa Kim Young-sam*, p. 294.

[14] *New York Times*, 16 September 1972.

[15] "Biographical Sketch of Kim Young Sam," released by the Korean Information Office, Embassy of the Republic of Korea, Washington, D.C., November 15, 1994, p. 2.

Assembly chamber. This was the first time a duly elected legislator lost his status by Assembly action. Subsequently, Kim was placed under house arrest for nearly a year.

Several years later the political arena was again swept by a series of stormy events triggered by President Chun's refusal to allow a constitutional amendment to reinstitute a direct presidential election, as well as his making Roh Tae Woo his handpicked presidential candidate in the 1988 election. The pent-up popular anger with the high-handed military dictatorship exploded across South Korea; continuous demonstrations by students, workers, middle-class citizens, and now the network of the civil society could not be contained by the coercive might of the regime. No one would belittle the courageous roles played by opposition leaders, particularly Kim Young Sam, in coordinating the mammoth demonstrations and marches of June 10, 1987, now celebrated as the "Democratic Struggle of June 10." However, it was the spontaneously demonstrating masses who constituted an unstoppable force that led to the "surprising victory" for reform and democracy promised in Roh's June 29 declaration. As the people led fierce struggles on the streets, ex-Generals Chun and Roh "surrendered," and the opposition leaders were the beneficiaries.

However, the two main opposition leaders, Kim Young Sam and Kim Dae-jung, once again—despite all the renewed pleas by numerous anti-dictatorship groups—could not agree to field a single opposition standard bearer in the 1987 presidential election. Such an idea overlooked the intense rivalry for the presidency that existed between the men and the mutual distrust left over from bitter personal rivalries of the past. In the end both Kims ran and both lost—once again.

Roh was the victor, winning 36.6 percent of the popular vote. Between the two Kims, they won some 55 percent of the total vote, meaning that one of them, with the support of the other, could easily have defeated Roh and restored the presidency to a civilian who had been "struggling to restore democracy." It was clear, then, that both Kims were driven more by personal ambition than by a commitment to restore civilian and democratic rule.

One might wonder about the extent and depth of Kim Young Sam's understanding of and commitment to democracy. In his long career there have been numerous short statements on urgent and specific—some even trivial—issues released for political purposes. For any substantive exposition of his thoughts on democracy, one could turn to his published books or collections of essays, always bearing in mind that they were also released by a career politician for political purposes. His books, some written during prolonged periods of house arrest, are *Urika kidael undŏkun ŏpta* (There are No Slopes We Can Lean Against), *Chŏngkwŏnŭn tchalko chŏngch'inŭn kilda* (A Regime is Short-lived but Politics is Long-lasting), *Sasipte kisuron* (A Treatise on Standard-Bearers in Their Forties), and *Nawa nae chokukŭi chinsil* (The Truth about Me and My Fatherland).

In most of these books, the essays are usually short, breezy, and eclectic. Kim touches on many topics, hopping around—as he was wont to do in conversation—without dwelling on a subject or developing a coherent theme. For instance, in *Nawa nae chokuŭi chinsil*,[16] he covers forty topics, offering essays such as "A Hymn for My Mother," "Democracy and National Security," and "Free Press and Opposition Parties." These and the other essays contain few penetrating insights or well-constructed analyses, but rather are long recitations of the political slogans of his day.

His more recent volume, *Minjuhwa kukukŭi kil* (The Path to Save the Nation Through Democratization),[17] is also a collection, of forty-four short essays on such wide-ranging topics as "My Twenty-three–Day Fasting Struggle" and "Democratizing Korea." The collection includes reproductions of publicity materials such as Kim's acceptance speech as president of the Unification and Democracy Party and press interview records. In "Democratizing Korea," rather than revealing his thoughts on democracy, Kim is evasive, declaring simply that democracy should be urgently attained in Korea "for the following reasons":

> the capitalist economic system cannot be properly developed and sustained unless it is accompanied with political democracy. . . . We must not forget that Asian and Central and South American countries such as Vietnam and Nicaragua . . . lost the opportunity to realize democracy. . . .
>
> Korea sacrificed dearly for democracy during the Korean War . . . in the April 19 (student) revolution . . . and the Kwangju incident. Korea has sacrificed more than any other nation in the name of democracy. These high-priced sacrifices can be repaid only through realizing democracy. . . . Third, realizing democracy is an essential task to restore Korea's relationship with friendly nations on the basis of true friendship and trust.[18]

Through such pedestrian declarations Kim justifies democracy as a means to an end, such as developing a capitalist economy (as though they are causally related) or improving relations with the United States and other nations (which maintain working relations with nondemocratic states). Kim did not write what might have passed as a sustained and well-developed treatise on democracy itself.

[16] Seoul: Ilwol Sogak, 1983.
[17] Seoul: Ilwol Sogak, 1987.
[18] Ibid., pp. 306–7.

Initial "Democratic" Reforms

When Kim took the presidential oath for a single five-year term on cold but bright February 25, 1993, it marked a number of firsts. Kim was the first civilian to be democratically elected in thirty-two years. This was the first presidential inauguration of a seasoned politician who could genuinely claim that he was a "fighter for democracy." It also meant the launching of a regime that was not burdened with questions about its legitimacy. In his twenty-minute inaugural address (evidently written in a different style from his prosaic essays of the past), Kim Young Sam, 65, declared:

> We are gathered here today to open a civilian and democratic era. . . . This government was made possible by the people's burning desire and noble sacrifices for democracy. . . .
>
> Deep in my heart, I have a dream of creating a new Korea. A new Korea shall be a freer and more mature democratic society in which . . . human dignity is upheld. . . .
>
> Today, however, we are suffering from a disease, a Korean disease . . . due to a value system that has been turned upside-down. . . . We must change and reform. . . .
>
> Our reforms must start with three urgent tasks: First, misconduct and corruption must be rooted out. Second, the economy must be revitalized. Third, national discipline must be re-established. . . . Immediate reforms shall start at the very top.[19]

He also proclaimed the need to establish a "new economy" to restore economic vitality:

> To that end, the government shall guarantee the autonomy and competition instead of regulations and protection of the economic sector. The creativity of the people shall be encouraged. The government will tighten its belt first. The people shall live frugally and save more. Luxury and waste shall be rooted out. Workers will have to sweat more to produce more. Enterprises shall win in international competitions through bold technological innovations.
>
> When the government and the people, the workers and the business work cheerfully together, our economy will be revived. This is the "new economy" I seek.[20]

[19] The full text of the inaugural address in Korea was carried in *Hankook Ilbo*, 26 February 1993, p. 4. The partial translation here is by this author.
[20] Ibid.

In the euphoric morn of having finally attained his lifelong ambition, Kim Young Sam equated the launching of the Seventh Republic with "the Second Founding of the Korean Republic." In his soaring rhetoric Kim set lofty standards to aspire to and also—probably unintentionally—to be judged by. To a detached observer, however, it was clear that his seemingly unbounded optimism was in fact bounded by a number of towering realities. He proposed building a more mature democracy on the political legacy of more than thirty years of military-dominated politics. During those years it had been a national obsession to attain rapid economic growth by whatever means, a fixation that degenerated to, and in time justified, each individual's pursuit of quick material gains by whatever means—even corrupt or immoral—available. When the national goal and human rights concerns clashed, the former took precedence. Just prior to Kim's inauguration the economic growth rate had slowed, and labor–management disputes were rampant. Huge, confident industrial–financial conglomerates, *chaebŏl*, were no longer submissive to the government. In this milieu Kim proposed the imposition of "national discipline" in a society that was expected to become freer and more democratic.

Kim's administrative and political capabilities were also seriously limited. True, he had been a skilled politician all his life. However, he had never "administered" anything larger than a party headquarters. What was not immediately apparent on his assumption of the presidency was that he owed much to his political maneuvers, such as the one that produced the dramatic but "unprincipled" merger in 1990 of the three parties. That meant that he owed his presidency largely to a conservative supercoalition. To the extent that Kim Young Sam won the presidency partly thanks to his political stratagem of joining Roh Tae Woo's ruling group, he remained a captive to his own maneuvers, at least in the early administration.

The twenty-five–member Kim cabinet as a whole, however, was refreshingly new. The first Roh Tae Woo cabinet of the Sixth Republic had retained many members of the last cabinet under Chun Doo Hwan's Fifth Republic, giving rise to the characterization of the Sixth Republic as "the 5.5 republic." Kim's cabinet, however, was almost completely devoid of members with direct cabinet-level ties to previous presidencies. Most of the Kim appointees were "progressive outsiders" and "reform-oriented men and women."[21] Four former university professors headed the National Unification Board and the ministries of foreign affairs, science and technology, and education. Among them, Professor Han Wan-sang was deputy prime minister of the National Unification Board. Han was a "progressive" political activist who openly protested military dictator-

21 *Korea Newsreview*, 6 March 1993, p. 5. Kil, "Political Reforms," p. 422.

ships. Consequently Han lost his professorship at Seoul National University twice and was imprisoned once, charged with Kim Dae-jung's "conspiracy to overthrow the (Chun Doo Hwan) government" in 1980. The minister of education, Professor O Pyŏng-mun, had experienced five years of unemployment after being forced out of his post at Chŏnnam University, charged with assisting student rioters in the Kwangju Incident of 1980. And for the first time, three women occupied cabinet posts simultaneously, heading the ministries of health and social affairs, environment, and political affairs.

What immediately attracted special attention was the appointment of another professor, Kim Deok of the Hankuk University of Foreign Studies, as the director of the Agency for National Security Planning (NSP), formerly the KCIA, which reports to the president's office. From the first director, Kim Jong Pil, on KCIA directors often wielded more power than a few cabinet ministers combined, and in the past most directors were appointed from military ranks or prosecutorial backgrounds. The KCIA and the NSP were often used by presidents for domestic political purposes rather than for gathering data on international matters, including North Korean affairs. President Kim was reportedly sprayed with acid by KCIA agents when he was an opposition leader; the other prominent opposition leader, Kim Dae-jung, was kidnapped in Tokyo by KCIA agents (Chapter 3). As a further indication of the downgrading of the NSP under Kim, its director was henceforth not to attend cabinet meetings. It was made known that Kim Deok, an expert on North Korea, was expected to downsize the NSP and its functions by eliminating domestic political intelligence gathering. Director Kim proceeded rapidly to reshuffle some 70 percent of top officials who had been appointed by the military regimes and 50 percent of the section chiefs. Together with abolishing the fourth bureau of the NSP, which had been conducting domestic political surveillance, he reduced the agency's local branches from twenty-two to six.

As if to underscore his determination to eradicate misconduct and corruption, the new president's top priority as stated in his inaugural address, Kim also made the widely praised appointment of Lee Hoi Chang as chairman of the Board of Audits and Inspections, another presidential agency. Lee, a former Supreme Court justice, was well known for his integrity and courage, as well as his intelligence. Emphasizing that the board was an independent constitutional organ, Lee declared that it would not bow to any political pressures and that there would be no "sanctuary" from the board's work. He quickly identified the main targets of the board's audits: government officials who handle taxation, loans, construction permits, land use, food, sanitation, the environment, and traffic.

To lead efforts in restoring economic vitality, Kim's second priority, Kim appointed Lee Kyŏng-sik, an able economist who was reputed to be scrupulously honest and untainted by any hint of corruption, as deputy prime minister of the Economic Planning Board. Lee was an early architect of the five-year economic development plans under Park Chung Hee, plans that became the blueprint for the rapid economic growth programs from the mid-1960s on. When Lee was a government official he brought home no more than his meager government salary, unlike many other officials who padded their incomes through illicit practices. Consequently, Lee's family lived in one of many "moon villages,"[22] shanty towns that spread ever upward on mountainsides and where "the moon rose first" but amenities were few and alleys were too steep and too narrow for vehicular traffic.

The average age of Kim's cabinet members was fifty-six, a youthful cabinet under a relatively young president, according to Korean standards. The appointees also included three practicing attorneys, in contrast with their notable absence in cabinets under former generals turned presidents. While welcoming the refreshingly moderate and intellectual character of the cabinet, some were concerned that a few members might be politically naive and lacking in administrative experience. However, the positive aspects generally stood out, and it was evident that President Kim had formed a cabinet designed to carry out his "reforms amidst stability."

The realignment of the military. With the launching of the cabinet, Kim enjoyed what official sources said was some 80 percent public approval. The first significant substantive reform measures he took were in the sector that held the naked power, namely the Korean military, now the only cohesive force that could still threaten the civilian government. Even before he was inaugurated as president Kim had clandestinely sounded out many top-ranking military officers, who assured him that there would be no danger to him personally or to his government if he "purged" the members of the *Hanahwoe* by removing them from their powerful positions in the military.[23] A complete roster of the *Hanahwoe* was made available by Colonel Paek Sŭng-do, formerly an aide-de-camp to Army Chief of Staff General Yi Chin-sam.[24] Barely two weeks after his inauguration, on March 8 the new commander-in-chief suddenly replaced Army Chief of Staff General Kim Jin-yong with General Kim Dong-jin. President Kim simultaneously dismissed Lieutenant General Sŭh Wan-su, commander of the notorious Defense Security Command, the erstwhile power base of

---

[22] *Hankook Ilbo*, 27 February 1993, p. 4.

[23] Yi Pyŏng-do, "Kwŏnryŏk taeidong: hanahwoe chekŏ makhu" (The Great Movement of Power: Behind the Scenes of the Elimination of the *Hanahwoe*), *Chugan Hankuk*, November 25, 1996, pp. 14–15.

[24] Ibid., p. 15.

Chun Doo Hwan when he seized the military and political power in 1979. The ousted generals' two-year terms had not been due to expire until December. The common element between the two generals was that they were members of the now infamous *Hanahwoe*.

The dismissals, early retirements, and demotions of these "political generals" continued quietly, from the top down. Included in this squeeze were those involved in the brutal massacres in Kwangju. When officers came up for regular promotions in October 1993, all *Hanahwoe* members were conspicuously denied promotion. Within nine months after the installation of the civilian government, some fifty of the highest-ranking officers were reassigned, including seven of nine four-star generals. By October twenty generals had been "retired." Eight non-*Hanahwoe* members were named division commanders, one after another. In time, 73.3 percent of the lieutenant generals and 68.3 percent of the major generals were reshuffled. The president also disbanded all private organizations in the military. These moves were called a "revolutionary cleansing" of the Korean military, which was thus firmly brought under the control of a legitimate civilian government. The position of the military was returned to its normal place in a civilian-led or democratic society.

However, the change was already beginning to create a new set of problems in a peninsula that remained divided. While most welcomed the elimination of the *Hanahwoe* "mafia" elements from the army, there were some indications that the military was demoralized and "withering" due to a combination of interrelated factors.[25] Until the end of the Roh presidency, the military had been guaranteed a route to power, or at least secure employment, particularly those from modest backgrounds. This was no longer the case. With almost universal attacks on the military-led governments and their excesses, the military itself was criticized by many. The morale of the military plummeted, and it had difficulty retaining young officers and experienced noncommissioned officers. The graduates of the regular military academy left after five years of mandatory service. In a country whose economy had been expanding dramatically, private-sector jobs were far more enticing to numerous noncommissioned officers, who constitute a vital layer in the large conscripted military. Watching these developments with increasing concern were a number of associations of retired generals, who form in the Korean context today ultraconservative right-wing forces and were generally uneasy about the reforms advocated by the Kim Young Sam government. One of these, the Starred Friends Association, included 189 multistarred retired generals.[26]

[25] A series of articles ran under the general theme "The Military Is Withering" in *Sin Dong-A* (February 1995): pp. 248–95.

[26] *Hankook Ilbo*, 30 November 1989, p. 13, and 8 December 1989, p. 5.

Highlighting the "democratic" heritage. On another front, with a mixture of hubris and hyperbole Kim boldly emphasized the legitimacy of his government and redefined a series of landmark events in the evolution of Korean politics. He designated 1993 the "year of the restoration of the history of the Korean people," suggesting that their history had been obscured by violent and oppressive events under military dictatorship. He now traced the legitimacy of his "civilian and democratic" government to the civilian tradition of the Korean government-in-exile in Shanghai, China, during the Japanese colonial occupation of Korea. Kim issued a special presidential statement claiming ties between his government and the exile-government in China.

President Kim also publicly redefined some milestones of the recent past through a series of public statements:

Traditional Designation	*Redefined Designation*
The April 19 Student Uprising	The April 19 Revolution
The December 12, 1979, Incident (led by Chun Doo Hwan)	Military coup d'etat-like incident
The May 18, 1980, Kwangju Incident	The Civil Pro-Democracy Uprising in Kwangju
The June 10, 1987, Great March	The June 10, 1987, Struggle for Democracy

Kim himself had organized and led the June 10, 1987, march that had demanded the democratization of Korean politics through a direct presidential election. Through a forced logic, he declared that "the struggle for democracy" in 1987 inherited the spirit of the March First Movement in 1919, a nationalistic demonstration for Korean independence from Japanese colonial rule. In the same vein Kim traced the root of his government to the April 19, 1960, student uprising, which resulted in the overthrow of the autocratic and corrupt Rhee government. He further identified his government with the Kwangju citizen-student uprising against the *Hanahwoe*-led "new military" that had seized power through an intramilitary coup. In the honeymoon period of his government he engaged in an audacious rewrite of the pedigree of his civilian and democratic regime, and also of modern Korean history in general.

Though his proposed visit to the burial site of the Kwangju victims during his presidential tour of Kwangju was thwarted by angry students there, Kim instructed that the honor of those who had been prosecuted by the military regime be fully restored. Under the president's constitutional authority to "grant amnesty, commutation and restoration of rights" (Article 78), the police records of 41,181 Kwangju citizens and students who took part in the May 18 uprising were expunged. Under Kim's authority

5,566 political prisoners were released and the conviction records of more than 500,000 political prisoners from the military regimes were wiped clean. Removed from wanted lists of the former regimes were 230 fugitives, and 102 who turned themselves in were forgiven. Under Kim's directives, teachers who had been fired for trying to form labor unions were restored to their former positions, and 2,046 students who had been expelled for their political activities from eighty-five colleges and universities were ordered readmitted.

The New Economic Development Plan

At the time of the birth of the civilian government, the overall Korean economy was stagnant, if not faltering. The competitive edge that Korea had enjoyed for decades, partly thanks to wages kept low by authoritarian regimes, had eroded because the politically uncertain Roh regime could not afford to appear antilabor. Under a civilian and democratic government labor disputes now could not be arbitrarily and brutally resolved by unleashing the dreaded *kongkwŏnryŏk* (the power of public authority), often in the form of thousands of riot police quelling either demonstrating workers or those physically occupying production facilities or managers' offices. At the same time, entrepreneurs were uncertain about the economic direction of the government headed by the unpredictable Kim Young Sam, and their ambivalence was reflected in the low rate of long-term investments in industrial plants and equipment at the beginning of the Kim regime. What big business and the workers did know was that Kim Young Sam had promised a new, revitalized economy as one of the regime's primary goals.

Within a month after Kim's inauguration, in March 1993 his government moved quickly to announce a 100-day new economic development plan while the seventh five-year economic and social development plan of the previous administration underwent revisions. During the 100-day period public utility fees such as charges for water and electricity were lowered to stabilize prices that would benefit ordinary citizens immediately, and producers were encouraged to keep as low as possible prices on twenty basic consumer items such as rice, beef, sugar, and milk. At the same time, the money supply was put under flexible governmental control to provide businesses with investment funds at low cost. As a result, the supply of funds for investment in industrial plants and equipment in 1993 rose some 15 percent from the previous year. These and similar other measures demonstrated the government's keen concern with bringing the economy out of recession, also part of a global economic downturn during that period.

The embodiment of the Kim administration's vision of a "new economy" to support his well-publicized vision of creating a "new Korea" was released at the end of June 1993 in the much-awaited five-year plan for a new economy.[27] The plan highlighted "reforms," "deregulation," and "internationalization." It emphasized reforms to promote "economic justice through fair income distribution," deregulation of economic activities to align the Korean economy for growing liberalization, and "globalization trends." The plan also laid out changes in the control of the money supply, credit control on large businesses, small and medium-sized business lending, and the liberalization of capital market and securities businesses, among others.

Kim's plan also included reforms to expand the fiscal ability of the government by increasing the average taxation burden from 19.4 percent in 1992 to 22.2 percent in 1997, and made various changes in the taxation system. Among other matters, the latter changes were aimed at reducing tax breaks for interest and dividend incomes, as well as raising the tax rate for stock transactions. These represented a step toward the reduction of the gap between the haves and the have nots. If they appeared disadvantageous to the rich, the long sections on deregulation significantly relaxed government control over financial and managerial matters, a move designed to please business conglomerates. The most significant aspect of the plan, however, was that it set up a definite timetable for reforms that in the past had only been talked about.

[27] "Document: Major Programs for New Five-Year Economic Plan," *Korea Annual 1994*, pp. 359–67.

✪

CHAPTER 7

Institutionalizing Political and Economic Reforms, 1993–1995

President Kim had repeatedly stated that the "upstream must be clean" to keep the "downstreams" of Korean government and society clean and free of corruption. As a lifelong politician he knew about collusive relations among politicians and businesses or any other favor seekers. He declared repeatedly that he himself would not accept a single won as political contribution during his presidency. This meant that he would stop the old pernicious practices under the presidents with military backgrounds—Park, Chun, and Roh—of accepting political "slush funds," which they audaciously called "ruling funds," and whose existence was an open secret. These funds had been quietly solicited and accepted by presidential secretaries at various venues, including the presidential mansion. Sometimes the presidents themselves accepted large donations at the end of brief private meetings with chairmen of the largest conglomerates.[1]

It was widely believed that President Park, who had seized power through a military coup and subsequently triggered rapid economic growth, had initiated the malignant practice, usually in exchange for the granting of special favors. Because the Korean economy took off during the Park era, competition among emerging entrepreneurs then became fierce, and as Park directly involved himself in economic areas, opportunities for soliciting "contributions of patriotic funds" were virtually limitless. It was common knowledge that Chun Doo Hwan, who had also seized power through an intra-army coup, amassed an astronomical sum

---

[1] Yang Kun-man, et al., "Hanguk pup'e kujoŭi simchangpu iyaki" (The Records of the Heart of Corruption Structure in Korea), *Wŏlgan Chosŏn* (March 1996): pp. 146–215.

in slush fund which he used unabashedly with "a generous hand" to boost his friends, to silence his opponents, and to influence journalists. Following Roh's nomination as presidential candidate, Chun himself provided enormous sums of money to the ruling party and to Roh for his campaign. At the same time, he was distributing money through intermediaries to opposition groups to divide them. Roh began the practice of collecting slush funds at the very beginning of his presidency, and when the heads of conglomerates were invited to private meetings with the president, they knew they had to come with money, usually in cashier's checks.

It has been recently revealed that Roh sent a colossal amount of funds to the ruling party to bankroll the successful presidential campaign of Kim Young Sam in 1992 while simultaneously giving a relatively modest amount to his opponent, Kim Dae-jung.[2] Kim Young Sam smugly maintained that he did not receive any money from Roh, although he said he "believed" that Roh gave large sums of money "directly to the (ruling) Democratic Liberal Party," of which he was the presidential candidate.[3] If Kim Young Sam's fine differentiation bemused many and infuriated his opponents, the campaign war chest of the ruling party made it possible for Kim Young Sam to run an exceptionally well-lubricated presidential campaign and attain his lifelong ambition, the presidency.

Anticorruption Measures

Disclosure of assets. It was against this backdrop that Kim Young Sam took the unprecedented step, only two days after his inauguration, of voluntarily disclosing not only his assets, but also those of his wife, his father, and his two grown sons—the total assets of his extended family.[4] The itemized assets included their homes, apartments, other real estate holdings, automobiles, fishing vessels, bank accounts—even their health club memberships. Total assets were reported as 1,778,226,070 won (approximately $2 million at the time), a comfortable level for Kim but not exactly extraordinary considering they included the assets of his retired father, said to have had a successful fishery. Indeed, the total was a credible figure; what was more striking was that the president had even decided to disclose his family's assets—and voluntarily. Coupled with this, Kim reiterated his pledge not to accept a single won as a political contribution during his presidency. For a president whose tenure was constitutionally limited to a single term, and therefore without any need to raise

---

[2] Ibid., pp. 149–54.
[3] *Hankook Ilbo*, 31 October 1995, p. 1.
[4] *Hankook Ilbo*, 10 March 1993, p. 4.

campaign funds for himself, this pledge was also believable. Newspaper editorials enthusiastically welcomed this surprising presidential initiative and urged other high-ranking officials to follow suit.

This single anticorruption initiative by a duly elected civilian president snowballed into a moral imperative. Mass media daily highlighted the move and built palpable public expectations for others to follow suit. The prime minister, cabinet members and other senior administrators, members of the National Assembly, and higher-level members of the judiciary hurriedly disclosed their assets in quick succession.[5] As expected, the media gleefully scrutinized these revelations in great detail, pointing out huge discrepancies between disclosed amounts and actual market values of many real estate properties based on records they researched. When it became apparent that some officials had evidently enriched their assets by abusing their government positions, public pressure quickly mounted for them to resign. Indeed, the speaker of the National Assembly, two cabinet ministers, five vice ministerial officials, and 242 senior administrators who had been long-time government officials left their positions voluntarily. Soon thereafter, an additional 1,363 were unceremoniously dismissed from their government positions for evident irregularities.

In their first year or so previous regimes had made temporary, "cosmetic" reform gestures such as the prohibition of weekday golfing—an exorbitantly expensive sport in overcrowded Korea—by government officials or their patronage of expensive restaurants or entertainment establishments. However, the Kim government now moved beyond, to institutionalize anticorruption provisions for officials. The government drafted the Ethics Law for Public Officials; the National Assembly promptly passed the legislation on May 20, 1993, requiring 1,063 high-ranking public officeholders to disclose their assets accurately and also stipulating that additional senior administrators register their assets.[6] Furthermore, these high-ranking officials were obliged to report annually any change in financial status. The law also expanded the legal grounds for "purging" military personnel found corrupt and, more significantly, belonging to any politically motivated private organizations within the military.

The real-name financial transaction system. Another significant reform executed about six months after Kim's inauguration was the imposition of the "real-name system" in financial transactions. By longstanding Korean practice, as in Japan, financial transactions under borrowed or false

---

[5] Na Yang-sin, *Kongjik cha chesan kongke* (Asset Disclosures by Public Officials) (Seoul: P'ulbit Publishers, 1993). The disclosures by 454 officials are reproduced on pages 279–319, followed with the author's analyses indicating that many officials reported minimal amounts for their real estate holdings, among other items.

[6] *Korea Newsreview*, 11 March 1995, p. 13.

names had been widespread. Such transactions made it possible for large amounts of untraceable monies to circulate, facilitating illicit collusion between politics and big business, and the funding of questionable real estate or stock transactions, among other matters. The practice also allowed the operation of a sizeable unregulated private money market, the so-called "curb market," which represented, according to an estimate, approximately one-fifth of the total currency in circulation in the mid-1980s.[7] Huge political "contributions"—bordering on extortion by military dictators or bribery by businesses—were made easy using these nameless "black" monies, the likes of which created the so-called "black mist" in Japan during the long period of Liberal Democratic rule.

It was, therefore, not surprising that regimes prior to Kim's had neglected to eliminate the practice of financial transactions under false names. A bill to ban such transactions had been drawn up in 1982, during the Chun era, but was evidently quashed at the highest level. Some hoped that the Roh government would initiate a real-name system to implement one of his eight-point "democratization and reform" declarations of June 29, 1987, which included a public pledge to trigger "bold social reforms to build a clean society." In fact, in the first months of the Roh regime the real-name system was publicly discussed again, but the idea quickly faded. It was said that the business sector feared a dampening impact on the economy. However, recent records (from the trials of Chun, Roh, and their cabals) reveal that Roh was receiving huge "donations" from the very first year of his presidency on. This turned out to be an important reason why the real-name initiative suffered a quick death once again, as it did under Chun.

President Kim surprised the nation on August 12, 1993, by issuing Emergency Presidential Order No. 16 to implement the Real-Name Financial Transaction System.[8] Kim declared that "without real-name financial accounts, a sound democracy cannot flower."[9] Obviously the preparatory work that went into the implementation of the comprehensive system was a tightly kept secret so as to maximize the salutary effects of the new system and minimize such possibilities as sudden withdrawals of deposits and the flight of funds out of the country, among others. Under the new system all financial transactions including securities

[7] Lee Tong Hun, "Monetary Aggregates in the Presence of a Curb Market," in *Korean Economic Development*, ed. Jene K. Kwon (New York: Greenwood Press, 1990), pp. 207–20. According to another source, in 1969 the size of the curb market "was said to have been 82 percent of total outstanding bank loans." Jung-en Woo, *Race to the Swift: State and Finance in Korean Industrialization* (New York: Columbia University Press, 1991), p. 113.

[8] *Hankook Ilbo*, 13 August 1993, p. 1. "Real-Name Financial Transaction System," *Korea Annual 1994*, pp. 72–75.

[9] *Korea Newsreview*, 21 August 1993, p. 14.

deals now had to be conducted under real names, meaning the name on the residence registration, the universal identification in South Korea and somewhat like the social security number for Americans. Business corporations likewise had to use the same name as on the business license and taxpayer registration numbers. This clearly was designed to assure the transparency of monetary transactions and property ownership while stopping tax dodging and tax avoidance on interests and dividends—South Korea had once been a notorious tax dodger's heaven. Initially the stock market and business transactions slowed down, as anticipated. However, it soon became evident that the new system, so boldly initiated by a new government within a half-year after its inauguration, was widely welcomed by most civic-minded citizenry, despite some unavoidable inconveniences and short-term uncertainties. Editorials in leading newspapers resoundingly endorsed the system.

Some 97 percent of false-name accounts were transferred to real-name accounts by the end of the grace period, apparently without causing significant financial dislocation. The financial market remained relatively stable, as did gold prices. However, when the real-name system created the inevitable economic shock wave, Lee Kyŏng-sik, deputy prime minister of economic planning, revised downward the 1993 projected growth rate from the original 6 percent to 4.5 percent. The overall growth rate in 1993 was about 5.8 percent, however. This compared favorably with the 5.0 percent rate in 1992 prior to the introduction of the real-name system. At that time the Korean economy was gradually turning upward, from a prolonged period of recession that occurred nearly simultaneously with the global economic slowdown. The per capita GNP in 1993 actually rose to $7,466, despite initial apprehension that the new system would dampen economic growth.

The new system, however, was not free of casualties. Many small and some medium businesses, the weak link in the Korean economy since the time of the Park government's favoritism toward large conglomerates, went insolvent and failed. Such businesses, habitually dependent on private money lenders who had prospered under the old false-name system, suffered mainly because they lacked the collateral to qualify for lower-rate bank loans. It was perhaps predictable that the "curb markets" would soon reappear because there were real needs in the Korean economy for them, such as for cash-starved small and medium-sized businesses. Overall, however, the real-name system, subsequently expanded to cover real estate transactions, has been seen as a lasting accomplishment of the Kim Young Sam government, despite subsequent ups and downs in its implementation and partial de facto rescission. A powerful principle of financial transparency was beginning to establish itself.

Legislative Reforms

Since the inception of republican Korea there have remained three huge and virtually perennial problems: assuring fair elections, regulating political funds, and implementing local autonomy. Of course, under military dictators these issues mattered little. After the "democratic reforms" of 1987, noisy promises were made to address these areas. But those who captured political power, including elected National Assembly members, took few decisive steps to curb unfair electoral practices, to assure transparency in the flow of often astronomical political funds, and to make the principle of local autonomy written into the 1948 constitution a concrete reality. Once ensconced in power, these officeholders made little effort to promote measures that might compromise their own or their successors' power or financial positions. Reform-minded Kim and many like-minded members of the Fourteenth National Assembly, elected in March 1992, finally broke this pattern. After ten months of intense debate in the National Assembly, ruling and opposition members together passed, in a rare display of harmony, three closely related laws on March 4, 1994. Kim then promptly signed them.

The Election Malpractice Prevention Act. The intent of the first of the three laws was made explicit by its title, "The Election for Public Office and Election Malpractice Prevention Act."[10] The lengthy law, with 277 articles and twelve addenda, was evidently the centerpiece of the "reform legislations." This law repealed the old and hitherto separate Presidential Election Act, the National Assembly Members Election Act, the Local Council Members Election Act, and the Election for Heads of Local Governments Act, and made the 1994 act applicable to all four categories of elections (Article 2). The integrated act represented thoroughgoing and often excruciatingly detailed amendments to existing election laws, which in the past were seldom strictly enforced, usually under the flimsy pretext of restoring postelection harmony. Article 1 of the new law declared: "The purpose of this Act is to contribute to the development of the democratic politics by making elections under the Constitution and the Local Autonomy Act to be held fairly in accordance with the free will of the people and the democratic formalities (sic) and by preventing any malpractice related to the election."

The all-encompassing law provided practically all known safeguards, many of which apparently had been gleaned from experiences in mature democratic societies, such as the United States and England, to ensure fair

---

[10] Republic of Korea government, *Kwanbo* (The Official Gazette), 16 March 1994, pp. 4–113.

and free elections in South Korea. In addition to normal procedural safe-guards the law prohibited, for instance, reporting on details and results of public opinion polls until "the time the voting is closed on the election day" (Article 108). The drafters of the 1994 law were evidently aware of criticisms of the American media's penchant for predicting winners on an election day, discouraging some West Coast and Hawaiian voters from voting. Though all Koreans live in one time zone, such a provision and the prohibition of "noisy speech and behavior" around voting places (Article 166) were indicative of the meticulous care the drafters took in writing this integrated election law.

Elections that don't cost candidates money and the public management of elections have long been goals advocated by reform-minded leaders. As a step toward these goals the letters of the new election law severely limited a presidential candidate's campaign spending to 20 billion won (about $25 million), governorship and mayoral candidates to 200 million won (about $250,000), and national parliamentary candidates' to 50 million won (about $63,000). Candidates for lesser offices could spend considerably lesser amounts. Under the old election laws spending limits were much higher. It had long been an open secret that many candidates actually spent much more than these limits, as monitoring was all but impossible before the institutions of the real-name financial transaction system.

Under extreme reform impulses, the law further stipulated that if a candidate exceeded spending by any more than a razor-thin margin of 1/200 of the limit, the election would be declared null and void (Article 263). At the same time, the "public management system" of electoral expenses was to have the national or local government treasury pay for printing and mailing costs of some campaign materials and expenses for public debates among candidates. It was common knowledge that these were trifling expenses in any election. Candidates were also encouraged to use public facilities free of charge. In view of the past widespread practice of political parties sponsoring mammoth political rallies to which participants, many of whom received daily cash payments, were mobilized by the busload, such rallies were now banned. Also banned were paid campaign workers; candidates were to rely solely on unpaid volunteers. The intent of the new law, to cleanse Korean politics of astronomical sums of "black money," was made abundantly—if naively—clear.

In a move unprecedented in Korean politics, the ruling party also agreed to relinquish a significant built-in advantage to have the integrated election law passed. Under the old election laws parliamentary seats for the national constituency were to be designated in proportion to the number of seats each majority party won. Under the new law the proportional representation seats were to be allocated to each party on the basis of the total number of *votes* each party garnered. The new system would favor minority parties because the ruling party, by definition, wins more *seats* than the minority, even with a slim vote margin from each single-member election district. Also, a provision in previous election laws that assigned 50 percent of proportional seats to the ruling party was abolished in a move to eliminate an unjust advantage to the ruling party.[11]

The new election laws also contained other provisions including a ban on any electioneering by government employees or organizations with business or other ties to the government, down to the platoon leader of the Homeland Reserve forces or heads of *ban,* the smallest neighborhood unit. If a judge refused to hear a suit for election law violations by any "government employees" defined most broadly or any suit charging candidates with "bribing" voters, those initiating the charge could request an appeals court to rule on the merits of the charge (Article 273). Indeed, the integrated election law promulgated on March 16, 1994, was intended to reform all election processes extensively and to prevent recurrences of corrupt and often violent elections in South Korea—if the law were effectively enforced. Elections envisioned in the 1994 law were light-years beyond the many past elections that had been bought or stolen and the elections in which thousands of soldiers lined up to cast premarked ballots under the watchful eyes of their commanders. This law made abundantly clear the collective wish of the nation to assure clean and fair elections—the very core of a democratic process.

The Political Fund Law. The second major legislation, promulgated on the same day, was the Political Fund Law,[12] which constituted amendments to existing political fund law. These amendments were closely interrelated with the Election Malpractice Prevention Act. Expanding the principle of the "public management of elections," which ideally would eliminate the need for an individual candidate's private money to run for public office, the law provided that subsidies from the state coffer to political parties be increased. The law also allowed an individual to contribute up to 150 million won (approximately $190,000) to political parties. Under the old political funds law, the limit had been 100 million won. In making political contributions individuals or support groups had to report their contributions to the Central Election Management Commission using commission forms and receipts. In essence, the law took a signifi-

---

[11] Myungsoon Shin, "Democratic Transition and Consolidation in South Korean Politics." Paper presented at "Democracy and the Reform Movement in Korea" at the Wohlstetter Conference Center, Washington, D.C., July 1995.

[12] *Kwanbo* (The Official Gazette), 16 March 1994, pp. 113–20.

cant step to make the flows of political contributions transparent and corruption free—but only if individuals and political parties observed the law.

The Local Autonomy Act. The third major legislation adopted in March 1994, the Local Autonomy Act,[13] was another landmark in the evolution of democratic politics in Korea. Article 1 stated: "The purpose of this Act is to strive for democracy and efficiency of local autonomous administration and to achieve balanced development of local areas and democratic development of the Republic of Korea by prescribing matters concerning type, organization and operation of local governments and the basic relations between the state and local governments."

Highlights of this act, with its 162 articles, include the following: (1) Local governments are classified into two types: (a) wide-area units (for special cities, large cities with direct ties with the central government, and provinces, or *to*), and (b) basic autonomy units (other cities, administrative districts of provinces, or *kun*, and wards of special or large cities, or *ku*). (2) The sizes of local assemblies depend on the size of each autonomous unit, ranging from seventy for the Seoul special city to ten for a *kun* assembly. (3) The term of assembly members is four years; they shall be in "honorary service" but receive a per diem travel and "meeting allowance" during assembly sessions. (4) When local government decisions are contrary to national laws, the central government in accordance with various national laws and procedures may request reconsideration, corrections, or suspensions. (5) Vice mayors of the Seoul special city and other large cities with direct ties to the central government and provincial vice governors shall be appointed from among national officials by the president.

It is clear that important units of local government are effectively penetrated by the central government. Even so, the revival of a local autonomy system as such was an important turning point in the evolution of Korean politics.[14] Though the central government is dominant in its control over purse strings, under Chapter VII of the new Local Autonomy Act local governments have considerable ability to collect local taxes, rents, and fees for the use of public facilities, and also to issue "local bonds by resolution of the local council within the limit approved by the Minister of Home Affairs." The national average of local governments' "financial self-reliance ratio" in 1995 was about 63.5 percent, ranging from a high of 97.3 percent for Seoul and a low of 28.5 percent for the poorest South Chŏlla Province.[15]

---

[13] Ibid., Law No. 4741.

[14] Chija chŏngch'i yŏnku hwoe, ed., *Hanguk hyŏng chibang chach'i ŭi ch'ŏng sajin* (The Blueprint for a Korean Style Local Autonomy) (Seoul: Kilbŏt, 1995), p. 11.

[15] Chong Mun-hwa, *Chibang chach'i* (Local Autonomy) (Seoul: Tasan Media, 1995), p. 135.

Local governments also have various enumerated ("entrusted" or dele-gated) functions under the new Local Autonomy Act. These functions in-clude the promotion of citizens' welfare, management of medical institu-tions, sewage disposal, support of local industries, and development. The lengthy enumeration in Article 9 also includes the establishment of day care centers, preschools, elementary schools, middle schools, high schools, and other kinds of schools of similar levels (no mention was made of college-level education, which is regulated by the central gov-ernment). The management of libraries, museums, performing arts cen-ters, and galleries is also included among the substantial "entrusted" tasks for local governments.

The *Segyehwa* (Globalization) Reform

While many South Koreans were still debating the possible impact of the three reform laws adopted by the Seoul legislature, a new term, *segyehwa*, suddenly emerged on the horizon. Riding the crest of a series of visible re-forms launched by his government, Kim announced in November 1994 his vision of *segyehwa* (globalization) for Korea against the backdrop of Sydney, Australia, where he held a news conference following his high-visibility participation in the Asia–Pacific Economic Cooperation (APEC) summit, in Indonesia. Kim's initial declaration stated that the globaliza-tion policy was "to brace the nation for cascading developments and sweeping changes in the world to build the Republic into a first-rate na-tion in the coming century," by opening Korea to the world "in *all fields, including political, economic, and social activities,*" and meeting "the global standards of excellence in *all* areas" (emphasis added).[16] Thus, Kim's ini-tial announcement was not much more than an expression of his ex-tremely expansive vision to "internationalize" Korea in all areas. Actually, the term *kukchehwa* (internationalization) had initially been used until it evolved into *segyehwa*.

Kim's subsequent remarks on *segyehwa* revealed his confidence in global-izing Korea, with an emphasis on the economy, as he declared in May 1996:

> Korea . . . has achieved success by pursuing an open economy and an open society. . . . Beginning in the 1960s, Korea began to pursue an outward-look-ing, open economic policy and has since seen its economy grow at an aver-age annual rate of some 8 percent in real terms. Today, the Korean economy is the eleventh largest in the world.

[16] The Embassy of the Republic of Korea, "President Kim's '*Segyehwa*' or Globalization Reforms," (Washington, D.C., February 25, 1996).

A rush hour in downtown Seoul. Numerous South Koreans have eagerly purchased automobiles, causing horrendous traffic congestion and air pollution in most cities in a heavily urbanized country. (The Korean Information Center)

Korea's annual trade volume last year amounted to $260 billion, the twelfth largest in the world. . . . To help boost economic cooperation between different regions of the world, Korea is actively participating in the activities of both the Asia–Pacific Economic Cooperation (APEC) forum and the Asia–Europe Economic Meeting (ASEM). Korea also plans to join the Organization for Economic Cooperation and Development (OECD).

Korea will be in the forefront of the move to implement the ideal of liberalizing investment and trade and will help lay a bridge between advanced and developing countries.[17]

Segyehwa was turning out to be an audacious and optimistic concept. Kim was still supremely confident in 1995 that Korea could reform successfully in all fields to bring all domestic endeavors to world standards, open the country to the world, cooperate and compete economically with all trading partners, and continue to forge ahead on the global scene. With a series of pronouncements and exhortations, the "civilian and democratic" government was setting nothing less than meeting a "global standard of excellence in all areas" as the national goal. In setting such a standard for the nation Kim, probably unwittingly, was setting a standard to assess himself and his administration and those that followed. In the past, many apologists for Korea's and the Korean government's shortcomings had attempted to explain them away, for example, haughty behaviors of government officials toward the people as acceptable according to Korean standards. Conversely, certain international procedures and standards such as safeguarding human and workers' rights were said to be unsuited to Korean realities. In a "globalized" Korea these apologies and excuses would no longer apply. The ideal of *segyehwa* included a commitment to accelerate efforts to reach the highest world standards of liberty, social justice, and quality of life.

The co-chairman of the Presidential Commission for Globalization, Kim Jin-Hyun, echoed President Kim's visions, and elaborated:

Our *Segyehwa* Policy will lay the foundation for the "Creation of a New Korea," a country that plays a pivotal role in world affairs of the 21st century.

Segyehwa stands for meeting the global standards of excellence in all areas by the government, private citizens, and various civil organizations. *Segyehwa* stands for an intellectual reform to change the attitude and be-

[17] "Document: Address by President Kim Young Sam of the Republic of Korea at the Seventh Annual Corporate Conference of the Asia Society: Toward the Globalization of the Republic of Korea" *Korea Annual 1996* (Seoul: Yonhap News Agency, 1996), pp. 363–64.

havior of the past one-dimensional economic development. *Segyehwa* stands for rising above class, regional, and generational differences.[18]

According to Kim Jin-Hyun, *segyehwa* ultimately had the ambitious goal of producing "an intellectual reform to change the attitude" in all the public and private sectors. This was a tall order indeed. However, initial recommendations made in December 1994 by the presidential commission were considerably more modest. These included lifting various restrictions on business activities in the country as well as overseas; simplification of government procedures for expediting loans to businesses engaged in exports and loans to small and medium-sized businesses; rapidly increasing foreign language skills among government administrators; and establishing a higher educational institution specifically for the purpose of training experts in foreign affairs, trade, and technology. To learn the globalization concept, in 1995 senior government officials were encouraged to enroll in special evening seminars and courses at a number of universities; some three hundred "graduated" from these programs. In addition, approximately seven hundred government employees were sent abroad for foreign language training as a part of a burst of such activity under the *segyehwa* banner. Other subsequent projects were to include building new ports, promoting Korean cultural activities both within Korea and abroad, encouraging tourism by foreign visitors, and inviting numerous international conventions to Korea.

The double-edged *segyehwa*. It was evident that globalization was double edged; it could benefit the country in the long run but would definitely bring some serious dislocations and hardships in the short run. This was probably why there were serious concerns raised against a premature and nearly full-scale globalization, as many were fearful that South Korea was not ready for a wide "open-door" policy either economically or politically. In March 1995 Korea formally applied for membership in the world's leading group of industrialized and largely democratic states, and the OECD decided in October 1996 to invite Korea to join, despite the the organization's reservations about Korea's pace of financial deregulation and its reforms of social and labor union legislation.[19]

Regarding the latter point, several OECD members expressed their view that far-reaching liberalization of the existing legislation would be required for Korea to demonstrate its commitment to the democratic

[18] Kim Jin-Hyun, "Preparing for the 21st Century: Korea's Globalization Policy and Its Implications for Future Korea–U.S. Relations," in *Korea's Turn to Globalization and Korea–U.S. Economic Cooperation,* ed. Yeomin Yoon and Robert W. McGee (South Orange, NJ: Seton Hall University, 1966), p. 4.

[19] *Hankook Ilbo,* 12 October 1996, pp. 1, 3–5.

rights of workers.[20] Their concerns were mostly about legal provisions banning plural labor unions in the workplace, a prohibition that had outlawed the competitive existence of labor unions; about prohibiting interventions by third parties in labor disputes, a practice that usually disadvantaged beleaguered unions and striking workers; and a ban on labor unions in most public sectors. All of these concerns were to become the key points of contention in the controversial passage of new labor union laws by the National Assembly in December 1996. In any case, South Korea became the second East Asian country after Japan to join the OECD, as its twenty-ninth member, when the National Assembly ratified accession documents in November 1997. Korea committed herself to abiding by international standards and procedures in economic cooperation and development, including in the areas of finance, securities, foreign investments, environment, transportation, and labor practices. Membership obliged Korea to liberalize its economy and completely open its domestic market, according to an agreed-on timetable. While rejoicing in the apparent recognition by the advanced and mostly democratic nations of the world of Korea's ability to meet global standards in not only economic but also political—particularly human rights—areas, some uncertainties remained regarding the implications of the membership economically and politically.[21]

In Korea serious reservations about OECD membership were reflected in heated debates on whether the country in balance would gain or lose by joining. The National Assembly ratified the accession agreement by a vote of 159 for and 101 against. This was clearly not a resounding endorsement. The split was along party lines; the ruling New Korea Party and the minority Democratic Party were in favor of the membership supporting President Kim's timetable of *segyehwa* whereas the two main opposition parties, the National Congress for New Politics and the United Liberal Democrats, were opposed to the measure, largely on the grounds that Korea was not quite ready for "unlimited economic competition" with advanced industrial giants including the United States, Japan, and Germany. Serious questions weighed heavily in many Korean minds, including whether Korean industries and finances could withstand open international competition, whether Korean businesses would be disciplined enough to restrain themselves to attaining a favorable trade balance when international trade restrictions were removed by refraining from importing unlimited amounts of expensive and "luxurious" consumer goods, and whether the "civilian

[20] *Korea Herald*, 11 September 1996, pp. 1, 3.
[21] Kim Joong-woong, "Korea's OECD Entry and the Road Ahead," *Korea Focus* 4, no. 5 (1996): pp. 61–64. An editorial in a leading daily paper was concerned about the "challenges" of the "OECD era." *Hankook Ilbo*, 12 October 1996, p. 3.

and democratic" government could persuade the economic sectors and the people to maintain sufficient economic discipline and health to sustain and nurture Korean democracy.

Local Autonomy and the 1995 Elections

Meanwhile, on the domestic scene all three of the reform legislations of March 1994 were put to the test in the first full-fledged local government elections of June 27, 1995, which gave birth to the very first full-scale local governments in Korean history. In this sense the evolution of Korean politics and government had indeed reached a new stage. Furthermore, to the extent that local autonomy and "self-government" are important to an individual citizen in his or her relationship with the level of the government which he he or she interacts directly, the events of 1995 had significance in the democratic development of Korean politics.[22]

The importance of the 1995 local government elections is all the more evident when one considers that local autonomy was an unknown concept in traditional Korea. A characteristic feature of the traditional governing pattern was aptly termed "the politics of the vortex" by one astute observer.[23] Briefly, the vortex was a powerful centralizing force in Korean society and politics that attracted with a gigantic magnetic pull the government, economy, education, culture, and most other worthwhile endeavors to its capital city. The centripetal force must be at work even today in Seoul, home to over one-fourth of the total South Korean population despite its proximity to the military demarcation line dividing the Koreas.

Local autonomy in perspective. In 1948 local autonomy was constitutionally mandated for the first time in Korean history in the original constitution's stipulation of "local self-rule" in Chapter Eight.[24] Article 96 provided the general principle that local self-ruling bodies should manage local administrative affairs and properties in accordance with laws to be subsequently adopted by the central government. Obviously the establishment of the principle of local self-rule was possible only in the first duly adopted "democratic" constitution. The 1948 constitution, drafted by a group of Koreans toward the end of the American military occupation of South Korea, was American inspired, according to Dr. Yu Chin-o,

[22] Cho Ch'ang-hyon, *Chibang chach'i ŭi iron kwa silche* (The Theory and Practice of Local Autonomy) (Seoul: Dong-A Ilbosa, 1991), Chap. 1.

[23] Gregory Henderson, *Korea: The Politics of the Vortext* (Cambridge MA: Harvard University Press, 1968).

[24] Kim Chŏl-su, *Hanguk hŏnbopsa* (The Constitutional History of Korea) (Seoul: Taehak ch'ulpansa, 1988), pp. 74–76, 551.

the most important member of the group.[25] The American "advisors" to the Korean constitution drafting groups were mindful of American history and the fact that there had been thirteen sovereign states before there was a United States. Similar inspiration had produced the 1947 Local Autonomy Law in Japan under American occupation there that made an explicit link between local autonomy and democracy in Japan.[26]

The first Local Autonomy Law was promulgated in Korea on July 4, 1949, essentially providing for two layers of local administrative organizations: (1) the first layer of *to* (provinces) and the Seoul special city and (2) a second layer of other cities, small administrative units of *ŭp* (towns) and smaller units of *myŏn* (subdivisions of counties) (Article 2). What was telling about the traditional nature of this law was that the provinces and the Seoul special city were both placed under the central government's direct control, and lower administrative units were under the control of provincial governments. Though the law also called for elections of local assemblies, various internal disturbances including the Yŏsu-Sunchŏn mutinies in 1948 and the Korean War made it difficult to hold local elections. It was not until April 25 and May 10, 1952, that local assemblymen were elected, first from smaller local districts and then from wider districts of provinces and the Seoul special city.[27]

If it was remarkable that local administrative elections were held at all in the midst of the Korean War, after the battle line stabilized more or less by the summer of 1951, it was notable that the elections were marked by an evident lack of ability and experience on the part of the citizens in electing their local representatives in accordance with acceptable democratic norms. When local administrative chiefs were elected similar patterns prevailed, occasioning troubled questions by many regarding the need for and suitability of local autonomy in South Korea, which is equivalent in size geographically to Indiana. Under these circumstances it was the Liberal Party, headed by President Syngman Rhee, that adopted on December 24, 1958, an amendment to the then-existing local autonomy law by substituting an appointment system of local officials for a direct election system.

When the Second Republic under Premier Chang Myŏn was inaugurated, the local autonomy law was again amended, this time to make the local assemblymen and administrative heads directly electable by the

[25] Yu Chin-o, *Hŏnbŏp kich'o hwoegorok*, pp. 48–51.

[26] Terry E. MacDougal, "Democracy and Local Government in Postwar Japan," in *Democracy in Japan*, ed. Takeshi Ishida, et al. (Pittsburgh: University of Pittsburgh Press, 1989), pp. 139–69.

[27] Chŏng Se-uk, "Hanguk ŭi chibang chach'ije wa minjuhwa" (The Local Autonomy System and Democratization in Korea), in *Hanguk chongch'i ŭi minjuhwa* (The Democratization of Korean Politics) The Korean Political Science Association (Seoul: Bŏpmunsa, 1988), p. 205.

people. This amendment of November 11, 1960, also drastically strengthened measures to enhance the possibility of fair, clean, and democratic elections of local officials. By the time fresh local elections were held in December 1960, however, the fervor for local self-rule had chilled and voting rates were visibly down—for instance, only 38.8 percent of eligible voters turned out for an important election, of the mayoralty of Seoul.[28] During the five months before they were ousted after the 1961 military coup, some local government officials also abused their positions for personal gain and as stepping stones in their search for central government positions, either elected or appointed.

As Park Chung Hee consolidated his postcoup presidency, he formally terminated local autonomy "until the unification of the fatherland is accomplished."[29] It was not until 1987, when the Sixth Republic under duly elected President Roh Tae Woo became operational, that a drive for local autonomy was renewed. The sixth item in Roh's famous democratization package of June 29, 1987, called for the resuscitation of a local autonomy system, and a newly amended local autonomy law was promulgated on April 5, 1988. However, this legislation—championed by the coalition of opposition parties in the thirteenth National Assembly, where an unprecedented phenomenon of yŏso-yadae (a small ruling party versus a large opposition) was in place—was vetoed by President Roh. It took prolonged renegotiations in the revamped Assembly to produce yet another amended local autonomy law on December 31, 1990. Based on this law, the elections of local assemblymen took place in the spring of 1991. However, the Roh government postponed the elections of local government heads until 1995; consequently, a functioning local government system was in effect aborted. At the inauguration on February 25, 1993, of the first duly elected civilian regime in thirty-two years, President Kim Young Sam pledged that he would strive to "create a new Korea" through "democratic reforms," including the establishment once again of functioning local governments.

The 1995 local government elections. The elections held in 1995 were direct electoral exercises throughout South Korea to choose 5,758 local officials from among 15,412 duly registered candidates. In terms of the numbers involved, the elections were unprecedented. Voters were to choose four groups of local officials: (1) wide-area government heads such as mayors of the largest cities and provincial governors, (2) heads of basic local units, (3) councilors for wide-area governments, and (4) councilors for basic local units. It was agreed among the government and opposition par-

[28] Ibid, p. 209.
[29] Kim, *Hanguk hŏnbopsa*, p. 576.

ties that all local officials would be elected in one sweep on June 27 for the sake of minimizing expenditures that might add to inflationary pressures, as well as to save time. At stake were the following[30]:

Fifteen heads of large-area autonomous bodies—the mayors of five major cities and the governors of ten provinces
230 heads of basic-area autonomous bodies—the mayors or commissioners of small cities and major city wards
970 councilors of five major cities and ten provinces, and
4,541 councilors of small cities, counties, and major city wards

The candidates nominated by political parties were:

1,050 members of the ruling Democratic Liberal Party (DLP)
712 members of the main opposition Democratic Party (DP)
244 members of the United Liberal Democrats (ULD, a new opposition party)

Political parties did not nominate candidates for the posts of councils in small cities and other basic units because the new Local Autonomy Act banned party nomination of such candidates so as not to overpoliticize local units at the basic level. For the most important prizes, the mayoral and provincial gubernatorial posts, the ruling party made nominations for all fifteen posts, whereas the opposition DP and ULD named eleven and nine, respectively. There were also numerous independent candidates, a phenomenon that led to some early speculation that the electorate was wary of established parties and that independents might sweep the June elections.

Brief summaries of the respective roles of "the three Kims," Kim Young Sam, Kim Dae-jung, and Kim Jong Pil, just prior to the 1995 local elections are in order here. These men were the best known and the most enduring Korean politicians and had interacted closely for decades, sometimes as allies and often as rivals. President Kim Young Sam needed a victory in the local government elections because they took place at about the midpoint of his presidential term. No matter how the ruling group attempted to downgrade the importance of these elections as a "midterm referendum," that aspect could not be denied. President Kim also needed a victory in the local elections in the summer of 1995 because his popularity rating, now that he had been in office for a little over two years, was plummeting.

---

[30] Chungang sonko kwanri ŭiwŏnhwoe (The Central Election Management Commission), *Cheil hwoe tongsi chibang sŏnkŏ ch'ongran* (The Complete Records of the Simultaneous Local Elections in the Entire Nation) (Seoul: Taejong munwha inswaesa, 1995), p. 91.

Kim Dae-jung had "withdrawn" from politics in 1992 after he was defeated by Kim Young Sam, his third such defeat in a presidential race. However, he remained the real power behind the scenes of the opposition Democratic Party. In fact, it was Kim Dae-jung, now chairman of the Asia–Pacific Peace Foundation, who provided a substantive issue for the June local elections through his "regional equal rights" argument. "In the past," said Kim, "politicians from a particular region have dominated Korean politics, deepening regional conflicts. The forthcoming local elections will end such regional hegemony by one region."[31] He was referring to the fact that all three successive presidents with military backgrounds—Park, Chun, and Roh—had hailed from villages near Taegu, North Kyŏngsang Province, a province that had benefited both economically and through high-level appointments of its citizens. Kim Dae-jung believed that the nation would be grouped into a number of regionally based power blocs in the wake of the June elections, putting an end to the longtime political and economic dominance by Kyŏngsang region. He was also reminding voters that Kim Young Sam was from South Kyŏngsang Province, and that his own native province of Chŏlla had been severely discriminated against since the early 1960s. He said that political realignments would be made possible when regionally based political parties won local elections and began sharing power among local parties on an equal basis while promoting regional cooperation. Kim suggested that such a development would remedy the pernicious effects of regionalism.

Kim Jong Pil also had a large stake in the local elections. Unlike Kim Young Sam, who had emerged from the three-party merger as the ruling party candidate for the presidency, Kim Jong Pil found himself eased out of the top party position in January 1995, when he was asked to announce his "resignation" from the chairmanship. If President Kim and his reform-minded followers could no longer tolerate the increasingly conservative stance of Park's onetime confidant, they miscalculated Kim Jong Pil's staying power as a political survivor, an identifiable standard-bearer of the "conservatives" from the eras of the Park, Chung, and Roh presidencies. He announced on February 21 the formation of a new political party, the United Liberal Democrats (ULD). Less than six months later Kim Jong Pil was leading his new party, opposing President Kim Young Sam's DLP, a fact that would have a far-reaching impact on the outcome of the local elections.

Another substantive issue, amending the constitution to institute a cabinet system of government, was advocated by Kim Jong Pil. Though Kim Jong Pil himself would not at the time openly link his advocacy with anything proposed by Kim Dae-jung, in the wake of the "regional equal

[31] *The Korea Herald*, 1 June 1995, p. 2.

rights" debates in the local election campaigns cabinet system advocacy took on the appearance of favoring rotations of the premiership not only among political parties but also among different regions.[32] Kim Jong Pil lamented that the voters in his native provinces of Ch'ungch'ŏng had become wearers of *hatbachi* (literally, cotton padded pants; figuratively, political impotents). Kim Jong Pil thus resonated Kim Dae-jung's charges of regional discrimination.

There were, of course, numerous concrete local interest issues, such as developing local industries and infrastructures for large-scale industrial and trading centers along the southwestern coastal lines, new harbors and airports, recreational spaces, and the like. However, the June election threatened from the beginning to become a nationwide midterm referendum on the Kim Young Sam administration,[33] thus overshadowing concrete local issues. Also, such issues as regional equal rights and the cabinet system of government were *national* issues in the 1995 local elections. Even a "local" election in Seoul attracted national attention. The contest in Seoul special city, the center of virtually all important activities in Korea, turned into a larger-than-local showdown and something of a microcosm of national electoral politics in the mid-1990s.[34]

From behind the scenes Kim Dae-jung persuaded Cho Soon to run for mayor as the candidate of the opposition party, which reluctantly accepted an outsider with the potential to win as its standardbearer. Cho, a well-respected economics professor at the prestigious Seoul National University (SNU), had served, among other posts, as deputy prime minister and minister of the Economic Planning Board under President Roh and as governor of the central Bank of Korea under President Kim. However, disagreements between Kim and Cho on the question of the autonomy of the Bank of Korea, which Cho had advocated, eventually prompted the two to part company.

The ruling party nominated Chŏng Wŏn-sik, also an SNU professor of education for decades and a former minister of education and prime minister under President Roh. Pak Ch'an-jong, a career politician since 1973 with a checkered background as a former assemblyman who had changed party affiliations several times, ran as an independent. There were six other minor mayoral candidates.

As a starting point Cho could count on the guaranteed support of Kim Dae-jung's numerous followers, many originally from the Chŏlla prov-

[32] Chŏngch'i kehyŏk simin yŏnhap chunbi uiwŏnhwoe, "6.27 sŏnkŏ wa chŏngch'i kehyok ŭi kwaje" (The June 27 Elections and the Tasks of Political Reforms) (Seoul: 1995), p. 33.

[33] *Korea Newsreview*, 1 April 1995, p. 4.

[34] For instance, *WIN: A Current Affairs Monthly* (June 1995): pp. 61–72, and *Sin Dong-A Monthly* (August 1995): pp. 173–82, 232–37.

inces and now residing in Seoul. A number of young volunteers enthusiastically campaigned for Cho, who proved a down-to-earth and tenacious campaigner.[35] Chŏng, on the other hand, enjoyed the financial and organizational backing of the ruling party and touted his administrative experience, but he did not seem comfortable in his campaigning role. He was overly formal and the picture of him wearing a pink dinner jacket that appeared in a Seoul magazine contrasted sharply with Cho's open-collar campaign poster.[36] Independent candidate Pak in turn relied on his relatively youthful appeal and the initially high public support that placed him way ahead of the others.[37]

Following a heated campaign at the end of which Kim Dae-jung campaigned actively for Cho, the latter emerged the decisive winner, with some 42.3 percent of the valid votes. Independent Pak was the runner-up, with 33.6 percent, and the ruling party's Chŏng received less than half the popular support Cho had mustered, only 20.7 percent. The humiliating defeat suffered by the ruling party candidate was nothing compared with the devastating ruling party loss in the election of ward chiefs of Seoul—the opposition party swept the election, winning twenty-three of twenty-five posts.[38]

The participation rate nationwide was 68.4 percent, a high point in local government elections.[39] More importantly, most observers agreed that the June 27 elections were clean, fair, and free of violence, particularly as compared to so many previous elections. The important outcomes are shown in Table 6.

It should be recalled that political parties did not nominate candidates at the level of basic-level councilors. Many observers highlighted the 5-4-4-2 ratio among the ruling and opposition parties and independents at the most significant level of large city mayors and provincial governors. At that level the ruling party was outnumbered by a 1 to 2 ratio if the opposition parties and independents were to be united on certain issues. At the basic-unit head level the ratio was 7 to 16. Overall, the strength of the ruling party versus the opposition plus independents was 1 to 2.1. This was a disastrous loss for President Kim's ruling party.

[35] Kim Jae-myŏng, "Chunghuhan sŏnbihyŏng kaehyŏcha: Cho Sun" (Cho Soon: A Courteous and Scholarly Reformer), *WIN: A Current Affairs Monthly* (June 1995): pp. 70–72.

[36] Kwŏn T'ae-dong, "Ch'ŏgni kŏch'in sosimpa kyoyukcha: Chŏng Wŏn-sik" (Chong Won Shik: A Former Premier and an Educator with a Conviction), *WIN: A Current Affairs Monthly* (June 1995): pp. 66–68.

[37] Song Ŭi-ho, "Mudangp'a sichang sinhwa kkumkkunun Pak Ch'an-chong" (Chan-Chong Park Who Dreams of an Independent Mayor), *WIN: A Current Affairs Monthly* (June 1995): pp. 74–76.

[38] *Segye Times*, 29 June 1995, p. 1.

[39] *Joong-Ang Daily News*, 28 June 1995, p. 1.

Table 6. Party affiliations of elected local government officials in 1995

Offices	No. to be elected	Democratic Liberal Party	Democratic Party	United Liberal Democrats	Independents
Head, wide-area gov'ts	15	5	4	4	2
Head, basic units	230	70	84	23	53
Wide-area Councilors	875	286	355	83	151
Total	1,120	361	443	110	206

Source: Chungang sŏnkŏ kwanri uiwŏnhwoe.

It was clearly undeniable that "anti-ruling party" and "anti-Kim Young Sam" sentiments were already rampant by the summer of 1995, in sharp contrast with Kim's approval rating of some 90 percent in early 1993. Knowledgeable observers pointed out three major reasons for the negativism.[40] First, it was believed that some two-and-a-half years after President Kim's inauguration there emerged many significant anti-Kim groups who had been adversely affected by Kim's vigorous reform measures. These included (1) military groups, for example, the former *Hanahwoe* members and their close allies who occupied powerful and lucrative positions in the government and semi-official organizations but were abruptly severed from them by the Kim government; (2) well-to-do businesses and their clients who were inconvenienced or who suffered financially from the imposition of the real-name transaction measures; (3) and numerous others who had been well connected and powerful under the three military regimes of Park, Chun, and Roh, harking back to the early 1960s. The mass media had welcomed the Kim government's reform measures as overdue corrective steps, but to those negatively affected by them Kim was a crafty and despicable enemy. They believed that Kim had duped them, Roh, and others by merging his party in early 1990 with parties led by Roh and conservative Kim Jong Pil. Having captured power through clever manipulations within the ruling party Kim now turned against them mercilessly, or so they said.

The second major reason for the ruling party's defeat in local elections was that most observers were now disillusioned by the Kim government's high-level appointees. He visibly favored those who had steadfastly supported him as an opposition leader for three lean decades. Understandably, those so-called *kasins* (literally, family subjects) of Kim Young Sam were not always the brightest or most politically adroit; Kim

---

[40] Kang U-sok Consulting Group, *6.27 Sadae sŏnkŏ paeksŏ* (The White Paper on the Four Great Elections of June 27) (Seoul: Chŏnbo yŏheng, 1995), pp. 358–60.

himself never had a reputation of being bright, well-educated, or well-read. Like Kim, his followers were as stubborn and determined as they were inexperienced in governing. As these eager novices surrounded President Kim, who also lacked administrative experience, they were nevertheless capable of launching several decisive reform measures that had been advocated by opposition parties at various times in the past. The reforms were initially welcomed by most voters. Even as they were carried out, however, the "ruling style" of the Kim regime as a whole began to trouble many observers.

The duly elected, "democratic" government appeared overly centered on the person of Kim Young Sam, so self-righteous and secretive. Some said that Kim had needed to be that way in the past to survive as an opposition politician under ever-suspicious military dictators. But Kim, now the president, often completely astonished even his closest official advisors with his "surprise shows," as cynics began to dub his bold measures. After he announced decisive steps to move *Hanahwoe* members from the military, for instance, Kim reportedly asked the chief of presidential secretaries: "Weren't you surprised?" In 1994 when the Kim government sent, without consulting among political parties in the National Assembly, shiploads of rice to North Korea, which was suffering from a major famine, many conservatives and anti-Communists, including millions of refugees from North Korea, had mixed feelings. But most South Koreans could acquiesce in the shipment on humanitarian grounds until the North Korean authorities humiliated a South Korean ship captain by insisting that the ship fly a North Korean national flag. When public opinion turned against the gift of rice, fanned by the mass media's sensationalized pictures of the ship in distress, one obvious option for the regime would have been to keep quiet until public indignation died down. Instead, Kim's self-righteous and imperious remarks were reported by the media as favoring more shipments "even if I have to buy rice from abroad."[41] Kim government's decisions, under these circumstances, now appeared arrogant, capricious, and undemocratic.

The third major reason for the unpopularity of the Kim government by 1995 was a growing perception that it was "operating much like an opposition party."[42] It is undeniable that Kim that long been in opposition, championing the cause of democracy in the name of opposing dictatorship, but some now wondered whether he had been using democratic rhetoric and justification simply as a means of establishing himself as an opposition leader. Was his advocacy of democracy a means to an end, or was democracy an end in itself? What would be the end for Kim and his

[41] Ibid., p. 360.
[42] Ibid.

government? As observers pondered this question, they recalled with some bitterness the merging of Kim's party in 1990 with those of Roh and Kim Jong Pil, whom Kim Young Sam had previously repeatedly denounced as the enemy of democracy in Korea. After Kim's election, however, the style of his presidency retained many aspects of an "imperial" presidency of old including his aloofness, his haughtiness, his secretiveness, and his penchant for solitary decision making following well-publicized retreats—alone. When Kim was just an opposition leader his politics did not directly affect many. But as president any surprise administrative decisions he made carried the government's full authority, exercised with a vengeance. Many of these decisions were perceived as "opposition" moves aimed at various powerful and organized interest groups, including many high-ranking members of the military, the ruling elites of the Third, Fourth, and Fifth republics, industrial conglomerates, and voters in the non-Kyŏngsang areas.

After the 1995 elections, analysts also pointed out that the most pronounced personality-based regionalism in voting was a prominent feature of the local elections. It should be added that President Kim was not the sole cause for this phenomenon—the other Kims were equally responsible. But Kim Young Sam's party did exceedingly well in his native South Kyŏngsang Province, winning sixty-two wide-area head and councilor posts over the opposition parties' zero. The opposition Democratic Party, closely identified with Kim Dae-jung, swept the posts in his native South Chŏlla Province, winning eighty-four seats, while the ruling party won but a solitary seat in the provincial council. Likewise, Kim Jong Pil's party won sixty-four posts in his native South Ch'ungch'ŏng Province, whereas the ruling party managed to elect only three provincial councilors and the Democratic Party just two seats in the same council. As Kim Dae-jung declared in his discourse on "regional equal rights," the country was clearly divided into three prominent camps and the Seoul special city, where the opposition Democratic Party emerged a lopsided victor with a total of 145 posts versus thirteen for the ruling party. Historically ruling parties had seldom been victorious in the capital city, but the 1995 ratio was unprecedented. If these patterns were to hold for both the 1996 National Assembly elections and the 1997 presidential election there would be mathematical bases for a potential Kim Dae-jung victory, should he declare that he was once again politically active.

The civil society and fair elections. Another notable phenomenon in 1995 was that there emerged at least 387 citizens' voluntary organizations, whose sole stated purpose was to promote fair elections.[43] The civil soci-

---

[43] Chungang sŏnkŏ kwanri uiwŏnhwoe (The Central Election Management Commission), pp. 125–26.

ety had been visibly activated. In fact, a small number of these private autonomous organizations had initially been formed by university professors during the limited 1991 local government elections. Hundreds of them now sprang up—as the saying goes—"like bamboo shoots after the rainy season" before the June 27 elections of 1995. They included among others fourteen religious groups, nine women's organizations, nine farmers' associations, and seventeen other citizens' volunteer groups. Together they formed the Consultative Conference for the Citizens Movement to Realize Fair Elections. The conference networked organizations scattered across South Korea and sponsored some sixty-eight public discussions with local election candidates, held six "seminars" to promote fair elections, distributed twelve publications, issued seven statements, received 729 complaints of election law violations, and sued forty-four candidates. The Central Election Management Commission noted that these voluntary associations clearly avoided partisan activities for or against any parties or candidates, instead concentrating their efforts on improving "the political consciousness of the citizenry" to promote fair elections.[44]

The members of most of these organizations were from the relatively well-educated middle class and were politically aware—neither pro- nor antigovernment in 1995—and had the leisure time and the wherewithal to sponsor and participate in their activities to promote fair elections.[45] These associations clearly signified that a "civil society"[46] in a broad sense was becoming energized in South Korea. That these civil associations promoted fair elections was yet another sign that the democratization of Korean politics was taking place. In this connection it might be added that a *Cultural and Social Directory*[47] lists thousands of autonomous, private, voluntary associations in Korea including the International Human Rights League of Korea, the Citizens' Coalition for Economic Justice, the Consumer Protection Association, the Korean Association for Conservation of Nature, the Korean Environmental Preservation Association, the Korean Freedom League, the Korean Council on Social Welfare, the Korean Senior Citizens Association, and *ad infinitum*.

[44] Ibid.

[45] It came out during a dinner in Seoul on June 15, 1996, that the middle-aged wife of a comfortably retired classmate of this author was just such a volunteer and had sponsored various election-related "seminars." With some pride she related that many other ladies of similar backgrounds were volunteering their time and effort in the interest of "democratizing" Korean politics.

[46] John Keane, *Democracy and Civil Society* (London: Verso, 1988); Jang Jip Choi, "Political Cleavages in South Korea," and Hagan Koo, "Strong State and Contentious Society," both in *State and Society in Contemporary Korea,* ed. Hagan Koo (Ithaca: Cornell University Press, 1993), pp. 13–50, 231–50.

[47] *Korea Annual 1995,* pp. 423–54.

In sum, that the first full-fledged, generally clean, fair local government elections were held in 1995 was a significant fact in itself. The ruling party was decisively defeated, but the president and the party accepted the election outcome, if somewhat begrudgingly. Ramifications included: first, the elections and the aftermath were an important landmark in the evolution for nearly half a century of democracy in South Korea. Second, these elections represented, among other things, the first test of the three interrelated democratic-reform laws of 1994 through which the ruling party had relinquished substantial built-in political advantages in the interest of refining and enhancing the democratic process in conducting elections, fund raising, and local administration. Third, for the first time the country had fully institutionalized local governments through democratic elections. Without prejudging (at this writing it is only three years after the elections) the actual operation of local governments, still significantly penetrated by and financially dependent to varying degrees on the central government, the Korean people now have concrete, proximate institutions that they elected. Their relationship with the elected governments should be different from the past patterns when officials were centrally appointed. Fourth, no matter how hard President Kim and his ruling party attempted to belittle the aspect of the 1995 elections as the midterm appraisal of the Kim presidency, no one could deny the negative impact of the elections on him, his government, and the ruling party, which had precious little time to regroup before the 1996 National Assembly and the 1997 presidential elections—important benchmarks in the democratic evolution of Korean politics.

✵

CHAPTER 8

Corruption, the Trial, and the National Assembly, 1995-1996

Corruption has been a perennial problem throughout the world[1], and indeed, "corruption is as old as government itself."[2] Plato expressed concern about "presents" (bribes) and Chinese and Indian rulers were beset by corrupt practices for thousands of years, as were Korean rulers and their people. Corruption persisted in a dynastic Korea in which few officials considered their power a public trust not to be abused for personal gain. Apparently few members of the ruling elite had a clear understanding of what was involved in being a steward of the commonweal. In the more than five hundred years of the Chosŏn dynasty, corruption was in a way built into the system itself in that the number of those who passed the state examinations, based mostly on a knowledge of Confucian classics far exceeded the number of government posts that legitimately needed to be filled. Attaining a government position was the ultimate goal for the best and the brightest of the *yangban* elites in an agrarian society where few other respectable career paths existed. This fact tended to sanction almost any means, often including bribery, to securing a government position.

Once appointed, many officials recouped their "investments" many times over through corrupt or exploitative means.[3] Even while they occu-

---

[1] Arnold Heidenheimer, *Political Corruption* (New York: Holt, Rinehart and Winston, 1970), Parts 2–4.

[2] Robert Klitgaard, *Controlling Corruption* (Berkeley: University of California Press, 1988), p. 7.

[3] For concrete examples of corruption and exploitation by government officials in the Yi dynasty period, see Yi Pyŏng-do *Hankuksa Taekwan* (A Comprehensive Survey of Korean History) (Seoul: Pomunkak, 1964), pp. 467–71.

pied government positions whose tenures were not at all protected or long, most officials' formal stipends were kept modest or low except for those officials considered specially "meritorious subjects." Many officials, both high and low level, grew greedy and regarded the common people as objects for exploitation. During the Yi dynasty the powerful had few qualms about their corrupt practices as the "three bonds" and "five relationships" of Confucianism, the national teaching during the Chosŏn dynasty, had said little about honesty, integrity, or public accountability. One Confucian relationship required "trust," but it was essentially a trusting relationship among friends of the elite, not vis-a-vis commoners or *ch'onmin* (the despised people). A culture of institutionalized corruption was therefore pervasive toward the end of the Yi dynasty.

A Culture of Corruption in Korea

This institutionalized corruption had been undergirded by what some call a "cultural trait" of the Koreans.[4] Like the Chinese and the Japanese, the Koreans had a long tradition of gift giving. Some were token gifts that were innocent enough, but when the gift was an expensive item presented to a powerful individual with the expectation of receiving a favor it was akin to a bribe. This type of a gift expected something in return; there were no expensive gifts without a purpose, which may be unstated but nonetheless understood or banked for the future. To receive a substantial gift and then refuse the requested favor was considered beneath the dignity of the receiver. This atmosphere of ill-defined mutual help was a longstanding way of life in traditional Korea.

In the First Republic, during the twelve-year tenure of Syngman Rhee, the aging president was personally abstemious, but his regime was not free of corruption in a new form. In an unaccustomed era of "democratic election" Rhee and his aides did not hesitate to bribe National Assembly members who were to elect him president according to the 1948 constitution. Likewise, many officials of the poor, infant republic whose salaries fell far short of providing living wages were also bribed by supplicants for government positions or favors. The Liberal Party, organized in 1951 by and for Rhee, began the unsavory practice of demanding and receiving huge "donations" from businesses both large and small for all manner of special considerations and favors, including tax reductions. Toward the end of the Rhee presidency the intricate tie among the government, the ruling party, financial institutions, and business—in a word, a pattern of

---

[4] Paul Crane, *Korean Patterns* (Seoul: Hollym, 1967), pp. 75–76, cited in Klitgaard, *Corruption*, p. 139.

"collusion"—began to appear. Businessmen knew that private fortunes could be made through cooperation with the ruling party. Political connections could be used not only for the acquisition of government-controlled foreign aid at favorable rates but also for purchasing government-owned property at a fraction of its real value and evading tax payments.[5] By the mid-1950s, when the Rhee regime no longer had to worry about effective checks by opposition parties, corruption was rampant.[6]

During the short-lived Second Republic, which made an effort to be more democratic than its predecessor, Premier Chang Myŏn's personal integrity was not questioned. However, desperate efforts at operating a government with a responsible cabinet system with the ruling party split in the middle often led Chang's assistants to bribe unwieldy assemblymen to accomplish anything. Those politicians who had opposed the Rhee regime for a long and lean period also became greedy once they were in positions of power, and as they were replacing the appointees of the Rhee regime at many levels of both the central and local governments, corruption and nepotism were increasingly evident. Government salaries for many employees were still at subsistence level in a country where the annual per capita income was $79 and some 24 percent of the available labor force was unemployed in 1960, when the Chang cabinet was formed.[7] Of course, there were officials who led lives of *ch'ŏngbin* (literally, clean poverty), but they were the exceptions rather than the rule.

Corruption of the former soldiers. Rhee and Chang, with aristocratic and upper-middle class origins, respectively, were not known for their acute senses of material insecurity. However, their successors, former Generals Park, Chun, and Roh, were from starkly different backgrounds. All three were from poverty-stricken farming families and had joined the army. That proved to be the path to the naked power with which the first two seized government, and the third managed to inherit it. Once each of the three men occupied the pinnacle of dictatorial power, his almost primordial obsession with material security led him to amass enormous riches, and, in Park's case, to a determined national effort at rapid economic growth. A byproduct of the government-led export-oriented growth was that a widespread pattern of collusion between politics and business and of kickbacks by businesses to the government was now firmly established.[8] In the case of both Chun Doo Hwan and Roh Tae Woo, once the men had tasted wealth they were driven to seek limitless material abun-

[5] John Kie-chiang Oh, *Korea: Democracy on Trial*, pp. 39, 46.
[6] Chu Sŏk-kyun, "T'am-o ron" (An Essay on Corrupt Officials), *Sassangge Monthly* I, no. 5 (August 1953): p. 178.
[7] Oh, *Korea*, p. 84.
[8] Klitgaard, *Corruption*, pp. 138–42.

dance—how much would be enough? Chun and Roh—egged on by their wives and relatives, according to many—sought such an unprecedented and egregious extreme of wealth it would put Ferdinand and Imelda Marcos of the Philippines to shame by comparison. As a military dictator, for instance, Chun held an almost absolute power that was accountable to no institution in the Fifth Republic, and he proved Lord Acton right by corrupting absolutely.

In the early 1990s it was a common belief that the election of Roh had been "bought" by Chun, who spent an astronomical amount in campaign funds to ensure his *Hanahwoe* cohort's election. Some thought it was partly to protect Chun himself after he left the presidency from investigation into his abuse of power and corruption while in office. It was also a common knowledge that Roh likewise received huge "donations" from big businesses beginning in the first months of his presidency and spent an enormous amount of money, delivered via the ruling party, on Kim Young Sam's election as president. Kim Young Sam all but acknowledged Roh's contribution when he demurred that he himself did not accept any money directly from Roh. This meant little, as Roh gave a large amount of money to Kim's party. Surprisingly, the leading opposition candidate, Kim Dae-jung, had acknowledged that he, too, received about $2.5 million from the Roh camp. If it would give such a gift to a sworn opponent of the military regimes, how much might the Roh group have given to the Kim Young Sam campaign? One critic of Kim called Roh's contribution to the Kim campaign the "original sin" of the Kim regime.[9]

Kim Young Sam detractors suspected that there was being built an illicit circle of mutual protection. They knew that Kim, who had risen to top leader in Roh's ruling party in 1990, had lived with much of the corruption in the ruling party. Even while the people applauded Kim's admirable disclosure of his family assets, the imposition of the real-name financial transaction system, and associated anticorruption measures, a dark suspicion lingered in many minds that the Kim presidency, in the beginning, had also been tainted by illicit political funds amassed by Chun and Roh or their unscrupulous sycophants. Kim's seemingly magnanimous and oft-repeated statement that Chun's and Roh's past deeds "should be left to the judgment of history" did not even amount to so much as slaps on their wrists, and the lingering suspicion deepened. At the same time, Kim's nonchalant, know-nothing attitude toward Chun and Roh profoundly dismayed many, particularly the Kwangju citizenry. When the public prosecutor's office, which traditionally had kowtowed to the chief executives, announced that it would not prosecute those who had executed "a successful coup d'etat" followed by the Kwangju mas-

---

[9] Kang Chun-man, *Kim Yong Sam Ideologie* (The Kim Young Sam Ideology), pp. 106–9.

sacre, the victims of Kwangju and their sympathizers were bitterly angered.

Huge accidents as signs of corruption.   It had been long speculated that engineering and construction companies had contributed large sums of money to politicians and political parties as bribes to win construction contracts and then cut corners and skirt construction and safety codes. It was feared that in due time the fruits of large-scale corruption would appear as mammoth construction failures and accidents. These apprehensions were proven shockingly true in the first years of the Kim government, much to the chagrin of the "civilian and democratic" government and those who supported it, though the seeds for these catastrophes had been sown years before. The people shrugged their collective shoulders at some relatively "minor" incidents, such as when a high-rise apartment under construction literally crashed to the ground after the top floor collapsed and brought all the other floors to the foundation in terrifying succession. Fortunately human casualties in the incident were limited because the building was still unoccupied. However, the collapse of the Sŏngsu Grand Bridge across the Han River, which flows through Seoul, was a truly astounding event. During morning rush hour on October 14, 1994, a 157-foot section of the bridge collapsed, killing thirty-two and injuring seventeen as six passenger vehicles and a bus plunged into the river. It was learned that the span on the fifth and sixth piers of the bridge had sheared away from the support structure. The Korean Society of Civil Engineers inspected the bridge and reported that the Dong Ah Industrial company had apparently cut corners on welding as a cost-saving measure. The bridge had been hurriedly built in 1979 during the Park presidency, which was then rushing numerous construction projects in the interest of rapid economic growth. The Dong Ah company had long been known for its generous political contributions. It subsequently paid huge indemnities to each of the families of the victims and also to the injured and a number of Dong Ah officials as well as the mayor of Seoul city, which was responsible for bridge safety inspections, were fired. But the people's faith and trust in construction projects and in those officials who were suspected of receiving bribes suffered. One foreign paper captured an important aspect of the incident when it reported "A Crisis of Faith: Is the New Korea Jerry-Built?"[10]

A similar disaster struck less than two months later, on December 8, 1994, again shocking the entire nation. This time an underground gas supply station exploded in a residential area near densely populated downtown Seoul, killing twelve and injuring more than sixty others, de-

[10] *New York Times,* 18 November 1994, p. A18.

stroying fifty-five houses and twenty cars. The gas supply station had been completed in 1992, the last year of Roh's presidency, by the Hanyang Corporation, which was also suspected of cutting corners to recoup money spent as bribes to win the construction contract. Another huge and tragic incident occurred when the five-story Sampoong Department store in a fashionable area of Seoul collapsed on June 29, 1995, killing 502 shoppers and injuring 937. Rescue operations for thirty-one missing, buried under layers of rubble, continued for a month. It was the largest man-made disaster in the nation's history. The building had been dedicated in 1989, the second year of the Roh presidency. A prosecution probe showed the collapse of the entire department store building was due to faulty framework. The nation was shocked to learn that Seoul city officials had been "bribed by the Sampoong owner to permit the department store's sloppy design and construction."[11] Some responsible persons were subsequently prosecuted, but public anger with those who collected large bribes and those offering them in connection with these and many similar incidents mounted.

Enormous public pressure was building to investigate the vicious cycles of corruption, disaster, and wrist slapping followed by corruption. An opinion survey found corruption led the list of "the most pressing problems in Korea."[12] The survey, conducted by the Yonhap News Agency in cooperation with the World Research Institute in January 1995, found 23.4 percent of 1,000 people who received the questionnaire felt that elimination of corruption was the most urgent task, followed by democratic rule (21.7 percent) and economic progress (15.6 percent).

Prelude to the trial. President Kim enjoyed an 80 percent approval rating in 1993, his first year in office. According to the Korea Gallup poll conducted in April 1995, however, some 44.9 percent of one thousand adults polled across the country approved Kim's performance record, while 37.7 percent did not approve them.[13] By the time of the June 27, 1995, local government elections, the Kim government's euphoric honeymoon period with the people was clearly over. If the ruling party's performance in the National Assembly elections turned out to be mediocre in 1996, the Kim government would likewise face difficulties in the all-important presidential election of 1997—unless the people's attention could quickly be deflected to some "spectacular surprises" and the sagging image of the regime improved. It was imperative that Kim, who was known for his ability to produce such "surprise shows,"

11 *Korea Annual 1996*, p. 204.
12 *Korea Newsreview*, 21 January 1995, p. 7.
13 *Korea Newsreview*, 30 December 1995, p. 5.

divert the people's attention to another engrossing drama even at the risk of opening a Pandora's box.

Meanwhile, the real-name financial transaction system had been detecting glacial movements of some huge borrowed-name accounts, and speculation was rampant that many of these belonged to Chun and Roh and their top-level henchmen, who were laundering the funds. The two former presidents, who were left unscathed by Kim's vague "judgment of history," appeared unconcerned and unapologetic about their past deeds. They increasingly renewed open contacts with their former cohorts and supporters, mostly extreme conservatives who had been in numerous influential positions while Chun and Roh held power for twelve years. Some observers speculated that they were clandestinely planning a "conservative" political comeback, probably through their proxies. It seemed that South Korea was experiencing a calm before a political storm. In this milieu, many political appointees in government and government enterprises and high-level bureaucrats took a *pokchi pudong* (literally, lying on the ground, making no move) approach.

The calm did not last long, however. One senior government party member hinted that there might be a huge secret fund "held by a former president." The comment was reported in the media but was so vague that it could not be pursued. Thereafter came a bombshell on the floor of a plenary session of the National Assembly. On October 19, 1995, Representative Pak Kye-dong, an opposition legislator, disclosed that Roh had a secret fund totalling 400 billion won, or about $500 million,[14] a staggering amount for a "slush fund" in a single person's possession in any country. Further, he substantiated the shocking exposure by adding that the amount was deposited in commercial banks under forty false-name accounts and then produced detailed copies of Roh's savings accounts. This disclosure in the National Assembly, with many members of the press in the balcony, immediately spread a shockwave through political circles and created a rapidly escalating chain reaction. The mass media had a veritable feeding frenzy for days since there were no forces to hinder the "free press" in the new era of "democratization." Questions quite naturally arose about the likelihood that Chun possessed similar slush funds. The natural outcome was that public demanded a full investigation of the allegations. Soon a former chief of security under Roh testified to prosecutors that Roh had indeed collected "funds for ruling," and the mass media again had a field day reporting on the testimony. The aroused public vociferously demanded action.

At a press conference on October 27, only eight days after Park's disclosure, a tearful Roh was compelled to "apologize to the nation" for col-

[14] *Hankook Ilbo*, 20 October 1995, p. 1.

lecting some $650 million in slush funds while in office. To the general public, whose per capita annual income reached just about $10,000 in 1995, the secret slush fund was a mindnumbing amount. When the news broke, the media reported sudden jumps in drunk drivers and withdrawals from savings accounts. Rates of work absenteeism also became abnormally high, and restaurants and bars enjoyed unusually full houses. A state of widespread despondency was palpable.

Roh's confessions also triggered demonstrations around the country demanding punishment for both Chun and Roh. A huge rally organized by opposition leader Kim Dae-jung demanded that Kim Young Sam prove that he had not accepted money from Roh's slush fund.[15] After prosecutors' further investigations into the large "donations" by Yi Kŏn-hi, the Samsung group chairman, and Chŏng Ju-yŏng, the honorary chairman of the Hyundai group, as well as ten other chairmen of the largest conglomerates, Roh became the first former president of Korea to be taken into custody, on November 25, 1995, on suspicion of accepting bribes.

Having watched these developments for weeks, President Kim made a stunning and sweeping announcement on the same day that a "special law" might be adopted to deal with the controversy over corruption as well as the military suppression committed under former governments.[16] This was truly an astounding about-face on the part of Kim, who had maintained from the early days of his presidential tenure that his predecessors would be judged "by history." He was now taking the position of "rectifying history" by prosecuting those who were corrupt and engaged in suppression. This new stance apparently broke a legal and political logjam, revealing much about the political and legal order in South Korea, specifically the relationship among the chief executive, the legislature, and the judiciary.

Before this point, under Kim's vague and do-nothing stance prosecutors had meekly decided in July 1995 that they could not prosecute those who led a successful coup d'etat. That decision, of course, profoundly disappointed the people, who had hoped that under the new government past wrongs by military dictators could be rectified in accordance with the law. Human rights advocates and relatives of victims of the Kwangju massacre, 398 in all, appealed the prosecutors' decision to the Constitutional Court. Two days after President Kim's about-face, on November 27, the court ruled that the decision by the prosecutor's office was wrong and that in fact those involved in the Kwangju massacre could be prosecuted "under a special legislation." The Court also declared that the prosecutor's reasoning that "a successful rebellion could not be a case of legal

15 *Washington Post*, 3 December 1995, p. A31.
16 *Korea Herald*, 26 November 1995, p. 1.

prosecution" was "erroneous" and also that the statute of limitations need not apply to a military mutiny that overthrew the constitutional order.[17] This surprise ruling opened the legal path to punishing those who had executed the December 12, 1979, coup and the Kwangju massacre led by Chun and assisted by Roh and their cohorts.

The opposition National Congress for New Politics (NCNP), headed by Kim Dae-jung, had attempted to have the National Assembly legislate Kwangju-related bills thrice and in vain. President Kim now declared that "the coup d'etat of May 17, 1980 (the Kwangju incident) tarnished the honor of the state and people as well as the pride of the nation, to the grief of all of us. . . . I will show the people that justice and law are still alive in this land."[18] Note the use of the first-person singular by Kim ("I will show . . ."). Those who speculated on the complete shift in Kim's position agreed that the president was attempting to "obtain an upper hand in political circles. Through the investigation of the Kwangju and related incidents, President Kim was believed to be trying to influence the fifteenth general elections (for the National Assembly) and the 1997 presidential election in the ruling party's favor."[19]

A special law to deal with the political bribery scandals, the May 18 Kwangju massacre, and the December 12 coup d'etat was hurriedly adopted by the National Assembly on December 19. The law paved the way for the prosecution to indict Chun, Roh, and other former army officers on charges of mutiny, treason, and bribery. Under the special law, the fifteen-year statutory limitations on former presidents Chun and Roh, who could not have been charged with any criminal offense during their presidential tenure other than treason, were suspended. Such a suspension troubled many legal experts, despite the obvious fact that Chun and Roh had been untouchable during their tenures. The special law also stipulated that statutory limitations would not be applicable to treason, mutiny, and massacre in the future.

The "Trial of the Century"

Standing trial along with Roh and Chun were fourteen military officers who had been directly implicated in the 1979 military coup and the 1980 Kwangju massacre. Fearing a catastrophic impact on the nation's economy, which appeared to be floundering, chairman of leading conglomerates who had donated huge amounts of money to Chun and Roh were not

[17] *Hankoo Ilbo*, 28 November 1995, p. 1.
[18] *Korea Annual 1996*, p. 48.
[19] Ibid., p. 49.

subject to physical detention; however, nine of them were formally indicted. Most of these conglomerate chairmen were hands-on chief executives; some were in distant parts of the world busily negotiating huge contracts with foreign industrial concerns even as they were being indicted.

Upon being arrested on December 3, 1995, a blunt-spoken Chun "angrily accused (President) Kim of using the arrest to protect himself politically" as his popularity plummeted, as evidenced by local election returns. Chun also bitterly accused Kim of having collaborated with what he called "rebellious forces," apparently referring to the 1990 merger of Kim Young Sam's opposition party with the parties of Roh and Kim Jong Pil. Chun was clearly reminding Kim of having benefited from an "opportunistic"[20] collaboration and accusing Kim of engaging in an another opportunistic about-face to punish Chun, Roh, and their followers for political reasons. Roh, who had been more deliberate than Chun when asked about his bankrolling of the 1992 presidential campaigns that resulted in the election of Kim Young Sam, simply replied, "I cannot comment on that." The financial aspect of the 1992 presidential election was one of the first questions that Roh was asked about upon his arrest, and has remained a key question since. It was clear that Roh's stance of not revealing details about the 1992 election was a card that he could play to his advantage vis-a-vis President Kim, who was an invisible but very real presence in the trial. Looking to the near future, Roh was also clearly aware of the provision in Article 79 of the constitution: "The president may grant amnesty, commutation and restoration of rights."

The public trials of the two former presidents and their codefendants began on December 18, 1995, in a relatively small courtroom in an imposing and heavily guarded courthouse in Seoul. Understandably, security was tight. Visitors with passes went through metal detectors twice, only to be checked again with handheld detectors before being admitted to the courtroom. When the chief judge of the three-judge panel called out, with no honorifics, "the accused, Chun Doo Hwan" and "the accused, Roh Tae Woo," the two men entered the room in short-sleeved, powder-blue prison garb. Three civilians, seated high on a dais, were now judging the once-powerful army generals and presidents—the symbolism was striking. In Korea, where the continental-law system has been the norm, there are no juries. There were a dozen defense attorneys, prosecutors, and scores of reporters and visitors in the austere courtroom, but one could have heard a pin drop.[21] The defendants had engaged the most prestigious and seasoned attorneys available; in comparison, the prosecutors appeared young, stiff, and maladroit. Chun's demeanor was haughty and dismissive, whereas Roh ap-

[20] "South Korea Judges Its Past." *New York Times*, 27 August 1996, p. A16.
[21] The author witnessed the trial on June 17, 1996.

peared relatively attentive. Naturally, most visitors' attention was focused on the two men; their codefendants seemed less significant.

Added to the expected bribery charges were treason and murder charges in connection with the December 12, 1979, coup and the Kwangju incident of May 1980.[22] While steadfastly maintaining that he had accepted donations but not bribes, Chun admitted during the trial that he sent some $240 million directly to Roh for his presidential campaign in 1987, including about $188 million that Chun personally delivered to Roh at his home in late 1987, according to testimony by the former presidential security chief.[23] It was also revealed that Chun had given an additional $70 million to Roh to celebrate his election and ease his way into the presidency. Chun subsequently admitted that he had spent an astounding $680 million in slush funds collected from forty-three conglomerates during his presidency, March 1981 to February 1988, and some $120 million since leaving the presidential office in 1988. Lingering suspicions that he was not revealing the entire amount were validated when prosecutors discovered some $8 million in cash in twenty-four boxes used to pack apples.

Chun remained vague on the identity of some 200 recipients of his largesse, just as Roh was silent on his financial backing of the 1992 presidential election. Chun's defense attorney intimated in a thinly veiled threat, however, that Chun might expose the recipients' identities if he were treated harshly, and Chun's wife made similar statements to journalists. A confirmation of the political nature of the trial, and probably of the influence of the Kim Young Sam government over the court, came on February 28 when the court abruptly postponed until April 15 Chun's second public trial. Chun or his defense attorney could explode a gigantic bomb by exposing, partially or fully, the list of the two hundred or so recipients of slush funds from Chun, just before the important elections of the entire membership of the National Assembly scheduled for April 11. Another indication of the Kim government's hand in the trial came when it was revealed that the prosecution discovered the $8 million in cash before the April 11 elections, a discovery whose announcement was not made until after the elections.

Roh also acknowledged that he had received donations—not bribes—amounting to roughly $575 million from thirty-five of the nation's leading industrial conglomerates during his presidency, February 1988 to February 1993. He stated that he recalled spending $175 million to help progovernment candidates in the 1988 and 1992 National Assembly elec-

[22] The text of the lengthy indictment was in *Hankook Ilbo*, 24 January 1996, pp. 1–3.

[23] *Chosŏn Ilbo*, 30 April 1996, p. 1. The dollar figures were calculated by dividing the Korean won by 800, as the dollar–won exchange rate of the period was approximately 1:800, with some daily fluctuations. Thus the figures might vary slightly from those cited elsewhere, but the magnitude of the figures remains.

tions. However, as to the key question of the amount of money he spent to have President Kim Young Sam elected as his successor he was evasive. He stated that his records on donations had been destroyed and that he could not recall the details. One could almost hear the collective sigh of relief from many political and business quarters in the nation's capital. President Kim's exclamations that "there will be no sanctuary during the investigation" now rang hollow.

As to the December 1979 coup, both Chun and Roh steadfastly maintained that they had been motivated by their "patriotic fervor" on the morrow of President Park's assassination, lest it should lead to internal chaos inviting another North Korean invasion. The trial revealed, however, that the Chun and Roh cabal had planned a careful scenario to seize control of the military through a lightening intra-army coup and then to capture the government. The proceedings also demonstrated how Chun and Roh and their *Hanahwoe* followers had completely subverted the regular military chain of command for purposes of seizing power. The Kwangju massacre of prodemocracy demonstrators was likewise explained away with an assertion that the violent uprising had threatened the restoration of order in the country following the assassination. In the course of the trial key questions surrounding the massacre, such as who actually issued the shoot-to-kill order and what were the levels of involvement by Chun and Roh, were strangely muted while attention was focused on the activities of their underlings, some of whom used the time-worn excuse of following orders from their superiors.

Nearly eight months after the opening of the trial, on August 5 the prosecutors summed up their cases in a lengthy prosecutor's statement.[24] In the opening section, "Significance and the Nature," the statement set historic and political perspectives, as well as the tone:

> We still vividly recall the events of sixteen years ago. . . . While mourning the tragic passing of a national leader (President Park Chung Hee), our hearts were filled with the expectation that *democratization* we eagerly desired could be realized. . . . We were concerned about the re-establishment of *a democratic constitutional order and a peaceful inauguration of a democratically elected government.* . . . *However, the events of 12.12 and the 5.18 incident shattered the peoples' hope for democratization.*[25] (Emphasis added.)

The highlights of the prosecutors' statement included the following facts: (1) The accused led a coup on December 12, 1979, in accordance with "a carefully premeditated plan" to seize power over the entire na-

---

[24] The full text in Korean was in *Hankook Ilbo*, 6 August 1996, pp. 6–7.
[25] *Hankook Ilbo*, 6 August 1996, p. 6.

tion illegally. (2) Chun and Roh "clearly engaged in amassing illegal wealth by abusing their power." In soliciting bribes from large conglomerates they used as bait the possibilities of their giving special consideration for arranging large loans with favorable conditions and of the reduction of or exemption from taxation. Though they called the bribes "political funds or ruling funds," Chun and Roh used substantial portions of these monies for private gain, purchasing real estate and making irregular loans to various enterprises. (3) The accused are criminals who murdered innocent citizens. To accomplish their schemes to seize power illegally, they first misused the troops, soldiers of the people, to trample down the Seoul Spring of 1980 that was hoped to give a rebirth to democracy, and subsequently created "an unprecedented tragedy of brutally suppressing the democratizing movement in Kwangju." (4) Chun and Roh led the nation to the path of institutionalized corruption and collusion between government and business. Their corrupt deeds at the top encouraged corruption among other officials and collectively "hindered the economic development of the nation and seriously damaged the order in the market economy that is based on justice and fair competition," leading to "the weakening of the nation's international competitiveness."[26]

On these bases, the prosecutors demanded the death sentence and life imprisonment, respectively, for Chun and Roh for mutiny, treason, and corruption. Article 87 of the Penal Code[27] provides that the "ringleader" of an insurrection "shall be punished by death, penal servitude for life, or life imprisonment." Article 5 of the Military Criminal Code[28] mandates a death sentence for any ringleader of a mutiny. Sentences ranging from ten years to life were sought against fourteen codefendants, mainly for helping Chun and Roh seize power; life imprisonment for both Hwang Yŏng-si (commander of the First Army Corps, implicated in the Kwangju incident) and Chŏng Ho-yŏng (special warfare commander, one of the most visible generals in Kwangju); and lesser punishments for the rest. The prosecution also asked the court to fine Chun some $277 million and Roh about $355 million for taking bribes while in office. Prosecutors called for "severe punishments" against the defendants, adding that the trial should serve as a historic milestone to show that law and justice were functioning in Korea. "We are convinced that by rooting out the wrong legacies of the past, we should prevent such crimes as the destruction of the constitutional order."[29]

[26] *Chukan Chosŏn* (The Choson Weekly), 19 August 1996, p. 16.
[27] Law Number 293, September 18, 1959.
[28] Law Number 1003, January 20, 1962.
[29] *Korea Herald*, 6 August 1996, p. 1.

Three weeks later the court pronounced its landmark ruling and sentences, applying both the Penal Code and the Military Criminal Code. The court's opening statement read, in part:

It is the judgment of the court that a severe punishment of the accused would be a historic cleansing of the stains left on the path of democratization in Korea and could prevent any recurrence of similar events in future generations.[30]

Standing grimly in prison garb, Chun and Roh were convicted of corruption and mutiny and treason for staging the 1979 coup. Chun was also found guilty of treason for the 1980 Kwangju massacre, but the court found insufficient evidence to find him guilty of actually murdering people for the purpose of treason. Chun was sentenced to death as ringleader of the mutiny and treasonous deeds, and Roh to twenty-two and a half years in prison, a lighter sentence partly in consideration of his role in a transition to democracy by submitting himself to "direct presidential election."[31] Of the fourteen other military officers, thirteen were sentenced to four to ten years, and one was found not guilty. Former Generals Hwang Yŏng-si and Chŏng Ho-yŏng, both directly involved in the 1979 coup and also heavily implicated in the Kwangju incident, each received ten years. The court found insufficient evidence to pronounce Hwang and Chŏng guilty of murder in Kwangju for the purpose of treason. Thus the trial found no one who actually ordered shooting in Kwangju.

The court also ruled that some $283 million and $355 million be confiscated from Chun and Roh, respectively, seemingly assuring their financial ruin if prosecutors indeed could unearth the large amounts of money the two were believed to be hiding. The business leaders who had bribed them were given suspended sentences. One, Lee Kŏn-hi, chairman of the Samsung Group, one of the largest companies in Asia, was sentenced to two years in prison, with a three-year reprieve. Another, Kim Woo Choong of the Dae Woo group, was given a two-year term, but the judges excused him from going to jail. Six other businessmen, including Chŏng Tae-su of the Hanbo Steel Group, were given lighter sentences that were suspended. The court evidently bent over backward to minimize damages to the reputations and credibility of these business leaders because the South Korean economy was then in a tailspin.

[30] *Hankook Ilbo*, p. 3.
[31] For a complete list of the sentences and a lengthy but "abridged" text of the judgment of the court, see *Hankook Ilbo*, 27 August 1996, pp. 1–10.

(From left to right) Former Presidents Roh Tae Woo and Chun Doo Hwan. The Generals-turned-Presidents were convicted by the Seoul District Court on August 26, 1996, to twenty-two and one-half years in prison and death, respectively. They were convicted of corruption in addition to mutiny and treason for staging the 1979 coup. Chun was also found guilty of treason for the 1980 massacre of Kwangju students and citizenry. For a "grand national reconciliation," however, they were pardoned by President Kim Young Sam, based on an agreement with President-elect Kim Dae-jung. Chun and Roh were on the dais when President Kim Dae-jung was inaugurated on February 25, 1998. (Joong-ang photograph)

The ramifications of the trial. Editorials in leading Korean papers at once "welcomed the historic sentences" that corrected "the logic of naked power"[32] and declared "a coup d'etat is guilty" and that the nation had "learned a lesson that even former presidents can be punished severely."[33]

---

[32] For instance, see *Hankook Ilbo*, 27 August 1996, p. 3.
[33] *Chosŏn Ilbo*, 27 August 1996, p. 3.

Major foreign newspapers also reported on the sentence in detail, some offering editorial opinions such as "Korea's democracy is stronger for beginning to deal honestly with a difficult past,"[34] and "South Korea is a model for many developing nations, and with good reason. . . . But some have expressed concern that the trials were designed more to improve the political standing of the current president, Kim Young Sam, than to uncover the truth about past abuses."[35]

Despite the evidently political calculations and involvements of the Kim government, it must be acknowledged that the trial was made possible under the "civilian and democratic" government. The lengthy trial had acquired its own momentum and logic under the watchful eyes of the media and the electorate. By all accounts, the three civilian judges proved to be focused, dignified, judicious, and, at least on the surface, unintimidated by any president, past or present. However, the outcome of the trial left many unanswered questions, such as the identifies of the two hundred or so recipients of Chun's slush funds, or the extent of the benefits presidential candidate Kim Young Sam might have realized in 1992 from Roh's funds. Despite Kim's declaration that there should be "no sanctuaries" in the investigations for the trial, there apparently were in fact safe havens at the highest levels regarding money, as well as in connection with the Kwangju massacre.

Predictably, the defendants appealed to the Seoul Appellate Court, hoping to have their sentences reduced; the prosecutors also appealed the case for the opposite purpose, seeking tougher sentences. As the appeals trial began on October 11, it became immediately clear that the defense attorneys were pursuing a strategy of appealing for the leniency of the court instead of challenging any evidence or the legal arguments on which the district court's sentences were based. The defense submitted that the prevailing patterns of collusion between politics and big business compelled conglomerate leaders to engage in the unsavory practices of "donating" money to capricious dictators to function under them. The defense also pleaded that the business tycoons' standing could not now be further jeopardized in the eyes of their domestic and international counterparts while the Korean economy continued to weaken. Compared with the eloquent arguments of the seasoned defense attorneys, stiff presentations by young and inexperienced prosecutors now appeared vengeful and strangely out of step with the rapidly diminishing public interest in the case, except on the part of the families of the victims of the Kwangju massacre. When the appellate court pronounced its ruling on December 16, 1996, it suspended or cleared the jail terms of the business leaders. It

34 *New York Times*, 27 August 1996, p. A16.
35 *Washington Post*, 27 August 1996, p. A10.

also commuted the death sentence of Chun Doo Hwan to life in prison, and reduced Roh's prison sentence from twenty-two and a half years to seventeen years. Likewise reduced were the sentences of the twelve other defendants who had been convicted with the two expresidents; for example, Chŏng Ho-yŏng, who was most visibly identified with the Kwangju incident, saw his sentence go from ten years to seven years. One foreign correspondent observed that the court reflected "the importance South Koreans place on political reconciliation and its effect on their economy."[36] The appellate court's sentences were automatically appealed to the Supreme Court, which has the authority "to make a final review of the constitutionality or legality,"[37] largely to review correct application of laws.

On April 17, 1997, the Supreme Court upheld the lower court rulings, confirming Chun's life imprisonment and Roh's seventeen-year prison sentence, as well as other lesser punishments. The highest court found that the lower courts' application of laws to the bribery charge against Chŏng Tae-su of the Hanbo Group was erroneous, and that he had not bribed the two former presidents. It was ironic that Chŏng was under arrest again even as the Supreme Court was clearing his name in connection with Chun and Roh. This time Chŏng was at the epicenter of a gigantic bribery scandal involving numerous highest-ranking officials of the Kim Young Sam administration, in both the executive and the legislative branches, and also strongly implicating President Kim's second son, Hyŏn-ch'ŏl. Also implicated were a few opposition party leaders suspected of receiving enormous bribes to persuade bankers to provide huge unsecured loans for one of Chŏng's subsidiaries, Hanbo Steel. Rampant corruption that the Kim government vowed to eradicate was evidently flourishing—and perilously close to President Kim himself.

Speculation now turned to whether President Kim, who had paved the way to "the trial of the century," would pardon and release the convicted before he left office in February 1998. But Kim, preoccupied with acutely worsening economic crises and seemingly under siege in his presidential mansion, from which his second son was charged with influence peddling, said nothing. In the end, Kim, the master politician, would likely base his decision on political calculation. That would include aiding a ruling party presidential candidate in the December 1997 election and making it more likely that he would eventually go free even after an anticipated investigation into his malfeasance in office.

Since 1948, no Korean president installed for a regular term had retired from office gracefully, and it was hoped that President Kim would be the one to break this disgraceful chain. A possible election advantage for a ruling party candidate in December 1997 from the presidential pardons of

[36] Kevin Sullivan, *Washington Post*, 17 December 1996, p. A14.
[37] Article 107 of the constitution.

Chun and Roh might be mollifying a sizeable number of conservative voters, particularly those old guards who had been affiliated with the military-led regimes. However, if Kim Jong Pil decided to run for the presidency, a likely prospect, the bulk of the conservative votes could be drawn to him. Resistance to the possibility of a pardon grew as prosecutors could not locate the illicit wealth Chun and Roh had been said to have hidden in the country and abroad. The amounts found fell far short of meeting the court-imposed fines, and the public was indignant about Chun's and Roh's defiant silence, as well as about the government's inability to locate the hidden fortunes that could ensure the former convicts would live luxuriously when pardoned.

In the end, the "trial of the century" that began in December 1995 and concluded in April 1997 failed, at least in part, to be the hoped-for catharsis of Korean politics. However, on balance, particularly from a historic perspective, the trial could be seen as part of Korea's painful effort at establishing a rule of law under a civilian government. The trial took place under a civilian president; certainly it would not have occurred under a president with a military background. Although the trial did not allow a complete cleansing of the accumulated misdeeds of the military-dominated past, the legal proceedings did mark a striking progress from the period of lawless armed terrors, such as during parts of the Park and Chun eras.

Two days after the December 18, 1997, presidential election, incumbent President Kim and President-elect Kim Dae-jung agreed to pardon Chun and Roh and twenty-three others who had been in prison since the trial. By then the country had signed the financial bailout agreement of December 3 with the IMF. The sweeping pardon was decided on for a "grand national reconciliation" to face the national crisis.[38] Chun and Roh were on the dais, conspicuously ill at ease, along with the other former presidents when President Kim Dae-jung was inaugurated on February 25, 1998.

1996 National Assembly Elections

As regular, fair, and routinized elections held in a competitive atmosphere are the essential hallmarks of a functioning democracy, the elections on April 11, 1996, to elect the entire membership of the fifteenth National Assembly were an important measure in gauging the progress "toward consolidated democracy" in South Korea.[39] The election for the fourteenth Na-

---

[38] For complete list of those pardoned and released, see *Hankook Ilbo*, 22 December 1997, p. 1.

[39] Juan J. Linz and Alfred Stepan, "Toward Consolidated Democracies," *Journal of Democracy* 7, no. 2 (April 1996): pp. 17–33.

tional Assembly had taken place four years earlier, in March 1992, the last year of the Roh presidency and about a year prior to the inauguration of the "civilian and democratic" Kim government. As such, the fourteenth Assembly was identified at least in part with the military-dominated period. It was expected that the fifteenth National Assembly would now be more than a "maid servant" of a strong executive—which had often been the case under strong-willed authoritarian chief executives such as Rhee, Park, and Chun. It was hoped that the new Assembly would play a significant role as a more or less equal partner with the executive and in carrying out far-reaching reform measures initiated by the civilian government. Whether the basic principles, the separation of powers and checks and balances—maintained as a feature in the Korean constitution—would be realized after the 1996 elections remained a central concern.

Keener-than-usual attention was focused on the 1996 Assembly elections because they came less than a year after the epochmaking local government elections of June 27, 1995, that had established the very first full-fledged local governments in Korea. Before 1995 heads of local units had been appointed by the central government; thus they were usually supportive of the ruling party candidates. A lead editorial in a major Korean paper emphasized the fact this was "the first general election in the era of local self-government."[40] Whether and how these local government units might influence Assembly elections remained important questions. Further, a clear-cut victory of the opposition groups over the ruling party of President Kim in the local elections a year before naturally sharpened the interest of observers in the outcome of the National Assembly election. A repeat victory by the opposition forces would definitely make Kim a lame duck with two of five years of his term remaining.

Because the local elections a year before had created the perception that the Kim government and the ruling party were bungling and bruised, the ruling camp was determined to recover its clout in the new Assembly. As part of the drive to present a fresh face to the voters, on December 5, 1995, the ruling party shed the old name, the Democratic Liberal Party, that had been chosen at the time of the now-infamous three-party merger of January 1990. As Kim was audaciously maintaining that his government was attempting to "create a new Korea," the ruling party decided to call itself the New Korea Party. Because there were few policy differences between the ruling and opposition groups on major national security and foreign affairs issues, most election differences were focused on domestic questions and personalities. The New Korea Party predictably highlighted political stability as its central election issue.

[40] "Chijache sidaeŭi ch'ongsŏn" (The General Elections in the Era of Local Self-Rule), *Hangook Ilbo*, 2 April 1996, p. 8.

The ruling party darkly foresaw political confusion and chaos, should the opposition groups win in the Assembly elections on the heels of the opposition victory in the local government elections. "Which do you choose? Stability or confusion? I expect you to make the right choice," President Kim declared at his party's national convention.[41] He warned the people that there would be no further reforms, many of which had been widely accepted by the electorate, if the opposition captured a majority of seats in the National Assembly. He further said a vote against his party could mean a vote for "social disorder and the paralysis of state affairs," like what the nation had experienced when the Assembly elections of April 1988 produced the phenomenon of *yoso yadae* (a small ruling party and a large opposition) in the National Assembly in the early years of the Roh administration.

As to the line-up of the other political parties before the Assembly elections, the main opposition party, the Democratic Party, had split into two factions immediately after the local government elections. Buoyed by the opposition victory in the local elections, which showed that the ruling party candidates were beatable, Kim Dae-jung, the most tenacious and ambitious opposition leader, lost little time in announcing on July 18, 1995, his return to the political arena from his self-imposed retirement. When Kim Dae-jung retired from politics, after his third unsuccessful bid for the presidency in 1992, Yi Ki-taek had inherited the presidency of the Democratic Party, although Kim Dae-jung remained a power behind the scenes, as president of the Asia–Pacific Peace Foundation. For more than three years Yi held the helm of the Democratic Party and consolidated his leadership position in the opposition party, instead of being content with temporary stewardship of the opposition party during Kim Dae-jung's absence.

On September 5 Kim announced the formation of a new party, the National Congress for New Politics. Demonstrating once again that Korean political parties had been largely based on personal ties between recognized "party bosses" and their followers,[42] or a boss–client relationship, fifty-three of ninety-five National Assembly members who had belonged to the Democratic Party bolted from it to join the new party headed by Kim Dae-jung. That left the crippled Democratic Party with just forty-two Assembly seats. Thus Kim Dae-jung emerged once again as the leader of the largest opposition group in the National Assembly. Kim Jong Pil had already formed the United Liberal Democratic party, in February 1995, only a month after being forced to resign his chairmanship of the govern-

[41] *Korea Herald*, 8 February 1996, p. 2.

[42] Yang Sung Chul, "An Analysis of South Korea's Political Process and Party Politics," in *Politics and Policy in the New Korean State: From Roh Tae-Woo to Kim Young-Sam*, James Cotton, ed. (New York: St. Martin's Press, 1995), pp. 20–21.

ment party. Finally, Yi Ki-taek was leading his hollowed-out Democratic Party in the assembly elections.

The three Kims. The 1996 elections were thus being contested among the four parties, three of which were led by the persistent "three-Kims," the fourth by Yi. What had approached a two-party system, comprising a ruling party born of the three-party merger of 1990 and the opposition Democratic Party, thus came to an end once again. Under the circumstances, an unusually large number of candidates, 475 of 1,352,[43] ran as independents. This was more than twice the number, 226, who had run for the Assembly elections of 1992, and indicated in part growing distaste with the decades-long domination of Korean politics by the aging Kims. The overall competition ratio between the total number of candidates and seats to be directly elected was about 5 to 1. The total number of seats in the Assembly was 299. Forty-six proportional representation or "national constituency" seats were to be allocated to each party receiving more than 5 percent of the popular vote cast in proportion to the number of votes each party garnered.

The ruling New Korea Party stressed "stability" as its key election issue, and Kim Dae-jung of the National Congress for New Politics made the nation's economic prosperity the principal issue for the Assembly elections. "Economic prosperity should come first if the nation is to join the ranks of world powers. Our party will put top priority on it if we win the April race," Kim Dae-jung declared at a New Year's press conference.[44] Positing an economy-first policy in the 1996 elections appeared, at first glance, a no-win stance because the overall economy in 1995 seemed on the surface robust, and traditional wisdom was that a strong economy would favor a ruling party. It was true that the Korean economy was pulling itself out of the stagnation of the early 1990s, when the economy had grown at rates of 5.0 and 5.8 percent, in 1992 and 1993, respectively, for example. The gross national product grew a hefty 8.7 percent in 1995, thanks to expanding exports due to the strong Japanese yen and brisk corporate investment in industrial plants and equipment.

Also, what was perhaps psychologically important was that per capita income exceeded the "magic" $10,000 mark for the first time ever in 1995. It was a heady moment, and Koreans boasted that the figure ranked thirty-second in the world. The proud Kim government began preparations for admission to the Organization for Economic Cooperation and Development (OECD). Kim did this despite caution from the opposition

[43] Central Election Management commission data as reported in *Chosŏn Ilbo*, 29 February 1996, p. 4.
[44] *Korea Herald*, 13 February 1996, p. 2.

parties that membership in the "rich men's club" of the world was premature for South Korea. Evidently buoyed by and confident about the competitive strength of the Korean economy, however, Kim savored his visible role in promoting a trade and investment liberalization regime under the Asia–Pacific Cooperation (APEC) forum.

In this optimistic atmosphere, no opposition leader except Kim Dae-jung dared make a major campaign issue out of the growing competitive weaknesses of the Korean economy. It was to prove soon Kim Dae-jung's accurate grasp of economic trends and his keen political judgment. High wages, the "proof of the prosperity," had been quietly but steadily eroding the Korean economy's competitive edge. Many Korean industries could no longer produce goods in Korea and export them abroad for profit. At the same time, imports had been significantly liberalized and contributed to sharply rising standards of living for many Koreans as high-priced foreign products became readily available. Conspicuous overconsumption, which had been a prominent part of the economic boom in South Korea in the 1980s, accelerated among many Koreans, who enjoyed the life of the nouveau riche. Those selling luxury goods discovered that the goods were snatched up when their prices were raised tenfold. Affluent Koreans were heard referring— presumably in jest—to visitors from the United States with prudent spending habits as "the beggars from America." In this milieu, better-educated Korean youths shunned employment in industries or construction, where hard work and long hours were the norm, and instead sought "softer" jobs in service sectors with a shorter, regular workweek. Imports had far exceeded exports since 1990, with the exception of 1993.[45] Not surprisingly, the trade deficit reached $8.8 billion in 1995; the government dismissed it as not serious because it represented only 2 percent of the gross domestic product.

It was under these disturbing circumstances that President Kim's ruling party appealed to the people to elect members of the New Korea Party to the National Assembly so as to maintain political and economic "stability." At the same time, Kim Dae-jung was pushing the "economy-first" policy. Alluding to some of the underlying but still largely unrecognized economic problems, and noting the mainly hidden plights of small and medium-sized businesses under the government policy of favoring the large conglomerates, Kim Dae-jung urged the government to extend credit to small enterprises suffering from the financial pinch. "It is sad to hear news of bankruptcies of small- and medium-sized companies, which are the pivot of our economy," Kim said. Most people working for large

---

[45] Republic of Korea, *Major Statistics of Korean Economy, 1996.* (Seoul: National Statistics Office, 1996), pp. 234–35.

conglomerates would not have agreed with the last part of his statement, but still he renewed his call to establish a ministry-level government agency to enhance and protect small and medium-sized businesses.[46]

Kim Dae-jung made a surprise public admission in October 27, 1995, regarding the bribery scandal then raging. He had clandestinely received two billion won, roughly $2.5 million, through intermediaries from former President Roh at the time of the 1992 presidential election. If this public admission by Kim Dae-jung very early in the investigation of the huge scandals involving the two former presidents was meant to be an indirect challenge to President Kim Young Sam to disclose how much he had received in campaign funds from Roh and his allies, the president steadfastly refused to accept the challenge. He held instead to an assertion that he had not personally received any funds from Roh and his lieutenants, who might have given money to the ruling party, of which Kim Young Sam was the presidential candidate. Kim repeated at every opportunity that he himself had received absolutely no political donations since assuming the presidency.

Kim Jong Pil's United Liberal Democrats attempted to become the rallying point for most "conservatives" with ties to the authoritarian regimes, including a number of former military officers in a country that had maintained one of the largest standing armies in the world. Kim Jong Pil also continued to advocate the adoption of the cabinet system of government. The Democratic Party, led by Yi Ki-taek, enfeebled by the mass defection of Assembly members who had followed Kim Dae-jung to form a new party, generally failed to carve out distinct election issues.

Overall, the Assembly election campaigns were a disappointment in terms of sharply defining concrete issues, and citizen participation at election rallies was lower than in the past, such as the fourteenth National Assembly elections,[47] or the local government elections a year before. Instead, the voters again tuned into the final contest among the aging three Kims—final at least in the sense that Kim Young Sam was completing his nonrenewable presidential term.

In a country in which 45.3 percent of the population was in the "youthful" age bracket of twenty to forty-nine, the three Kims were definitely "old" in 1996: Kim Young Sam was sixty-nine; Kim Dae Jung, seventy-one; and Kim Jong Pil, seventy. Attaining the age of seventy used to be considered *kohui* (rare from the ancient times) in Korea, where mandatory retirement from most professions was once fifty-five. Only about 2.5 per-

---

[46] *Chosŏn Ilbo,* 7 March 1996, p. 1.

[47] For comparable week-long periods just prior to elections, campaign rallies in 1996 drew about a third of the participants of those for the previous National Assembly elections. For a comparison of daily totals, see *Hankook Ilbo,* 8 April 1996, p. 7.

cent of Koreans were alive in the seventy and older group. According to a survey conducted by the Ministry of Home Affairs, some 46 percent of the 31 million eligible voters in 1996 were in their thirties and forties. Another poll of 13,000 Seoul voters conducted by the *Joong-Ang Ilbo,* a mass-circulation newspaper, revealed that 58 percent of the respondents in that age bracket said they would vote in the assembly elections.[48] Those in their twenties and thirties accounted for fifty-six percent of all eligible voters. Kim Young Sam, the youngest of the three Kims, had advocated a "generational change" in political leadership, at least in terms of age. This was, of course, a welcome stance among younger political aspirants and voters.

To enhance the possibility of this transition, the ruling New Korea Party inducted to leadership positions three younger politicians. Lee Hoi Chang (born in 1935), prime minister for a brief tenure in the Kim government, joined the New Korea Party on January 24 following a well-publicized meeting with Kim at the presidential mansion. He was given the first position on the ruling party's "proportional representation roster" for the fifteenth National Assembly to be formed after the April elections, thus guaranteeing Lee a legislative seat. Lee, a former appointed judge and premier, was considered a political outsider with no experience in party politics,[49] but Kim chose him to be chairman of his party's campaign headquarters for the assembly elections.

Pak Ch'an-jong (born in 1939), a "slick tongued"[50] politician active since 1971 and known to be a "maverick" for changing his party affiliation several times, was also recruited into the ruling party on January 16 after meeting with Kim. Pak was named chief campaign manager in charge of Seoul and its environs. He had been an unsuccessful candidate for mayor of Seoul in the 1995 local government elections.

Finally, Lee Hong Koo (born in 1934), another former prime minister under Kim, was recruited on February 13 and made permanent advisor to campaign headquarters. President Kim presented the three with letters of appointment at a ceremony held at the presidential mansion, giving the maximum publicity to the recruitment of these "big three," young faces compared with the aging three Kims.

Though neither Kim nor the new appointees said a single word about the presidential race in 1997, it was immediately clear that the political stature of the three younger politicians would be enhanced if the ruling party won in the assembly elections—particularly in and around the politically savvy metropolitan Seoul, where ruling parties traditionally fared

[48] *Korea Newsreview,* 9 March 1996, p. 14.
[49] *Korea Herald,* 15 February 1996, p. 2.
[50] Ibid.

poorly. Lee Hong Koo was given the second spot on the proportional representation roster. Pak was given the twentieth slot. The New Korea Party hoped to garner enough popular votes to appoint seventeen to twenty-one proportional representation members.[51] To assure twenty-one of forty-six proportional representation seats, however, the ruling party had to muster some 39 percent of the popular vote, according to a calculation of voting pattern and proportional representation records since 1980. This was an unlikely percentage in 1996, when four parties, albeit of unequal strength, were competing. The ruling party had received 38.5 percent of the popular vote in the 1992 National Assembly elections, when the contest was essentially only between the ruling and the main opposition parties.

Kim Dae-jung, the "perennial" presidential aspirant, put himself at the fourteenth spot on the proportional representation roster of his National Congress for New Politics. This, too, was a perilous range as the main opposition party, organized less than six months earlier, needed to garner 26 percent of the popular vote for Kim Dae-jung to occupy an assembly seat. In the 1992 election the unified opposition Democratic Party had received 29.2 percent of the popular vote. Kim Jong Pil, president of the United Liberal Democratic party, decided to run in his "safe" home district of Puyo, where three others nominated by the other parties were also running.[52]

Toward the end of the officially allowed sixteen-day campaign period, parties began resorting to shrill words and personal attacks—verbal mudslinging but no physical violence of any kind. Overall the campaigns were relatively orderly and no great surprises were expected. However, about twenty days before election day another financial scandal exploded in the face of the ruling party. The major opposition party, the National Congress for New Politics, exposed on March 21 that Chang Hak-ro, Kim's confidante for twenty years and now a close personal assistant to the president and the first lady as head of the first annex office to the presidential mansion, had received roughly one million dollars in bribes for influence peddling after Kim was in office. Initially the president's office denied the charge. Following investigations by the prosecutor's office, however, Chang was fired, prosecuted, and imprisoned.

This was a major embarrassment for the ruling party and its leader, Kim, whose loudest pronouncements had been that his government should be squeaky clean. Kim himself may have kept his word, but the

[51] It actually received enough popular votes to entitle it to appoint eighteen proportional representation seats.

[52] For a complete list of the 1,047 candidates in all 253 election districts and a full list of the 163 nominees of the four parties for forty-six proportional representation seats, see *Hankook Ilbo*, 27 March 1996, pp. 5–6.

Chang scandal, erupting so close to the president rekindled the lingering suspicion in many voters' minds that corruption might be continuing just below the surface, and at a very high level. One editorial lamented the scandal so close to the president and the first lady and speculated that financial scandals might be widespread in the Kim administration.[53] This was predicted to be an important variable in the election campaign, a variable that was expected to reduce the votes for the ruling party candidates. However, the Chang scandal was hardly of the magnitude to shock South Korean voters, who were by now becoming inured to relatively "minor" misdeeds.

As campaigns for the Assembly election heated up, numerous observers noticed that the well-heeled ruling party had opened a floodgate from its seemingly unlimited war chest, reputed to be several times larger than the leading opposition party's. Torrents of money flowed from ruling party candidates to influence potential voters, in clear violation of the Political Fund Law of 1994. Candidates used every loophole and often completely ignored the law. It was putatively a "fair" election, but in fact was a "money feast" for ruling party candidates.[54] It was even charged that envelopes containing large-denomination cash flowed freely into the palms of Central Election Management Commission members.[55] It was also subsequently alleged that the Election Management Commission had looked the other way when complaints were brought against ruling party candidates while it pursued those against opposition candidates. The decision to win the Assembly elections at any cost, even sacrificing the reform laws passed in 1994, was evidently made at the very top, which was still smarting from humiliating defeats in the local government elections. Local governments were now but minor nuisances to the Kim Young Sam government, but still the government was doing all it could to avoid an opposition majority in the fifteenth Assembly.

The largest shock wave, however, came from an unexpected external source six days before the elections, reflecting the ever-precarious nature of the larger political–military environment in and around divided Korea. On the night of April 5 hundreds of armed North Korean soldiers entered the northern sector of the joint security area at the truce village of Panmunjom, which was under joint control by the United Nations Command

---

53 *Chosŏn Ilbo*, 22 March 1996, p. 3.

54 An Yong-bae and Yi Ho-kap, "Kŏtturon kongmyŏng sŏnkŏ, sokuron tonpan sŏnkŏ" (Fair Election on the Surface, but Money-Run Elections), *Sin Dong-A* (June 1996): pp. 152–61. In the same June issue, *Sin Dong-A*, a respected opinion journal published by the *Dong-A* daily, carried three additional "special feature" articles on the assembly elections allegedly swayed by big money.

55 Pak Song-won, "Sŏnkŏ kwanri wiwŏnhwae kkachi p'akodŭn donbongtu" (Money Envelopes Penetrating even the Central Election Management Commission), pp. 174–79.

and the Communist North. This was in clear violation of the Military Armistice Agreement signed on July 27, 1953. This unnerving armed incursion into such a closely watched spot on the demilitarized zone was repeated three times, and on the third occasion the North Korean troops staged field maneuvers in the buffer zone for more than two hours. The buffer zone separating the two Koreas, two-and-a-half miles wide, is the most heavily fortified border in the world. More than one million North Korean soldiers and 650,000 South Korean troops, bolstered by 37,000 U.S. troops, faced one another across the tense demilitarized zone only thirty miles north of Seoul. President Kim placed the South Korean military on its highest level of readiness, and the U.S. forces also put themselves on a higher state of surveillance.[56]

These North Korean incursions and puzzling withdrawals followed the announcement by North Korean officials that they would no longer honor the terms of the armistice agreement. The North had advocated direct United States–North Korean negotiations looking toward a formal peace treaty to replace the 1953 agreement, essentially a cease-fire arrangement between the Communist armies (of the People's Republic of China, called "the Chinese People's Volunteers," and North Korea) and the United Nations Command. Washington and Seoul, on the other hand, repeatedly had urged the North to negotiate peace with the South, but intermittent direct contacts between the North and the South were in vain. In April 1996 it appeared that the "hawkish" factions of the increasingly dysfunctional regime of North Korea, whose economy faced virtual bankruptcy, timed the military incursions for President Bill Clinton's stopover at Cheju Island, where he had scheduled a brief meeting with President Kim. Clinton was to visit Japan and Russia, and his stopover on April 16 at the offshore island had been announced on March 29. Clearly the timing of the Clinton visit had little to do with legislative elections in South Korea. American officials quickly "discounted" the idea that P'yŏngyang was trying to influence the National Assembly elections in the South.[57] It was more likely that the North, not known for its knowledge of international politics, had miscalculated that the military incursions just before the Clinton visit could nudge the United States to engage in direct peace talks with the North to stabilize the military situation in the Korean peninsula. In any case, after the Cheju meeting South Korea and the United States formally proposed a four-party meeting with North Korea and China to discuss the establishment of a new peace regime on the Korean peninsula. White House spokesman Mike McCurry characterized the North Korean incursions as a "minor incident."[58]

[56] *New York Times*, 9 April 1996, pp. A1, A11.
[57] Ibid., p. A11.
[58] *Washington Post*, 18 May 1996, p. A16.

Table 7. April 11, 1996, National Assembly election results

Party	NKP	NCNP	ULD	DP	IND	Total
District seats	121	66	41	9	16	253
Proportional seats	18	13	9	6		46
Total seats	139	79	50	15	16	299

NKP, New Korea Party; NCNP, National Congress for New Politics; ULD, United Liberal Democrats; DP, Democratic Party; IND, Independent.
Source: Central Election Management Commission.

Within South Korea, however, the incursions were a major event. Not surprisingly, South Korean papers reported them for days on their front pages with banner headlines and large pictures, complete with diagrams of the Panmunjom joint control area where the incursions had occurred. President Kim lost no time in calling a National Security Council meeting, and loudly asked the United States to urgently dispatch AWACS surveillance planes to monitor North Korean troop activities.[59] Obviously taking advantage of the unexpected "national crisis" in the final stage of the campaign period, the ruling party urged voters to assure national security and "stability" by supporting ruling party members. As voting took place on April 11, it became evident that the "North Korean variable" had clearly influenced at least those voters living in the provinces contiguous to the military demarcation line. In postvote interviews many stated that they had cast their ballots in favor of those legislators who would support stability, the ruling party's campaign theme. The voter participation rate in the election was the highest in Kyŏnggi and Kangwŏn Provinces, adjoining the military demarcation line, at 80 percent. According to the Central Election Management Commission, the overall participation rate was 63.9 percent, or some 20.1 million of 31.5 million eligible voters.

The Fifteenth National Assembly. When the votes were tallied for the first Assembly formed during the civilian and democratic government, the strength of various parties in the legislature was as shown in Table 7.

The most significant fact was that the ruling party had averted a major setback. That party was initially eleven seats short of a majority, but this was not as serious a loss as the disastrous election defeat in the local election of a year before. One astute foreign observer[60] agreed with many Ko-

[59] Ibid., p. A1.
[60] Andrew Pollack, *New York Times,* 12 April 1996, p. A3.

rean commentators that the saber rattling by North Korea might have helped President Kim's party. Most voters in the Kyŏnggi and Kangwŏn Provinces, contiguous to the demarcation line, supported ruling party candidates. It was also believed that millions of voters who had roots in North Korea supported the stability theme and thus the government party.

The ruling party also scored an election first. The New Korea Party emerged victorious in the capital city, Seoul, which has historically been called "the citadel of the opposition" for being critical of the regime in power. Seoul, many of whose residents have roots in North and South Cholla Provinces, was considered a stronghold of Kim Dae-jung—until the votes were counted. In the capital city the New Korea Party won twenty-seven seats, the National Congress for New Politics eighteen, the Democratic Party one, and one independent was elected. While the ruling party received some 34.5 percent support nationally, it was supported by some 36.5 percent of voters in Seoul, where voter participation was a low 60.0 percent, some 3.9 percent lower than the national rate. Further, some of the most prominent candidates of the main opposition party of Kim Dae-jung—Chŏng Dae-ch'ŏl and Yi Chong Ch'an—lost their bids in Seoul districts.

Analyses of voting patterns in Seoul clearly revealed that the division among opposition groups—specifically, the split caused by Kim Dae-jung of the erstwhile main opposition Democratic Party when he reentered politics in 1995—resulted in their defeat. In all but two of twenty-seven districts where the ruling party emerged victorious the combined vote totals garnered by opposition parties were larger than the winning votes of the ruling party.[61] The groups led by Kim Dae-jung, Kim Jong Pil, and Yi Ki-taek split votes opposed to the party led by Kim Young Sam. It was believed that many sophisticated Seoul voters were now showing their anti-old-politicos sentiment.

Another probable indication of voter disillusionment with politics dominated by the old party bosses was that only 106 of 203 incumbent assemblymen who ran again, or 52.2 percent, were reelected from direct election districts. Nearly half the directly elected fifteenth National Assembly members were freshmen. Further, in a qualitative sense, a greater number of better-educated professionals than before were elected, including those from legal backgrounds, universities, and mass media, while those with military backgrounds faded.[62] Nine university professors, all with doctorates, were Assembly freshmen.

[61] "Tukchip: 15dae Taekwŏn chŏngkuk" (A Special Issue: The Political Arena Prior to the Fifteenth Presidential Election), *Chukan Chosŏn*, 29 April 1996, p. 18.

[62] *Hankook Ilbo*, 25 April 1996, p. 6. For a complete list and pictures of those elected, as well as their educational levels and occupations and votes received in all districts, see *Hankook Ilbo*, 13 April 1996, pp. 10–11.

Despite these potentially significant harbingers of change, the regional politics of the three Kims were still very much in evidence in 1996. Candidates of the Kim Young Sam-led New Korea Party were defeated, with a solitary exception, in the Cholla Provinces, the home base of Kim Dae-jung. Those candidates nominated by Kim Dae-jung's National Congress for New Politics were successful in the Cholla Provinces and in a part of the Kyŏnggi Province, but failed to win a single seat in the Kyŏngsang Provinces, Kim Young Sam's stronghold.

In the end, the New Korea Party fell eleven votes short of a majority. However, this was a tolerable election result for the ruling party, compared with the outright defeat in the local elections a year earlier. Customarily the party in power, with numerous perks at its disposal, could entice independents and even members of minor opposition parties to forge a working majority in relatively short order. Thirty-nine days after the elections the ruling New Democratic Party had recruited enough independents and a few defectors from the opposition Democratic Party and the United Liberal Democrats to secure 150 sets, a simple majority. Ignoring indignant protests by Kim Jong Pil, who suffered the most defections from his party, as well as by Kim Dae-jung, who was attempting to form a political alliance of the "two Kims" against the "third Kim" and his party, the New Korea Party's door remained open to "welcome in" (yongip) additional assemblymen into its fold.

After the elections the political flirtation between Kim Dae-jung (DJ) and Kim Jong Pil (JP) intensified, conjuring up the image of a new set of "strange bedfellows." The delicate relations between the two old Kims were quickly dubbed "the DJP alliance." Their two parties did not merge, but their 1996 alliance against Kim Young Sam's ruling party was reminiscent of the 1990 three-party merger. If the 1990 merger had been a strange embrace of a beleaguered minority President Roh, his bitter long-time critic, who was burning with ambition to succeed Roh, and a political survivor from the 1960s who shared that ambition, the "DJP alliance" of 1996 was motivated by a single but mutually exclusive goal: capturing the presidency in 1997.

✪

CHAPTER 9

A Leadership Crisis and the Economy, 1996–1997

The arrogance of government power again reared its ugly head just as the politics and economy of South Korea were facing internal and external challenges. With the accomplishment of some visible reforms and the attainment of a majority in the National Assembly, the Kim administration seemed to grow overconfident in its political capabilities. It was ironic that this attitude change came about just as the limits of the government's capabilities were becoming obvious to many observers in dealing with political and economic developments in and around Korea. The changes included increasingly keen international competition in the era of the World Trade Organization (WTO), which became operative in 1994 and obliged Korea to adopt import–export liberalization and free-trade policies. Korea's membership as of 1996 in the Organization of Economic Cooperation and Development (OECD) also meant challenging opportunities for the country, as well as far-reaching obligations for Korea to meet international standards in numerous economic interactions with other member states. These obligations included a promise to reform Korea's labor laws, which had been enacted during the period of state-directed rapid economic growth.

When the dust settled after the 1996 National Assembly elections, the second nationwide election in as many years, there was a perceptible sense of weariness and disillusionment with the "civilian and democratic" government. It was widely felt that the ruling party, with its close collusion with *chaebŏl*, which did not spare any money to assure a conservative majority in the Assembly, clearly violated the spirit and letter of the 1994 reform laws that dealt with fair and clean elections and campaign spending. At the euphoric inauguration of the Kim Young Sam administration some three years before there had been a great—undoubtedly an unrealistic—surge of expectation that the new regime marked a clean and decisive departure from the oppressive and authoritarian rule of the past. It was also hoped that corruption and injustice under the military-dominated regimes would be eradicated, and that the deepening chasm between the fabulously rich entrepreneurs and the unsung heroes of the Korean political and economic transformations—the largely silent working men and women—would be narrowed. By 1996, when most people knew that the ruling group, closely allied with *chaebŏl*, had spent astronomical amounts of money to win the National Assembly elections, there was a rueful realization that the real difference between those elections and the past was that the government was now headed by a professional "civilian" politician. Kim's ruling style was turning out to be essentially self-centered, self-righteous, and "imperial," just as past leaders had been. A "civilian authoritarianism" had emerged. It was also obvious that corruption and irregularities in most sectors of society were largely unchecked despite some spectacular "purges" and "surprise shows," but the political and economic positions of the larger public showed little improvement.

Simmering Labor Issues

The disillusionment was most keenly felt among working men and women. The relative socioeconomic standing of the labor groups that contributed steadily, working exceptionally long hours often under less than ideal conditions, showed relatively little improvement as compared, for instance, with the lot of the high-ranking government officials, who continued to enjoy numerous perks including chauffeur-driven luxury automobiles, and dozens of *chaebŏl*, who became world-class tycoons. An example of the latter is Chŏng Ju-yŏng of the Hyundai Group, who was reported to be the forty-seventh richest man in the entire world, and Yi Kŏn-hi of the Samsung Group, the forty-eighth according to *Forbes* magazine.[1] Although the state, entrepreneurs, and labor unmistakably constituted the three main actors of Korean economic success, the latter appeared perennially underappreciated and marginalized in what some now called a "*chaebŏl* republic," as distinguished from the military republics under Park and Chun. The working people were not always silent, however. Labor activism was quite visible during many worker strikes, some of which formed temporary alliances between labor and

[1] *Hankook Ilbo*, 15 July 1997, p. 2.

student activists, and through the annual *ch'unt'u* (spring struggles) between labor and management to renegotiate wages and benefits. Labor's massive participation in antidictatorship demonstrations in the early summer of 1987 unquestionably contributed to political pressures leading to the "democratic transition" of 1987 under Roh. Admittedly, a causal relationship is difficult to establish, but a measurable indicator was the number of labor disputes. When Chun took power in 1980, 407 cases of labor dispute occurred. Under Chun's iron rule the number of disputes remained in three-digit figures; in 1986, for example, there were 276 cases involving nearly 47,000 workers. However, the frequency of disputes, often involving labor strikes, skyrocketed to 3,749 cases involving more than 1,262,000 workers in 1987. That was the last year of the Chun era and was also the year of the massive "people power" demonstration that led to the "surrender" of General Roh, who submitted to the people's direct presidential election. The frequency and number of workers involved in labor disputes remained extremely high for three more years, until 1989 as shown in Table 8.

The most common causes of these disputes included delayed payments of wages, wage increase demands, and demands for the betterment of working conditions. For instance, in the explosive year of 1987 there were forty-five disputes caused by delayed wage payments, 2,613 cases demanding more wage increases than management was willing to grant, and 566 cases demanding an improvement in working conditions. Even after the 1987 "democratic" reforms opened doors to rapid liberalization for many including political activists, the press, and academics, labor issues remained largely unresolved and working men and women were still repressed under the existing labor laws.[2] Roh's famous eight-point "democratization and reform" package of June 29, 1987, was silent on labor issues. This was probably due to the fact that through various means, including the huge "political donations" that were later proven to be unadulterated bribes to Roh and key Assemblymen, powerful business interests kept the Roh government probusiness and antilabor outright.[3]

Erstwhile allies of labor such as student activists seemed to forget labor's contributions to democratic reforms, as student activism lost many political issues with the reforms that began in 1987–1988 and have accelerated since 1992–1993. During the campaigns for the 1996 National Assembly elections, largely a contest among national security-oriented, conservative groups mostly supported by big business money, the labor interest remained a nonissue. The three Kims who were still the decisive

[2] Eun Mee Kim, *Big Business, Strong State*, pp. 120–23.
[3] Sin Kwang-yong, "Hanguk nosa kwange wa chŏngch'ijŏk chŏnhwan" (Labor–Management Relations and Political Transformations in Korea), *Sasang Quarterly* (Summer 1997): pp. 182–93.

Table 8. Occurrence of labor disputes

Year	Number of disputes	Workers involved	Working days lost
1979	105	14,258	16,366
1980	407	48,970	61,269
1981	186	34,586	30,948
1982	88	8,967	11,504
1983	98	11,100	8,671
1984	113	16,400	19,900
1985	265	28,700	64,300
1986	276	46,941	72,025
1987	4,749	1,262,285	6,946,035
1988	1,873	293,455	5,400,837
1989	1,616	409,134	6,351,443
1990	322	133,916	4,487,151
1991	234	175,089	3,271,334
1992	235	105,034	1,527,612
1993	144	109,577	1,308,326
1994	121	104,339	1,484,361

Source: National Statistical Office, *Major Statistics of Korean Economy* (March 1996): p. 140.

actors in the assembly elections, largely ignored labor. President Kim was preoccupied with securing a majority in the Assembly by whatever means necessary after having lost the local government election a year before, and the ruling party relied on huge contributions from large businesses, which evidently opened up a torrent of money to the ruling party and its candidates. Kim Dae-jung, once champion of the downtrodden, now consciously struck a centrist—even a probusiness—stance as he tried to tone down his image as a firebrand liberal to appeal to a wide segment of voters at the center and the right. Kim Jong Pil took pride in being "the true conservative" whom the followers of authoritarian leaders of the military-dominated republics should support. The military-led regimes had been notoriously antilabor to maintain the international competitiveness of Korean industries by keeping workers' wages low. Thus, three years into civilian rule labor continued to be an "orphan."

Worse still, it became increasingly noticeable after the Assembly elections that the marginalization of labor was not just a benign neglect of labor. Labor collectively was turned into a villain responsible for a multitude of economic ills, with a long series of government and mass media reports suggesting that the high wages of Korean workers were the chief culprits robbing the competitive edge of the Korean economy. The government-run Bank of Korea darkly warned on August 28, 1996, that the cost effectiveness of the Korean economy was then at its lowest since 1993, a report that was carried on the front page of the mass circulation *Choson Ilbo* with an alarming headline reading "Economy Faces Serious

Recession."[4] Other dailies quickly followed suit. At about the same time it was widely reported that the average hourly manufacturing wage in 1995 was $7.40; corresponding figures for the other "Asian Tigers" were $7.28 for Singapore, $5.82 for Taiwan, and $4.82 for Hong Kong.[5] It was also reported that between 1990 and 1994—the last two years of the Roh regime in "democratic transition" and the first two years of the "civilian and democratic" Kim government—Korea's average hourly manufacturing wage grew by 73.1 percent, "the fastest growth rate in the world."[6] That rate was followed by Hong Kong's rate of 48.5 percent, Singapore's 43 percent, and Taiwan's 39.4 percent. For the same period the average hourly manufacturing wage grew 11.4 percent in the United States and 7.6 percent in Japan. These alarming reports tended to mute the fact that during the most recent economic boom cycle in the early 1990s, the Korean labor market had experienced almost "full-employment" and labor shortages in manufacturing sectors. Unemployment declined from 2.8 percent in 1993 to 2.4 percent in 1994, and finally to 1.9 percent in 1995. In this virtual full-employment environment, wage negotiations between labor and management each spring produced large wage increments, despite the low frequency of labor disputes since 1990.

An economic crisis and labor. When the economy took a sharp downturn in 1996 and the government and mass media, some of which are owned or heavily influenced by *chaebŏl*, appealed to citizens to "tighten the belt,"[7] the top priority was curtailing the wage increase rate. Antilabor reports continued steadily in the *chaebŏl*-controlled media. At the same time, some articles highlighted the onset of a "mass layoff era,"[8] which would mean a sharp reversal from the near complete employment picture of only a couple of years before. Newspapers featured stories of pathetic middle-aged middle managers suddenly being laid off, marginalized, and utterly demoralized. Toward the fall of 1996 there was a veritable flood of bleak economic news such as: "Korea's economy fails to attain soft landing," "current account deficit widens: shortfall amounts to $17 billion," and "nation's foreign debt rising sharply: expected to hit $140 billion." Under the last headline it was reported:

[4] *Choson Ilbo*, 8 August 1996, p. 1. The paper carried the Bank of Korea report using the term *pulwhang* (recession or depression). This would be equivalent to the *New York Times* or the *Washington Post* warning on the front page of an imminent recession.

[5] *Korea Trade Focus*, no. 75 (October 1996): p. 1. According to this report, the comparable figure for Japan was $23.66, much higher than $17.20 for Germany.

[6] Ibid.

[7] *Hankook Ilbo*, 4 September 1996, p. 5, in a feature story titled "Comprehensive Measures to Face Economic Difficulties."

[8] For instance, Kim Su-kon, "A Mass Layoff Era," *Choson Ilbo*, 21 September 1996, p. 5.

anticipated total foreign debt level in 1997 represents about 27 percent of the nation's gross domestic product (GDP), a sharp rise from the 22.9 percent estimated last year. . . .

At the end of last year, Korea's short-term foreign debt level accounted for about 4.6 percent of GDP, nearly approaching the 5.6 percent recorded by Mexico in 1994, when the Latin-American country started to slide into an economic crisis.[9]

It was in this crisis milieu in the economic sector—so reminiscent of a similar crisis at the end of the 1980s—that the Presidential Commission for the Reform of Industrial Relations, headed by Prime Minister Lee Soo Sung, was formed. The commission worked for months but had failed by November 1996 to hammer out a labor–management agreement on the proposed revision of existing labor laws, some dating back to 1953. The blue-ribbon commission was made up of representatives of labor, management, and independent members drawn from academia, the media, and other civic organizations. The select body strived to arrive at a compromise version of proposed labor law reforms, but labor and management remained deeply divided over a number of major thorny issues. These included the recognition of multiple labor unions at a single workplace; allowing third-party intervention in labor disputes, a practice that would tend to favor labor because management is usually able to arrange for outside help; management's right to lay off workers, which had not been widely recognized in large enterprises due to the concept of "life-time employment," particularly during the boom decades; the elimination of the practice of keeping full-time union leaders on company payrolls, a practice that also grew largely to keep labor peace or to shorten the length of worker strikes during periods of rapid economic growth; and the legal recognition of "no pay for no work" during labor strikes to end the longstanding practice of paying striking workers.[10]

Obviously these were issues of great interest to both management and labor. Because the presidential commission was dissolved in November 1996 without a clear agreement on the final draft amendments to labor laws, and because there was an obvious need to reform these laws, the task was referred to the National Assembly.

Labor laws and unions. The first Korean labor laws were promulgated in 1953 under President Rhee to protect the workers, whose total number

[9] *Korea Newsreview,* 22 March 1997, p. 28.
[10] Yi Hak-ch'un and Sin I'ch'ŏl, *97 kejŏng nodongbŏp haesŏl* (Commentaries on Revised Labor Laws of 1997) (Seoul: Bŏpyul hengjŏng yŏnkuwŏn, 1997), Chap. 2.

was minuscule in the last year of the Korean War. These laws were written apparently to counter North Korean propaganda that claimed the North was a "workers' paradise." They were not in response to existing labor–management needs in South Korea at the time, but were largely translations of similar laws enacted in Japan under the "democratic" ("MacArthur") constitution of 1947.[11] Since the Korean economy under Rhee had remained stagnant and limping for the balance of the 1950s and production was largely limited to some light industries, management—even if it wished to—could not afford to meet the exaggerated benefit provisions for labor under the various labor laws, and the workers had little ground to claim any such benefits.

In 1963, after the military coup led by Park, labor laws were drastically amended to allow draconian interventions by the state, which was single-mindedly promoting government-led rapid economic growth at any cost, particularly to labor. Some 29.9 percent of the labor force was still either totally or partially unemployed in 1963, and any job was a precious commodity. The government-sanctioned Federation of Korean Trade Unions (FKTU) was readily manipulable by the Korean Central Intelligence Agency and remained "unfailingly loyal" to the Park regime.[12] The FKTU in many minds was synonymous with cooptation by the authoritarian regime. Workers were kept toiling long hours in generally appalling working conditions. Strikes by desperate workers, often occasioned by such basic grievances as delayed payment or non-payment of wages, were met resolutely by the government, which usually declared strikes detrimental to national security and therefore illegal under the National Security Laws that were supposed to deal with Communist infiltration and subversion. Still, in 1965 Korea joined the International Labor Organization (ILO), partly to secure better treatment for the more than twelve thousand Korean workers who went abroad seeking better employment in West Germany, Vietnam, Thailand, Malaysia, Sweden, and elsewhere.[13]

Following the imposition of the *yusin* (revitalizing reform) system in 1972, collective bargaining and collective action by labor were banned. All labor disputes became subject to government arbitration, which usually supported management. When arbitration attempts failed, the government all too often unleashed the *kongkwŏnryŏk* (literally, the power of the public authority), which concretely meant hundreds or thousands of well-

[11] Lee-Jay Cho and Kennon Breazeale, "Changes in the Social Structure," in *Economic Development in the Republic of Korea*, eds. Lee-Jay Cho and Yoon Hyung Kim (Honolulu: East-West Center Book, distributed by the University of Hawaii Press, 1991), pp. 599–600.

[12] Ogle, *South Korea*, p. 159.

[13] Yonhap News Agency, *Korea Annual 1966*, pp. 201–3.

trained riot police.[14] The per capita annual income, which had remained in the triple digits from 1963 to 1976, $100 and $797, respectively, jumped to $1,008 in 1977 thanks to sustained economic growth under President Park. Still the average wage for workers in June 1987 was 89,121 won, slightly below the government-calculated "monthly living cost" of 90,880 won for an "urban worker household of five persons."[15] The unemployment rate, chronically high for decades, however, had fallen sharply, to 3 percent. Nearly all of the economically active South Koreans were now employed, and the Park government boasted of the economic "Miracle on the Han."

As Chun Doo Hwan seized the government in 1979–1980, the FKTU continued to be shamelessly servile to the harshly authoritarian Chun regime, which maintained a stern policy of controlling wage level and inflation at any cost. Predictably, industrial workers seeking a more equitable share in the nation's vaunted economic growth, as well as more democratic and human rights for labor, began to organize "unauthorized" unions such as the Cho'ngge Garment Union and the Council for Promotion of Workers' Welfare. Fourteen such dissident labor unions formed by 1983 as a counterpart to the FKTU. The rival National Federation of Labor Unions (NFLU) was also born; it later changed its name to the Korean Confederation of Trade Unions (KCTU). This era marked the birth of the sometimes militant *minju nodong undong* (democratic labor movement), thus sowing the seeds for the politically explosive issue of plural labor unions in a single workplace.

Predictably, the labor minister labeled some of the unauthorized unions Left leaning and reminded them that the existing labor laws stipulated that any third party—other than the management and a union under the government-controlled FKTU—guilty of instigating labor disputes was to be imprisoned for up to five years and face heavy fines. The labor minister also demanded that "underground" labor unions disband. Still, the number of dissident unions grew steadily. By early 1997 the "democratic union" claimed 896 separate unions and some 490,000 workers under its umbrella.[16] In the era of democratization of Korean politics, democratic labor unions could no longer be suppressed. The Korean Confederation

---

[14] The use of riot police to break up labor strikes continued even under the civilian government. For instance, when workers went on strike at the giant Hyundai Motor company in May 1995, one thousand police stormed the tent sites of striking workers and arrested 292 "militant members." Hyundai Motors asserted that the strike was detrimental to the nation's economy, and the Kim Young Sam government accepted the argument. *Korea Herald*, 20 May 1995, p. 1.

[15] Yonhap News Agency, *Korea Annual 1978*, p. 202.

[16] Mun Kap-sik, "'Nodongge ŭi silsae': Kwon Yŏng-kil wiwŏnjang kwa kŭ ch'kkundŭl ŭi silch'e" ('The Real Force in the Labor World': Realities of Chairman Yong-kil Kwon and His Confidants) *Wolgan Chosŏn* (May 1997): pp. 338–39.

of Trade Unions was one organization among many officially consulted by the Presidential Commission for the Reform of Industrial Relations in its inconclusive effort to recommend labor law reforms. Thus the government recognized de facto the federation of "democratic unions."

Lengthy labor bills containing many changes from existing laws and practices—changes that both management and labor recognized as necessary—were introduced to the National Assembly on December 10, 1996. By that time the ruling New Korea Party controlled 157 of 299 votes, a slim but secure enough majority to pass revised labor bills. Introduced with the labor-related bills, however, was a bill to revise the law governing the Agency for National Security Planning that was aimed at strengthening the intelligence agency, as well as several other minor bills dealing with economic welfare measures. Unlike the slowly growing precedents of cooperation between the ruling party and the opposition in the National Assembly, such as the passage of three important reform laws in 1994, confrontational postures regarding these bills quickly became evident in 1996. A real but unspoken reason for the bellicose stance taken by the ruling party and the main opposition party headed by Kim Dae-jung was the proposed revision to the laws governing the intelligence agency. The agency's authority to investigate cases involving instances of praising the North Korean regime and practices, encouraging subversive activities, and not reporting on the people engaged in such activities, were deleted at the outset of the civilian government. However, the extremely short bill proposed along with the labor law revisions would restore these authorities, which in the past had been all too often used against domestic political opponents of the government. The ruling party insisted on the restoration. The opposition parties were alarmed but did not wish to emphasize it lest they look soft on Communism—still a dangerous position to take in South Korea. Repercussions from the incursion of a North Korean submarine into South Korean waters in September 1996 were fresh in many minds, as the alarming incident and the massive reaction by the South Korean military created yet another wave of anxiety in the South. In this milieu the opposition parties dared not scuttle the bill proposing to strengthen the intelligence agency.

Some powerful organizations, particularly the Korea Employers' Federation, representing *chaebŏl* interests, and other conservative forces, launched an allout campaign to have the government-drafted bills enacted promptly "to save the economy," which was continuing to weaken at the end of 1996. The opposition Assembly members, realizing they did not have the votes to block the passage of these bills, now resorted to familiar obstructionist tactics. They physically blocked some entrances to the Assembly hall and the residence of the Assembly chairman to prevent him from presiding over Assembly meetings. While the physical paralysis of the Assembly continued for a week, some members of the ruling party demanded extraordinary action, the kind of action that no doubt needed the approval of the party chairman, President Kim.

On December 26, at 6 A.M., 155 ruling party members met for less than seven minutes and passed a dozen bills before adjourning. The meeting was presided over by the vice chairman. The "New Korea Party-style sneak attack in the predawn hours"[17] was coordinated like a military operation as the New Korea Party members assembled at four downtown hotels and were bused into the Assembly parking lot, to arrive there simultaneously at 5:56 A.M. No opposition members or reporters were present. The tyranny of the majority—a slim majority in this case—was brazenly perpetrated once again, leaving another blot on the record of this supposedly democratic government. Many of the ruling party members did not even have time to read the final versions of the lengthy labor bills,[18] but sleepily stood up to approve in the half-empty chamber—with no debate, no press, no visitors, and no witnesses. Yet the leadership of the ruling party had made a last-minute change, just hours before the predawn session, that would ban the formation of plural unions until 2002, whereas the original government bill was to allow democratic unions in 1997.

The outmaneuvered opposition Assembly members subsequently howled their protest in vain in the empty Assembly building. Also outraged at the undemocratic parliamentary procedure by the ruling party were the mass media and the people, who later read detailed reports in both domestic and foreign media. Labor unions—both the government-approved FKTU and the militant KCTU, in a rare collaboration—promptly resolved to launch nationwide strikes. For about three weeks South Korea was swept by waves of strikes, large and small, ranging from Hyundai Motors to Korea Telecom to subway engineers. What was striking was that these strikes appeared well disciplined. It soon became evident that the strike leadership, provided largely by the militant or democratic KCTU paid keen—almost expert—attention to public opinion.

The democratic confederation chairman, Kwon Young-Gil, age 56, emerged as a forceful but sophisticated leader of what could have been chaotic strikes nationwide. A graduate of the agricultural college of Seoul National University, Kwon was a former reporter for the *Seoul Sinmun* and also chairman of the national union of journalists.[19] Having effectively demonstrated that the combined forces of KCTU and FKTU could

[17] *Choson Ilbo*, p. 3. The mass circulation daily lamented in its lead editorial that the Kim Young Sam government had resorted to "despicable tactics" that were no different from those used by the military dictators of the recent past.

[18] *Kwanbo*, 31 December 1996, pp. 6–75. Law numbers 5,244, 5,245, 5,246, 5,247, and 5,248 were promulgated by President Kim on December 31, 1996.

[19] Mun Kap-sik, pp. 342–47.

bring the country's economy to a grinding halt, Kwon and the other leaders showed that they could discriminately flex their muscle. The leadership clearly attempted not to antagonize the middle class and inconvenience the working people—those who had to ride subways. Subways ran regularly during rush hours, even during the national strike. Both public opinion and editorials in *chaebŏl*-owned and -influenced newspapers condemned the Kim government for its arrogant and capricious handling of the labor laws and the law to strengthen the intelligence agency. The insensitivity of the regime was demonstrated when the government issued arrest warrants for the democratic confederation leader and others. Strike headquarters were quickly moved to the Myŏngdong Catholic Cathedral, a time-honored "sanctuary" for antidictatorship fighters.

At the same time, the media soon noted that it was the labor leaders who showed restraint and common sense. An "in-depth analysis" of the labor disputes concluded that "well-educated labor activists with experience on worksites constituted the nerve center" of the national strikes.[20] The government and the powerful *chaebŏl* interests had won a pyrrhic victory in the National Assembly, but they had lost the war in the arena of public opinion, which no power in Korea could now ignore. Still, President Kim and his prime minister vowed repeatedly not to yield. However, Lee Hoi Chang, a permanent counsellor in the ruling party and a known aspirant to the ruling party's presidential nomination in 1997, broke with the party and publicly stated on January 16 that the issues should be reconsidered. Two days later President Kim met with Stephen Cardinal Kim, the respected Catholic primate, in a well-publicized meeting. This became a signal that the Kim government was about to abandon its haughty and rigid stance and have the disputed laws that had been duly promulgated by the president reconsidered by the National Assembly.

On March 10 the Assembly nullified the labor laws it had passed in December.[21] It then passed revised labor laws based on compromises between the ruling party and the opposition.[22] The highlights were the following:

> The formation of more than one umbrella union was formally recognized, but the actual formation of multiple unions at a single worksite would not be allowed until 2002.
>
> Third-party interventions in labor disputes were not allowed.

[20] Ibid., pp. 328–29.

[21] *Kwanbo*, 13 March 1997, pp. 5–6.

[22] *Kwanbo*, 13 March 1997, pp. 6–51. These laws were the basic labor law, Law No. 5309; the laws governing labor unions, Law No. 5310; the labor commission law, Law No. 5311; and laws related to labor participation, Law No. 5312.

From 1999, management could lay off workers for "managerial emergencies," subject to workers' legal challenges. Management could now move workers from a nonstriking worksite in the same corporation to a worksite that was on strike.

From 2002, management would no longer be obliged to pay full-time labor union officials.

Management would no longer be obliged to pay striking workers in most cases.[23]

On balance the final versions of the labor laws made it abundantly clear that there were no prolabor voices in the National Assembly,[24] and the powerful management gained much more than labor. The democratic labor unions scored some symbolic victories, but the laws approved on the basis of collaborations in March by the ruling and opposition parties "showed few differences from those advocated by the Korean Employers Association."[25] A KCTU leader declared "the revised laws are nothing but a product of political negotiations that disregarded the basic rights of workers."[26] Many realized anew that there was no Labor Party in a heavily conservative National Assembly, and wondered if labor might run a candidate in the 1997 presidential election if it found no other candidate it could support. In March the National Assembly side-stepped the controversy regarding the laws governing the intelligence agency,[27] one of the bills adopted in the predawn rump session of December 26, 1996—in effect leaving the intelligence agency strengthened. However, the greatest loser was the government, which had engaged in what Koreans call "snatcher tactics," a term of contempt applied to purse snatchers and pickpockets. This was surely not the first time that ruling powers had engaged in these tactics; authoritarian regimes of the past had resorted to more heavy-handed measures.[28] However, the people's profound disillusionment in 1996–1997 was caused by the shocking realization that the "civilian and democratic" government in this instance had acted no differently from past practice. Of course, the wrongs of December were corrected in March, but the deep sense of disappointment lasted.

---

23 *Choson Ilbo*, 11 March 1997, pp. 1, 12, 13.
24 Ch'oe Chang-jip, *Hanguk minjujuŭi ŭi iron* (Theories of Democracy in Korea) (Seoul: Hangilsa, 1993), pp. 263–91.
25 Sin Kwang-yong, "Hanguk nosa Kwange," p. 199.
26 *Korea Newsreview*, 15 March 1997, p. 6.
27 *Kwanbo*, 31 December 1996, p. 76, Law No. 5,252.
28 A similar incident had occurred as recently as May 11, 1991, when the Roh government railroaded a law strengthening the intelligence agency through the National Assembly in forty seconds. *Hankook Ilbo*, 11 May 1991, p. 3.

While the nation was preoccupied with labor law controversies and worker strikes, the Hanbo Steel Industry, the second largest steelmaker in South Korea went bankrupt on January 23 under the sheer weight of a $6 billion debt, mostly in bank loans. Prosecutors accused Chung Tae Soo, the Hanbo president who had been linked to a series of financial scandals under military-led regimes, of bribing the highest-ranking government officials, political party leaders, and others to pressure various bank presidents to provide large preferential loans at rates favorable to the Hanbo Group. What was shocking even to the people who had long been inured to collusive relations between the government and *chaebŏl* were the early revelations in investigations into the Hanbo bankruptcy that several of the closest confidants of President Kim were directly implicated in receiving large bribes. These included a former top presidential political strategist and the former cabinet ministers of home affairs and construction. Some quickly dubbed the sordid affairs "Hanbogate." To make the situation worse, it came shortly after a defense minister and a labor minister had been convicted of taking bribes. Some thirty high-ranking officials and politicos, a few from the opposition camps, were soon implicated in the Hanbo scandal. The worst, however, was yet to come.

Two opposition politicians publicly charged that President Kim's second son, Hyŏn-ch'ŏl, was deeply involved in the Hanbo bribes and in influence peddling at the highest level. This was an unprecedented and serious charge against a son of a sitting president, particularly in a Korean context, which emphasizes family responsibilities. Under the watchful eyes of the mass media, prosecutors summoned the president's son on February 21 for questioning. However, the prosecutor's office, which had been too often proven subservient to the president,[29] released Kim Hyŏn-ch'ŏl after questioning him for a single day. Influential mass-circulation dailies, including *Hankook Ilbo*, promptly observed that the prosecutors were again engaged in a whitewash and that "suspicions lingered" about the president's son.[30] In a closely watched televised statement on February 25 marking the fourth anniversary of his administration, President Kim publicly "apologized"[31] to the nation for the fact that those close to him were involved in scandal. He was also obliged to refer to the possible involvement of his son in the Hanbo scandal and pledged that Hyŏn-ch'ŏl would be "legally liable" for any wrongdoing. In a typically Confucian

[29] Min Pak, "Min chŏboriko kwŏnryŏke t'uhang han 'munmin kŏmch'al,'" ('Civilian and Democratic' Prosecutors Who Have Turned Against the People and Surrendered to Power), *Sin Dong-A* (April 1997): pp. 248–65.

[30] *Hankook Ilbo*, 24 February 1997, p. 6.

[31] "President Kim's 'Apology,'" *Chosŏn Ilbo*, 26 February 1997, p. 3.

manner he added: "Like all fathers, I regard my son's failings as my own failing. . . . It was my fault that I failed in teaching him to behave prudently and carefully in all matters."[32] If the high-profile admission of his and his son's "failings" were a calculated ploy to elicit public sympathy, the move backfired. Although President Kim's honesty and morality had been questioned by few at his inauguration some four years earlier, the public's appraisal of his trustworthiness had been radically revised by early 1997. The public was now wary of his empty promises to eradicate the corruption that now swirled around the presidential secretariat, his cabinet, and himself.

The old question of the campaign funds for Kim's successful presidential election of 1992 was raised anew at this embarrassing moment by the United Liberal Democrats (ULD), the party headed by Kim Jong Pil, who was in a position to know about the avalanche of money that flowed into the ruling party, which had been born of the three-party merger of 1990. The ULD and other sources focused on some $75 million allegedly "delivered to Kim Young Sam by Chung Tae Soo"[33] of the Hanbo Group and some $375 million reportedly given by former President Roh. If established, these amounts alone would have meant tens of times more than the legal spending limit in a presidential race. Kim Dae-jung joined the fray when his secretary announced to the media that Kim Dae-jung had been offered "a substantial sum" by the Hanbo Group in 1992 but refused it. Korean conglomerates had been known to give some money—usually a fraction of the amount given to the ruling party—to the opposition as an "insurance policy, just in case," and also to prevent or minimize investigations into their questionable dealings.

Predictably, the National Assembly launched a televised hearing on the Hanbo affairs and on Hyŏn-ch'ŏl's involvements. Though the Assembly questioned forty-two witnesses, including the president's son, for twenty-five days, these hearings were largely inconclusive. This was so in part because Chung Tae Soo had been a master at keeping quiet about disbursements of money that were sometimes delivered by a chauffeur in cardboard boxes used to pack apples, and also because National Assembly members lacked the investigative abilities or authority to penetrate the conspiracy of secrecy ruling party members were not eager to crack. Most witnesses simply denied the allegations, and Assembly members failed to produce any evidence. By May 2, when the unproductive hearings ended, however, they had established the precedent of questioning the son of an incumbent president. This would have been unthinkable un-

[32] Kim Jae-hong, "Kim Yŏng-sam ui chŏngjik sŏng kwa munmin chŏngkwŏn ŭi todŭk sŏng" (Questions About Kim Young Sam's Honesty and the Ethics of the Civilian and Democratic Regime) *Sin Dong-A* (May 1997): pp. 168–79.

[33] *Chosŏn Ilbo*, 25 March 1997, p. 2.

der presidents Park, Chun, or Roh. The parliamentary hearings also established that the president's son had pulled many strings in important personnel appointments at high governmental levels and in the nomination process of candidates in the 1996 National Assembly elections. All of this influence peddling carried bribery implications.

The aroused public demanded thorough investigations and severely criticized the prosecutor's office, which was seen as kowtowing to the chief executive once again. The prosecutor's office decided to grill the president's son for three more days before arresting him on May 19, formally charging him with taking some $3.6 million in bribes from businessmen who sought his influence in obtaining government contracts and licenses. Prosecutors announced that the younger Kim had hidden large sums of money in 100 bank accounts, and that prosecutors had found $7.3 million in these accounts. Obviously much remained to be discovered by the prosecutors. The younger Kim was also charged with evading $1.5 million in taxes on payments he had received from businessmen and office seekers. Prosecutors led the president's son to a room full of media representatives who were reporting extensively on the Hanbo case, but Hyŏn-ch'ŏl remained tight mouthed while he was photographed before being whisked away to a tiny prison cell.

The trial of the president's son began on July 7. If convicted, he could have faced five years in prison plus fines.[34] Meanwhile, the Seoul District Court, which had been trying Chung of the Hanbo Group and ten others directly implicated in the scandal sentenced Chung to fifteen years in prison on June 3. The others sentenced to serve prison terms included a former home minister in the Kim cabinet, a political strategist and personal confidant of President Kim, and an opposition National Assembly member.[35] (At this writing Chung is still in jail, and Hyŏn-chŏl's appeal is still pending.)

Incidentally, the Hanbo and Hyŏn-ch'ŏl affairs meant to a few foreign observers, among other matters, that (1) "corruption seems deeply rooted in (the) still fledgling democracy,"[36] (2) the trials provided proof of democratic advances; increasingly free media, which have educated the public about the amazing sums of cash flowing through politics, and (3) a "more independent court system that has broken away from the oppressive control of the president's office. Even a few years ago, it seemed unimaginable that the president's family could be investigated."[37] It was evident that from the disgraceful affairs and partisan political wrangling there

---

[34] *New York Times*, 18 May 1997, p. 6. *Washington Post*, 8 July 1997, p. A10.
[35] *Choson Ilbo*, 3 June 1997, pp. 1, 2–3.
[36] Andrew Pollack, *New York Times*, 18 May 1997, p. 6.
[37] Mary Jordan, *Washington Post*, 5 June 1997, p. A26.

gradually emerged a picture of a slow but continuing political evolution toward democracy, particularly in contrast with the heavily authoritarian era under the former army generals.

A paralyzed presidency. Meanwhile, the popularity and credibility of President Kim hit a nadir. The Kim government was palpably paralyzed in recurring avalanches of problems, which came perilously close to crushing the regime. Even before the predawn "passage" of the labor and other bills by a nearly half-empty National Assembly, a *Kukmin Ilbo* newspaper survey on December 10, 1996, revealed that only 17.7 percent of respondents thought that President Kim was "doing a fine job," while some 40.8 percent called his performance poor.[38] More surprising was the result of an April 11 survey conducted by *Dong-A Ilbo* that showed that President Kim was "popular" among only 3.7 of the respondents, a rating even lower than the 6.6 percent of Chun Doo Hwan, now in prison.[39] What was alarming to some Korean intellectuals was that the same survey found Park Chung Hee to be most popular of all South Korean presidents, with 75.9 percent approval. A series of other facts, including a respectable turnout at the anniversary commemoration of the death of Park, an increasing number of visitors to his birthplace, and the popularity of his new biography, was referred to as "the Park Chung Hee syndrome." A Seoul political scientist dismissed this syndrome as a temporary reaction to a series of "gloomy" events in the second half of the "civilian and democratic" regime.[40] However, it was hard to deny that some Koreans felt nostalgic about a tightly ordered but well-functioning Korea that was accomplishing rapid economic growth under President Park.

The Economic Cataclysm

Some observers of the Korean economy agree that there have been cyclical upturns and downturns, as in many other economies. Since the early 1970s the average length of the economic cycle in Korea has been about fifty months: an upturn for about thirty-one months and a downturn for approximately nineteen months. According to these calculations, a business cycle peaked in late 1995,[41] the second year of the Kim administration, when the downturn began. A prevailing assumption, particularly by

---

38 *Chukan Hankook,* 13 January 1997, p. 3.
39 Kim Jae-hong, p. 169.
40 *Choson Ilbo,* 19 May 1997, p. 19.
41 Chung Un-chan, "A Diagnosis of the Korean Economy," *Korea Focus* (March–April, 1997): p. 61.

the government economy team, was that the economy would begin its cyclical upturn in late 1997, an important presidential election year.[42]

Signs of the recession were obvious. While the nation's industrial output in June 1995 was 10.2 percent over that of a year before, the same output was up by only 3.8 percent by June 1996, the lowest since February 1994 according to a National Statistics Office release on July 30. The current account deficit, partly due to a slowdown in exports and plummeting semi-conductor and steel prices in the world market, reached $9.3 million in the first half of 1996, according to a Bank of Korea (BOK) announcement on July 29. The figure was the largest first half-year deficit since 1950, when the nation began compiling data on balance of payments. Even as the BOK announcement was being made, a dozen top leaders of the largest *chaebŏl* were being tried in Seoul District Court, charged with bribing former presidents Chun and Roh. When the court found them guilty on August 26, 1996, the impact of the sentences, though suspended to minimize the negative effect on the nation's business and industries, resonated throughout the business community and revealed serious structural problems in the Korean economy. If anyone was not convinced of the seriousness of the problem, a disappointing export performance, much of which depended on the largest conglomerates, resulted in a trade deficit of $3.7 billion in January, 1997, the largest monthly deficit ever.

The government and the conglomerates. Most of the *chaebŏl* were initially the creatures of the state-led policy of rapid economic growth that began in the mid-1960s under Park. Gradually, however, some of these conglomerates, including Daewoo, Samsung, Hyundai, Lucky-Goldstar, and Ssangyong, became extremely rich and powerful in the 1970s and 1980s because they conformed to the state's policy of emphasizing heavy and chemical industries. As they became world-class conglomerates—five top big business groups controlled more than 75 percent of total sales in gross domestic product in manufacturing in 1987[43]—they became "allies" of the state rather than servants, single-mindedly pursuing rapid economic growth. Naturally, their political influence over and collusion with the state grew.

From the early 1960s on, for about three decades, the two most powerful groups in South Korea were the military, which dominated the government under Park, Chun, and Roh, and the *chaebŏl*, which controlled

---

[42] Han Seung-Soo, "Challenges and Choices Facing the Korean Economy," *Korea Economic Update* (April 1997): p. 2. Han was vice premier in charge of the economy during the Kim administration. Interview by author, Seoul, June 21, 1996.

[43] Eun Mee Kim, *Big Business*, p. 183.

the economy. With the advent of Kim's civilian government the military was contained, but the *chaebŏl* became even more powerful. Rather than being reined in, their power grew inexorably. Political leaders appeared insensitive to the monstrous growth of the *chaebŏl* while small and medium-sized businesses steadily lost ground as the conglomerates relentlessly expanded their operations. Gradually political leaders became "prisoners of the *chaebŏl*," and even the "100-Day Plan for a New Economy" promulgated by the Kim administration at its inception and "subsequent reckless deregulation carried out in the name of globalization, have only added to the *chaebŏl's* power."[44]

For more than three decades the government had exercised control over industry, largely through the nation's banks, by determining which industries and conglomerates should get preferential loans. In time, however, loan screening became less and less efficient and more and more corrupt. Some entrepreneurs, having bribed powerful government officials or politicians, received huge loans at favorable rates from banks under pressure from these powerful people. Many engaged in ambitious and often competitive expansion with borrowed funds, as well as in scandalous and risky rent-seeking activities, including speculation in real estate. Such loans were thus often used for purposes quite removed from the core businesses, heating up what some called a "bubble economy." In the late 1980s the prices of Korean assets, especially land and stocks, skyrocketed, as they did in Japan. As Korea became economically confident and joined the OECD, the bubble continued to grow. The Koreans overconsumed and the *chaebŏl* expanded their tentacles like octopuses, as some Korean commentators observed, usually at the expense of small or medium-sized businesses, which could not get bank loans for want of collateral or political clout. Meanwhile, the government created more bureaucracies,[45] presumably to regulate these activities but sometimes creating more bureaucrats to be bribed. It was reported that one needed approval by forty-four bureaucrats to build a single factory in Korea, while ten were needed in China.[46] Coupled with rapidly rising wage levels in Korea and straightjacketed by increasing bureaucratic hurdles in an uncertain political climate, many *chaebŏl* turned to foreign directed investments, which grew rapidly. Total Korean foreign investments were $1.26 billion in 1993, $2.30 billion in 1994, $3.07 billion in

---

[44] Chung Un-chan, "Diagnosis of the Korean Economy," p. 70.

[45] According to a report by the presidential secretariat, the total number of civil servants has increased by 5.4 percent since the inauguration of the Kim government in 1993, despite Kim's campaign promise to trim the number. It now stands at 934,248. *Choson Ilbo*, 26 August 1997, p. 1.

[46] Ibid., 7 January 1997, p. 2.

1995, and $4.13 billion in 1996.[47] Some 50 percent of that amount was held by manufacturing companies, usually making inexpensive cars or electronics and marketing them in developing countries.

The collapse of the Hanbo Group with its $6 billion bank loans on January 23, 1997, was inevitable once the economy went into a serious recession. But the recession this time proved to be more severe and protracted than expected by those who watched regular cyclical changes, as the economic woes appeared to be manifestations of long-accumulated structural problems in the Korean economy. These problems included the modest level of technological development partly due to the low level of investments for decades while Korea was boasting the "miracle" of rapid economic growth in research and development, 0.29 percent in 1973 and 2.32 percent of GNP in 1993.[48] One inevitable upshot was that Korea's ability in 1996 to make state-of-the-art technology was about 10 percent of Japan's and some 4.7 percent of that of the United States. Further, Korea paid about $2 billion a year in royalties and patents to foreign enterprises, creating a significant drag on the economy.[49] The structural problems also included the monstrous growth of a limited number of mega-*chaebŏl* that believed in the survival of the strongest and the largest, instead of the fittest. These superconglomerates were no longer content to monopolize the economic sector, but were increasingly dominating the political, cultural, and educational communities. In at least one instance the honorary chairman of a super-*chaebŏl*, Chŏng Ju-yŏng of the Hyundai Group, made a direct attempt in 1992 at wresting the presidency from those who were ignorant about the economy. In the 1960s, 1970s, and a good part of the 1980s the government was dominant and had at least a consistent policy of pursuing growth, but the Kim Young Sam government became schizophrenic and inconsistent. On the one hand it advocated equitable and democratic income distribution and some welfare measures while trying to encourage (no longer direct) economic growth. In a few short years it lost the confidence of both the conglomerates and the people. When the Hanbo Group collapsed early in 1997, the central Bank of Korea had to lower bank reserve ratios and expand the money supply to minimize the impact of the collapse of this conglomerate, only the fourteenth-largest *chaebŏl*.

It was hoped that a domino phenomenon would not occur. But by April 1997, some subsidiaries of the Jinro, Sammi, and Dainong groups had failed to honor their bills and promissory notes. The nationwide dishonored-bill ratio reached its highest level in fifteen years. The government-

[47] Bank of Korea data, *Far Eastern Economic Review* (May 1, 1997): p. 44.
[48] National Statistics Office, *Major Statistics of Korean Economy 1996.3*, p. 284.
[49] According to the Committee on International Economic Competitiveness, funded by five Korean conglomerates. *Choson Ilbo*, 7 January 1997, p. 2.

orchestrated device of a bankruptcy prevention pact among major banks barely sustained these conglomerates as they abruptly shut down most of their weak subsidiaries, adding more bodies to the sea of mass layoffs. The number of bankrupt companies increased from 1,268 in March to 1,318 in April,[50] meaning that about forty-four enterprises went insolvent each day in April due to heavy debt-repayment obligations. According to Bank of Korea figures, the amount of defaulted bills in the first four months of 1997 rose by 50.6 percent from the same period in 1996. Though the dishonored-bill ratio was 0.25 percent of the total economy, because a dozen or so giant *chaebŏl* that controlled the largest portion of the nation's wealth remained stable, such a seemingly cold and indifferent calculation by a government-run institution did not fully explain the plights of companies not able to meet accumulated debt loads. Nor did it explain the psychological effects of reading about failed heads of businesses committing suicide. It was no surprise that United States and European banks stopped loans to Korean banks and stepped up bids to withdraw loans extended to Korean banks. The Bank of Korea decided on June 23 to extend $1 billion in emergency loans to twenty-one domestic banks to ease financial difficulties caused by the critical shortage of foreign currency needed for international payments.[51] This round of emergency loans marked the third time in 1997 that the central bank had bailed out the nation's major banks. Similar loans of $1.5 billion in February and $1 billion in March had been extended immediately following the Hanbo and Sammi group insolvencies.

Meanwhile, the morally crippled and discredited President Kim appeared preoccupied with the arrest and public trial of his son. Kim, president of the ruling party, now seemed powerless to assert any restraining influence over the several ambitious "dragons" of the party, engaged for months in fierce competition and mud-slinging in their attempt to win the nomination for presidential candidacy for the December election. It appeared that the sick economy was the least concern to the government and the ruling party. Under these circumstances the Ministry of Finance and Economy reported that tax collection in the first half of 1997 fell 2.8 percent short of the target and projected a 3.0 percent shortfall for the second half. This was the first time in fifteen years that tax collection fell short of the projection, and if the problem indeed continued into the second half of the year, the national treasury might be empty by the end of the year.[52] Still, the government-run Bank of Korea floated a report that the country's registered current account deficit began to fall in April "due

[50] *Korea Herald*, 30 May 1997, p. 12.
[51] *Korea Herald*, 23 June 1997, p. 12.
[52] *Choson Ilbo*, 30 June 1997, p. 9.

to the bolstered competitiveness of Korean products in world markets"[53]—a point that was not fully explained. The Bank of Korea also foresaw the economy rebounding in the fourth quarter of 1997—a cyclical view that was held by the optimistic economic team of the Kim government, which was hoping that the 1997 presidential election would take place when the nation's economy was improving. For most other observers, however, that government, from which the people had expected so much at the end of the military-dominated era, appeared to be facing political, moral, and economic bankruptcy in the final year of the Kim presidency.

The Road to the 1997 Presidential Race

The paramount role played by Korean chief executives has been one of the most outstanding features of Korean politics. Each Korean chief executive to date has left a defining mark, both positive and negative. Down to the Seventh Republic under President Kim Young Sam, each republic has been coterminus with the chief executive's rule, except for the Fourth Republic under Park Chung Hee, who had engineered in 1972 the *yusin* reform that enabled him to stay in office indefinitely. After Korea was "liberated" from Japanese colonial domination and became an independent nation it was common for the Korean father of a bright son to say that his son would one day become the president of the country. The ultimate ambition of some of the best and the brightest—and even the not-so-bright—was oriented toward the highest political office, and they would use almost any means to attain it.

Presidential fervor is hard to comprehend when one considers the fact that most former South Korean presidents did not enjoy happy endings; in fact, they were often tragic. President Rhee was ousted by a massive student uprising and died a lonely exile in Hawaii. President Park was shot dead at a dinner party. Presidents Chun and Roh were tried and convicted like common criminals, although pardoned while serving their prison sentences. Yun Po-sŏn presided over the Second Republic as a "figurehead" with a cabinet system of government for less than a year, only to be shunted aside by Park's military coup. Whether President Kim Young Sam would escape the fate of Chun and Roh, who were tried and convicted during Kim's presidency, remains to be seen at this writing.

Kim Dae-jung had pursued the presidency ever since he first ran, unsuccessfully, in 1954 at the age of twenty-nine for a National Assembly seat in Mokp'o, a southwestern port city in his native South Cholla

[53] *Korea Herald*, 30 May 1997, p. 1.

Province.[54] He was endorsed by labor unions, which had little power at the time,[55] and lost the bid but later won the Assembly seat six times and has tenaciously stayed in politics ever since. He was a "liberal" on the political spectrum until recently, when he repositioned himself visibly and sometimes awkwardly toward the right, obviously to attract more votes from the middle.[56] Since the Korean War, and more recently in view of the virtual collapse of the Communist North Korean system, voters on the Left have nearly disappeared. From a different direction came Kim Jong Pil, who, at the age of thirty-five, was a key leader in Park's 1961 military coup. He has stayed tenaciously active in politics ever since,[57] and has been the self-anointed champion of conservative voters and those affiliated with military-led regimes. Along with President Kim, these two Kims are the venerable (or infamous) "three Kims."

One Kim has been president, and the other two Kims did everything to prolong the "Kim era" for another five-year presidential term. Kim Dae-jung lost his presidential bid thrice—in 1971 to Park Chung Hee, in 1987 to Roh Tae Woo, and in 1992 to Kim Young Sam—but decided in 1997 to run for a fourth time, at the age of seventy-two. Kim Jong Pil, seventy-one years old, lost his first bid for the presidency in 1987 but did not abandon his presidential ambition in 1997. These two Kims engaged in a prolonged public flirtation to field a single opposition candidate—one Kim, but each one referring to himself. The two Kims seemed to believe that the 1997 presidential race might be the last hurrah for each of them, and both appeared obsessed with wresting the highest office from the ruling party candidate. The Kims are determined survivors who obviously believe in the old Korean maxim of *ch'ilchŏn p'algi* (literally, stumble seven times, but stand up eight times) to attain one's goal.

The Kims. In fact, Kim Dae-jung declared his "retirement" from politics immediately after he conceded defeat in the 1992 race. He lost no time, however, in reentering the political arena shortly after the ruling party was decisively defeated in the June 1995 local government elections and in September formed a brand new party, the National Congress for New Politics (NCNP), to be headed by himself. It was a foregone conclusion that Kim would be nominated by the party to run for the presidency, and 3,223, 77.5 percent, of 4,157 convention delegates nominated him to be the opposition party's standard bearer on May 19. His only rival, Chŏng Dae-

---

54 Kim Su-yong, *Kim Dae-jung: Kŭйi sengaewa chŏngch'i* (Kim Dae-jung: His Life and Politics) (Seoul: Tongbang Ch'ulpansa, 1986), pp. 40–41.

55 Kim Dae-jung, *Hengdong hanŭn yangsim ŭro* (With a Conscience in Action) (Seoul: Kummun dang, 1985), p. 60.

56 Interview by author, Ilsan, Korea, June 12, 1997.

57 Sŏk Ch'ŏn, *J. P. nun yŏngwŏn hada* (J. P. is Eternal) (Seoul: Immundang, 1987), p. 364.

ch'ŏl, age 53, garnered only 907 votes, 21.8 percent. In accepting the nomination Kim declared that he would ensure the complete independence of the National Assembly and the governing party from the presidential mansion in the interest of further promoting democracy in Korea, and that he would meet with North Korean leaders to help lead the stumbling Communist nation to a soft landing.[58]

Predictably, the third Kim, Kim Jong Pil, was nominated on June 24 by the United Liberal Democrats, an opposition party he founded in February 1995 only about a month after he had been eased out of the chairmanship of the government party. He received overwhelming support from 3,190 convention delegates, readily defeating a nominal opposition by little-known Han Yŏng-su, who received only 554 votes. Kim Jong Pil declared in his acceptance speech that he would press for a constitutional amendment to adopt a responsible cabinet system, "an imperative of our time."[59] He continued, in a sweeping statement: "Only a parliamentary government system can free us from dictatorship, corruption, chaos, regional factionalism, which all stem from the presidential system."[60] Unimpressed by the nominations of the two Kims, Professor Byong Kook Kim, a political scientist at Korea University in Seoul, noted that "people see the two Kims as part of the corrupt establishment, and they want something new."[61]

A competitive nomination. If the open and competitive nomination of presidential candidates is a sign of a genuinely democratic process, the *kyongson* (competitive selection) of a presidential nominee conducted by the ruling party marked a sharp departure from past practices in Korea or the happenings in the opposition party conventions, where nominees were designated by party bosses. Both the National Congress for New Politics and the United Liberal Democrats in fact anointed the two heavyweight veteran politicians their nominees at well-orchestrated "coronations" to enable the two Kims to run for the presidency. In contrast, the nomination process by the New Korea Party marked a historic first in the troubled evolution of democratic politics and established a precedent of nominating presidential candidates through a fiercely competitive process.

When the requisite registration by candidates for the NKP nomination was completed by July 3 there were seven competitive aspirants who were dubbed the "seven dragons." All of them were much younger than the three Kims, whose average age was seventy-one; the average age

---

[58] *Korea Newsreview,* 24 May 1997, pp. 8–9.
[59] *Choson Ilbo,* 25 June 1997, p. 1.
[60] Ibid.
[61] *Washington Post,* 25 June 1997, p. A22.

among the seven hopefuls was fifty-eight. The competition for the government party's nomination was indeed fierce, but largely above board. When Lee Hoi Chang appeared to be pulling ahead of the rest of the pack, allegedly taking advantage of his position as chairman of the ruling party, various coalitions attempted to drag him down. These contests of will, political strength, stamina, and undoubtedly considerable financial resources led some pundits to call the competition "dog fights on a mud field." Throughout the fierce competition, however, President Kim kept a credible "neutrality" stance and silence—unlike some of his predecessors.

When the convention delegate votes were counted on July 21, Lee Hoi Chang had received 41.12 percent of 12,104 votes, and Rhee In-Je had garnered 14.71 percent. Lee Han-Dong, a "conservative heavyweight," was third, with 14.66 percent, and the rest received far less—all the way down to 1.95 percent. Because the front runner failed to receive majority support there was a run-off ballot between the top two as per the party constitution, and Lee Hoi Chang emerged a clear winner. Of the 11,544 valid ballots cast for the run-off, Lee received 6,922 votes, or about 60 percent, and Rhee garnered 4,622 votes, or 40 percent. In the end there was no question about Lee's clear-cut victory in the first open and competitive nomination convention ever held by a government party in Korean history.

In his acceptance speech Lee declared his three main policy goals: (1) furthering the development of the democratic system of government, (2) strengthening economic health and international economic competitiveness, and (3) promoting the peaceful unification of the country. He emphasized that Korean politics should become a "transparent, low-cost and high efficiency system," eliminating "money- and secret-room politics."[62]

Even after the nomination of the three presidential candidates, there remained a few dark horses. Cho Soon, the first elected mayor of Seoul, remained a presidential aspirant.[63] Before the nominations of Kim Dae-jung, Kim Jong Pil, and Lee Hoi Chang, some political commentators had naively speculated about the two Kims' agreeing to field Cho as a winnable panopposition candidate. This was an unrealistic expectation on the part of those who knew little of the undying obsessions of the old career politicians in their advanced age. A respected economics professor, Cho was the former vice prime minister in charge of the economy under President Roh, and was the only possible presidential aspirant with known expertise in the economy, although some conglomerate heads were leery of his "balanced economy" and "economic fairness and eq-

[62] *Hankook Ilbo*, 22 July 1997, p. 1.
[63] Interview by author, Seoul, June 22, 1997.

uity" leanings, which had been evident when he was vice premier. Cho formally announced on August 13 that he would run as the candidate of the Democratic Party, which had been enfeebled when Kim Dae-jung formed the National Congress for New Politics and a mass exodus of National Assembly members following him to the new party resulted. Cho declared that he would "stabilize the price and wages, and restore a balance in economic structures." He vowed to "become an economy president who would show the path to observe sound economic principles that would not be compromised by political considerations."[64]

The Korean Confederation of Trade Unions (KCTU), the "democratic" and second largest umbrella union, nominated Kwon Young-Gil, age 56, as the fifth presidential candidate. Kwon had emerged as an intelligent and disciplined leader of the dissident labor confederation that had acted decisively but responsibly during the nationwide strike in early 1997. By becoming a candidate Kwon would make labor, which had long been marginalized in Korean politics, far more visible than ever.

In the crowded presidential arena, Lee Hoi Chang's popularity plummeted drastically after the July 21 convention with the persistent charge by opposition parties that his two sons had evaded military service supposedly on the grounds that they were "underweight." In a country that has maintained a large conscripted army, the evasion of universal military service by many sons of the rich and powerful on debatable grounds has been an extremely sensitive issue that has touched many raw nerves.

A survey taken by *Choson Ilbo* on August 30 and a few other opinion polls indicated that Governor Rhee would take the lead if he ran as an independent.[65] Rhee was supported by 31.7 of *Choson Ilbo* survey respondents in a five-way race involving Rhee, the two Kims, Lee, and Cho Soon. According to the survey, Kim Dae-jung would take second place, with 25.2 percent, Cho Soon would be third, with 16.5 percent, Lee fell to fourth, with 15.2 percent, and Kim Jong Pil would be last, with 7.9 percent. A few other opinion polls, which were reported frequently during the months immediately preceding the December election, also indicated that ruling party candidate Lee was irreparably harmed by the issue of the avoidance of "compulsory" military service by both of his sons.

Despite public warnings by President Kim and ruling party candidate Lee, Rhee announced on September 14 that he would leave the ruling party and become the sixth candidate, representing the New Party of the People, which would be formed to back him. Utterly disappointed were

[64] *Choson Ilbo*, 29 August 1997, p. 6.
[65] www.chosun.com, 31 August 1997.

those who believed that the open and competitive nomination of a candidate by the ruling party constituted another hopeful sign that democratic politics was slowly being consolidated, and also those who hoped that "trust" would gradually be restored to the political arena at least at the most visible level of presidential elections. All the contestants in the nomination process of the ruling party had signed solemn pledges that they would abide by the outcome. Thus, the preliminaries to the 1997 presidential contest left many questions; the final outcome was unpredictable.

✪

CHAPTER 10

The Economic Crisis and the Presidential Election, 1997–1998

With the high-profile trial of President Kim Young Sam's son and the collapse of Hanbo Steel, among other woes that seemed to be surfacing with disheartening regularity, the Kim government appeared severely befuddled, dispirited, and immobilized from early 1997 on. On February 25 President Kim felt compelled to issue a televised "apology to the nation," mostly for his son's illegal activities. This was the third open apology he had made during his presidency, which was four years old. Kim had issued a formal apology to an angry nation on December 9, 1993, for his failure to stop the opening of the rice market to foreign imports contrary to his election pledge. The second apology was made on October 24, 1994, after the collapse of the Sŏngsu bridge across the Han river. Kim was sarcastically dubbed an "apology president,"[1] and clearly became a lame duck a full year before his term was to expire in February 1988. From early 1977 on the Kim administration, as well as the nation as a whole, was preoccupied by the December 1997 presidential election, through which the opposition headed by Kim Dae-jung now seriously threatened to capture power from the long-entrenched ruling camp. It was at this juncture that an economic collapse came, the width and depth of which few had anticipated.

Economic Paralysis and the IMF Bailout

During the 1960s, 1970s, and 1980s, the Seoul government constantly kept a watchful eye on and—often—control of the economy, while it engaged

---

[1] An editorial in *Choson Ilbo*, 26 February 1997, p. 3.

in an unbalanced rapid-growth strategy that relied heavily on foreign capital. The Korean government, single-mindedly leading the rapid economic expansion, guaranteed the repayment of foreign loans made to policy-directed industries, from which former presidents Park, Chun, and Roh had received huge "political contributions" or bribes. The central Bank of Korea subsequently assumed loan guarantee responsibilities. As Korean industries gradually acquired international credit standing, however, the government and its central bank stopped extending payment guarantees. Nevertheless, Korean companies slyly kept suggesting to foreign lenders that "the government would in effect guarantee repayment, while encouraging these lenders to think of Korean industry—especially of the *chaebŏl*—as immune to bankruptcy."[2]

Since the elections of Roh Tae Woo in 1987 and Kim Young Sam in 1992, both with no knowledge of or conviction in economic policy matters, the economic sector dominated by super-*chaebŏl* essentially had charted its own way. Having joined the Organization for Economic Cooperation and Development (OECD) in 1996 against the judgment of some thoughtful critics that it was probably premature, the *chaebŏl* became even more emboldened and cocky—some say reckless. The conglomerates accumulated more foreign debt for more reckless expansion in the name of economy of size and diversification into numerous ventures far removed from their core businesses. Typically, a Korean *chaebŏl* had an average of 6.1 operations in "related" areas but some 57.1 "unrelated" businesses in 1995; in the United States a typical conglomerate operated 45.2 businesses in related and 19.2 operations in unrelated areas.[3] At the same time, Korean commercial banks also allocated more than 40 percent of their overall loan volume to lending still dictated by government officials. These were some aspects of the continuing massive collusion between the government and business and the "*chaebŏl* game."[4] One inevitable consequence of the game was the accumulation of a staggering amount of foreign debt by major conglomerates, as compared with their equities, as shown in Table 9 on page 222.

The "*chaebŏl* game" and the falling dominoes. What was becoming increasingly troublesome was the debt-to-equity ratio of many Korean conglomerates, which competed for sheer size, often with borrowed money. In the United States the average ratio seldom exceeds 150 to 200 percent—most

2 Cho Dong-sung, "Korea's Economic Crisis: Causes, Significance and Agenda for Recovery," *Korea Focus* 6, no. 1 (1998): p. 18.
3 Peter M. Beck, "Revitalizing Korea's Chaebol" (paper presented at a conference on "The Persistence of Korean Culture in a Changing World," May 15–17, 1998), University of South Carolina, p. 17.
4 Ibid., pp. 18, 21.

Table 9. Korea's total external liabilities (in billions of dollars)

	End of 1996	End of November 1997	End of December 1997
Long-term debt	57.5	72.9	86.0
Short-term debt	100.0	88.9	68.4

Source: Ministry of Finance and Economy.

blue-chip companies keep their ratios below 150 percent—but average debt-to-equity ratio for the thirty largest Korean *chaebŏl* reached 450 percent in 1996, when the comparable ratio in the United States was 160 and in Taiwan 86 percent. Even this figure, however, exaggerated their capital holdings because the affiliates of rapidly diversifying conglomerates invested in each other's stocks, inflating the values of their major stock holdings, or engaged in cross-holding of shares. After an adjustment for these widespread cross-holdings and mutual debt payments it was estimated that the real debt-to-equity ratio ranged from 690 to 880 percent at the end of 1997.[5] This put practically all of the highly leveraged conglomerates in extremely precarious financial positions, where they were susceptible to economic and political fluctuations.

Worse still, in periods of instability companies sought short-term, high-interest loans, so-called "hot money," from both foreign and domestic banks. On the putative strength of the Korean economy, vaunted as the eleventh largest in the world, many Korean banks had received long-term foreign bank loans and made quick profits in turn by lending these funds to Korean companies as short-term loans. This economic "house of cards," with the cross-holding of shares and cross-payment of debts among numerous affiliates of conglomerates, was built on shifting sand and buffeted by domestic and international disturbances. With the political leadership crisis in the Kim government, rapidly rising wages coupled with falling productivity by Korean labor in too many overbuilt factories, and a prolonged economic crisis abroad, economic paralysis in Korea was just waiting to happen. A wide-ranging economic storm was already sweeping across Southeast Asia from Thailand, Indonesia, Malaysia, and the Philippines to Hong Kong. These were markets for Korean goods, and Korean businesses had been investing heavily abroad, particularly in Indonesia. Worst of all, the Japanese economy from which Korea borrowed capital as well as technology was in the middle of a seven-year slide and had suffered increasingly severe stagnation since 1991.

[5] *Hankook Ilbo,* 28 March 1998, part II, p. 1, citing Korean Stock Exchange sources, and Cho Dong-sung, "Korea's Economic Crisis," p. 22.

A chronology of the rapid and seemingly unstoppable succession of falling conglomerates is as follows[6]:

January 23, 1997—The Hanbo Steel Corp., South Korea's second largest steel maker, defaults on loans.

January 24—Seoul stock market index drops 2.8 percent on the Hanbo news.

March 19—Sammi Steel, a unit of Korea's twenty-sixth largest conglomerate, defaults on loans. The Sammi failure triggers four successive days of losses on the Korean stock exchange.

April 21—Jinro, South Korea's largest distillery, collapses under a mountain of debt and is placed on a bailout program by its creditor banks.

July 15—The Kia Group, the eighth largest conglomerate, becomes the latest candidate for a bank bailout after it fails to make loan payments.

October 2—Ssangbang Wool faces a debt default.

With each loan crisis the value of the Korean won against the U.S. dollar and the stock market index plunged. Amazingly, however, the key government agency, the Ministry of Finance and Economy, remained unperturbed, at least on the surface, perhaps still hoping that the Korean economy as a whole was "fundamentally sound" and would somehow muddle through another cyclical downturn. Simply astounding was the news that Finance–Economy Minister Kang Kyŏng-sik and presidential Economy Secretary Kim In-ho apparently had suppressed and buried reports their subordinates had submitted warning of an approaching foreign loan crisis. Kang reportedly said that the president should not be further troubled while "the country was already disturbed with the Hanbo scandal" in which President Kim's son had been criminally implicated.[7] Exactly when the President became aware of the international loan crisis remains uncertain as of this writing.

The IMF bailout. In any case, on November 18 the Bank of Korea finally urged the Finance–Economy Ministry to seek an IMF bailout loan to avert a national bankruptcy as the Korean won sank to a record low of 1,013 against the dollar. At the beginning of 1997 the average rate had been in the mid-800s. Disgraced Minister Kang, who allegedly had vowed never to turn to the IMF for a bailout during his tenure, resigned and was replaced by Lim Chang Yuel. The government then announced that it would indeed apply for a bailout from the IMF.[8] When the announcement

---

[6] www.koreaherald.co.kr, December 3, 1997.

[7] *Hankook Weekly*, 26 January 1998, p. 9, and *Hankook Ilbo*, 12 May 1998, Part II, p. 1. It is believed that some responsible officials, ultimately including former President Kim Young Sam, may be investigated by the prosecutor's office and/or the National Assembly.

[8] *Wall Street Journal*, 25 November 1997, pp. A2, A10.

shocked the nation, November 21, it was less than a month before the presidential election, scheduled for December 18. Frantic negotiations between the Korean government and the IMF took place before Michel Camdessus, IMF managing director, arrived in Seoul on December 3 to sign a bailout package for $57 billion. The package involved not only the IMF but also a number of governments, including those of the United States, Japan, and Germany. The following were highlights of the package.[9]

Restructuring and reform measures
Troubled financial institutions shall be closed or, if are deemed viable, restructured and/or recapitalized. The government has already suspended nine insolvent merchant banks (on December 2, 1997). . . . All support to financial institutions will be provided according to pre-established rules, and recorded transparently. . . . Financial statements of large financial institutions will be audited by internationally recognized firms. . . . The schedule for allowing foreign entry into the domestic financial sector shall be accelerated, including allowing foreigners to establish bank subsidiaries and brokerage houses by mid-1998.

Corporate governance and corporate structure
The government will not intervene in bank management and lending decisions. Remaining directed lending will be immediately eliminated. . . . Measures will be worked out and implemented to reduce the high debt-to-equity ratio of corporations.

Labor market reform
The capacity of the new employment insurance system will be strengthened to facilitate the redeployment of labor, parallel with further steps to improve labor market flexibility.

What troubled many Koreans most were the following provisions under the heading of "capital account liberalization," coupled with the aforementioned stipulation that allowed foreign banks to establish their subsidiaries and brokerage houses by mid-1998: "The present timetable for capital account liberalization will be accelerated by taking steps to liberalize foreign investment in the Korean equity market by increasing the ceiling on aggregate ownership from 26 percent to 50 percent by the end of 1997 and to 55 percent by the end of 1998. The ceiling on individual foreign ownership will be increased from 7 percent to 50 percent by the end

[9] www.koreaherald.co.kr, December 5, 1997. For the full text of the agreement in Korean, see *Choson Ilbo*, 10 December 1997, p. 12.

of 1997. . . . [Steps will be taken to] allow foreign investors, without restriction, in the domestic money market instruments . . . [and] allow foreign investment, without restriction, in the domestic corporate bond market."

One explanation offered for these provisions was that they conformed to established practices among members of the Organization for Economic Cooperation and Development (OECD), which Korea had joined in 1996. However, it was natural for many Koreans to feel apprehensive that the Korean economy might soon be dominated and hollowed out by foreign investors and banks that were incomparably stronger than their Korean counterparts. Fanning this fear were reports that many powerful foreign investors, such as George Soros of the Soros Foundation, were sending scouting groups swooping down to the "bargain basement" of South Korea to sweep the Korean stock market when prices hit the bottom.

The nation and the political arena, which had been preoccupied for months by the December 18 presidential election, were simply stunned. Having hurriedly read the bailout agreement, Kim Dae-jung, the front runner since late summer, openly demanded renegotiations with the IMF on terms that he felt would rob Korea of its economic sovereignty and impose an "economic trusteeship" over the country. He was immediately and sharply attacked by the ruling camp candidate, Lee Hoi Chang, who said that Kim was damaging the credibility of the Korean government at a critical moment, as it faced imminent "sovereign insolvency." It was revealed that Korea had a hard currency reserve of only about $8 billion, although up to $15 billion in troubled loans were due by the end of 1997. Lee's implication was that Kim was currying the favor of the voters, who felt humiliated by the agreement, at the risk of national bankruptcy. Under the circumstances, President Kim Young Sam, who had been nearly invisible while the country was buffeted by the IMF storm, called a meeting of Kim Dae-jung, Lee Hoi Chang, Rhee In-je, and himself. That meeting produced a brief document bearing the four men's signatures. The document, dated December 13, stated, among other things, that the men would abide by the agreement to "enhance the international credibility of our nation and to stabilize the financial market at the earliest opportunity."[10]

On Christmas day a $10 billion package of emergency loans was hurriedly shipped to Korea to stave off the immediate collapse of the cash-starved economy. The South Korean stock market and currency immediately rebounded a day later, and on the same day Japanese banks, which held the largest share of nearly $100 billion in short-term debts, announced they would roll over the short-term debts to long-term liabilities. This set a pattern of wholesale rollovers of foreign loans into longer-term

[10] *Choson Ilbo*, 15 December 1997, p. 1.

loans at much higher interest rates, given the evidently higher risks. Large U.S. banks announced that they would join in rolling over the Korean loans, as did banks in Canada, Italy, and Germany.

At the same time, the National Assembly enacted a wide-ranging set of measures to reform the country's financial system in accordance with the IMF guidelines. An advisory committee on financial reform headed by Park Seong Yawng, the knowledgeable chairman emeritus of the Kŭmho Group, had been working on a similar reform package since early 1997. A financial reform bill languished in the National Assembly—until the IMF broke the logjam.[11] Further, the Korean government renewed its assurance that it would ensure payment of debt liability loans to Korean commercial institutions. With these steps it became unlikely that foreign banks would have to write off any loans to Korean banks, in contrast to what happened in the Latin American debt crises in the 1980s, when banks lost billions in uncollectible debts.

Overall, Korean responses to the IMF bailout have been responsible and determined. Negative impacts of the IMF bailout, of course, were immediate and predictably grim. Every day many marginal banks and moderate-sized enterprises went bankrupt, creating an army of the unemployed numbering more than 1.5 million at this writing. With a not-so-subtle nudge from the newly elected and reform-minded President Kim Dae-jung, structural reforms of the *chaebŏl* began to take place, albeit at a glacial speed and with considerable resistance. Understandably, labor has been restive, making some noises about striking in January, but apparently cooler heads prevailed, even when a new labor law allowing worker layoffs went into effect in February. The labor situation remains extremely volatile and will probably become explosive with mass layoffs.

Meanwhile, the industrial sector jumped into high gear with an almost patriotic fervor. One prime-time TV newscast began with the coverage of a Hyundai freighter loaded with cars headed for a foreign market. Another newscast featured workers at the Anam Group busily producing semiconductors day and night for export even during the lunar New Year holidays, traditionally one of the most important holidays when practically all Koreans get together with their families and relatives to pay homage to their elders and celebrate. Soon, the trade figure for March posted a record $3.74 billion surplus, contrasted with a $1.7 billion deficit the year before. The trade surplus in the first quarter of 1998 was $8.58 billion, compared with a $7.33 billion deficit during the same period in 1997.[12] However, some expressed concern that raw materials in stock for

[11] Kwak Young-sup, "Reform of Financial Industry Gains Momentum," *Newsreview,* January 11, 1997, p. 27, and *Korea Herald,* 17 June 1997, p. 1.

[12] *Korea Herald,* 2 April 1998, p. 1.

the production of goods for future exports would soon run low, and that the trade surplus might not be sustained for long.

What was symbolic of the Korean people's spontaneous resolve to free themselves of the "IMF era" as soon as possible was a gold collection campaign sponsored by many civic and religious groups. Tens of thousands of citizens, young and old, voluntarily brought their gold bracelets, medals, decorative items, and family heirlooms to gold collection centers. In January alone South Korea exported $698 million worth of gold, making the precious metal the second largest export item behind electronics, or 16.1 percent of the total January export.[13] This in turn brought down the world gold price. In March Korea again shipped $300 million worth of gold to the world market. The gold collection campaign, which has gathered more than $2 billion worth of gold thus far, was unheard of in other countries in similar financial straits such as Indonesia or the Philippines. However, how long the citizens' voluntary drive could be sustained remained a question as there was a finite amount of gold buried in people's dresser drawers.

The newly installed Kim Dae-jung government, which had focused on the economic paralysis, announced an economic recovery package carefully coordinated with both international agencies and domestic groups.[14] The package aimed, among other things, at lowering high interest rates, preventing corporate bankruptcies, increasing funds for the unemployed, and accelerating employment through public works projects. At the same time, foreign investor confidence in the economic future of Korea appeared to be slowly improving, albeit unsteadily and unpredictably, as many Koreans and their government were responsibly coping with the economic crises. The IMF itself was reported to have forecast, in a prepublication "outlook" made available to the Ministry of Finance and Economy, that South Korea might begin to pull itself from the economic paralysis by 1999, when economic growth could resume, as compared with a negative rate in 1998.[15] It should be noted that the IMF has made many miscalculations in the past regarding economic conditions in many countries, and could do so again.

The Election and the Transfer of Power to the Opposition

By the time the economic storm was brewing at the end of November the political arena was bracing for a showdown in the December 18 presiden-

---

[13] www.koreaherald.co.kr, February 9, 1998.

[14] *Korea Herald,* 3 April 1998, p. 1.

[15] *Korea Herald,* 14 April 1998, p. 1.

tial election. In early November, the two Kims, Kim Dae-jung and Kim Jong Pil, who had been engaged in an elaborate courting game, managed to patch up their differences, which dated back some thirty-six years, and formed an alliance between the National Congress for New Politics (NCNP) and the United Liberal Democrats (ULD). Kim Dae-jung would be the single presidential candidate for both parties and, if elected, would designate Kim Jong Pil prime minister, with a strengthened office of the premier of what would be a power-sharing "coalition" government. Since the April 11, 1996, National Assembly elections the NCNP had held seventy-nine seats and the ULD forty-nine. Subsequently, Pak T'ae-jun, age 70, a retired army general and legendary chairman emeritus of the Pohang Iron and Steel company, was also brought into a troika.

To an observer, who immediately recalled the infamous three-party merger of February 1990, the carefully crafted text of this new agreement of 1997 read like a prenuptial agreement among three septuagenarians to capture and share power.[16] Thanks to the 1990 merger, Kim Young Sam had emerged as president in 1992, and Kim Dae-jung, by now a thoroughgoing pragmatist who had lost three presidential bids, was learning from history. The agreement also stipulated that during Kim Dae-jung's presidential term the constitution would again be amended to convert the current presidential system into a parliamentary one, a change that Kim Jong Pil had long advocated. A political science professor in Seoul wrote:

> This agreement . . . is one of the most glaring examples of the rather sorry state of South Korean presidential politics. The two Kims maintain that their alliance is the only way to effect a transfer of power from the government party to the opposition, something that has never happened in South Korean politics and that is badly needed for the consolidation of Korean democracy. This may be the case. However, more to the point, it illustrates better than anything else that South Korean politics do not revolve around ideological or political issues. Former nemeses can now join hands to attain the presidency and even change the constitution to fit their interests and ensure their political survival and longevity.[17]

Largely to counter the so-called DJT alliance (among Kim Dae-jung, Kim Jong Pil, and Pak T'ae-jun), Lee Hoi Chang, the ruling party candidate, and Cho Soon, the Democratic Party candidate whose popularity was the lowest among major candidates, likewise joined forces in mid-

---

[16] *Hankook Ilbo*, 1 November 1997, pp. 1, 3.

[17] Chaibong Hahm, "An Election without Issues," in *The 1997 Korean Presidential Elections*, eds. Chaibong Hahm, Robert A. Scalapino, and David I. Steinberg (New York: The Asia Society, 1997), pp. 11–12.

November. They agreed that Cho would give up his candidacy, accept the presidency of the ruling party, to be renamed the Grand National Party (GNP, or *Hannaradang*), and support Lee as presidential candidate. Thus, about a month before election day the presidential contest became a three-way race among Kim Dae-jung, Lee Hoi Chang, and Rhee In-je.

A distinct phenomenon during 1997, partly reflecting the free and open political climate, was the mushrooming of public opinion polls. Authoritarian regimes of the past had allowed only a few pollsters to operate until the late 1980s. More than fifty polling companies—most notably Gallup Korea, Korea Research, and A. C. Nielson—were taking the public pulse on numerous issues, including the popularity of presidential candidates. That Kim Dae-jung established a leading position in many polls in late August, an unprecedented event for an opposition candidate, while Lee Hoi Chang's popularity plummeted with the information that his two sons had managed to evade military service. In a strange turn, Rhee In-je justified his decision to run as a candidate despite the outcome of the competitive nomination of the ruling party candidate by alleging that Lee had become unelectable, according to the polls. In fact, Rhee split the ruling camp beyond all hope of repair. Even when Lee's popularity improved steadily so he occupied second place, behind Kim by 2.1 percent but ahead of Rhee by the same amount one month before the election day, Rhee hung in the race.

Overall, the 1997 presidential election was the most violence free and least expensive contest ever, and was closely watched by many civil society groups. An important new development in 1997 was the introduction of a series of televised debates among the three leading candidates that "helped improve the nation's election culture by replacing the traditionally expensive massive outdoor rallies."[18] In many of these television appearances Kim Dae-jung appeared eloquent, quick with facts, and presidential, while Lee sometimes seemed stiff and labored, albeit with a vast command of pertinent information. Rhee was certainly most youthful and energetic, but often appeared to be sloganeering instead of debating.

As Kim Dae-jung maintained a comfortable lead over Lee, knowledgeable observers were concerned about the recurrence of the unfair practices all too often perpetrated by the ruling camp in the past. Sure enough, two major attempts at ruining Kim's candidacy were made. The first came in a public accusation by Kang Sam-jae, secretary-general of the ruling New Korea Party (NKP), shortly before it changed its name to the Grand National Party. Kang declared that Kim, the perennial opposition leader, had stashed away the incredible amount of $74 million in slush funds. The NKP, headed by Lee, one of the most famous lawyers in the

18 www.koreaherald.co.kr, December 16, 1997.

country, promptly filed a complaint with the public prosecutor's office, which had almost always been subservient to the incumbent president, to investigate possible bribery and tax evasion. In a country with fresh memories of the slush fund scandals involving former presidents Chun and Roh, now both in prison, the charge had a ring of truth to those who disliked Kim. Critics of the NKP saw the move as just a desperate attempt to torpedo Kim Dae-jung's candidacy. In a major surprise move, however, Prosecutor-General Kim Tae-joung announced on October 22 that the prosecution was "suspending the probe until after the . . . presidential election," because it would be "technically impossible to complete the investigation before the presidential election."[19] Though the stated reason was technical, the real reason appeared to be political. The prosecutor-general, too, must have been reading opinion poll results indicating that Kim was the leading candidate and also that an investigation would likely lead, in fairness, to a similar investigation of President Kim Young Sam's campaign spending in 1992.[20] The investigation was quietly dropped after the election.

A far more sinister attempt to destroy the Kim Dae-jung candidacy was made in early December by the Agency for National Security Planning (NSP), the successor to the KCIA, apparently in consort with leaders of the Grand National Party. In essence, the scheme included an unscrupulous Korean residing in the United States who allegedly received at least $250,000 from the NSP to spread vicious rumors at press conferences in Tokyo, Beijing, and Seoul alleging that Kim Dae-jung had received funds from elements of the North Korean regime. Reports from these press conferences were to be immediately and widely disseminated in South Korea. This was the continuation of the so-called *pukp'ung* (northern wind) campaign that had plagued and sabotaged, in one form or the other, Kim Dae-jung's past presidential campaigns.[21] However, the South Korean news media were far more sophisticated in 1997 than in the past; the NSP could not force the media to report on these happenings. As a side note, after Kim's election as president, Kwŏn Yŏng-hae, director of the NSP, who allegedly had masterminded the elaborate anti-Kim operation, attempted suicide while being interrogated by the Seoul district prosecutor's office. Kwŏn was subsequently indicted for violating the election law banning the NSP from meddling in domestic politics. In an apparent move to redeem its image the agency decided to change its name to the

[19] www.koreaherald.co.kr, October 22, 1997.

[20] In any case, Prosecutor-General Kim Tae-joung was quite visible at the reception given by President Kim Dae-jung immediately after his inauguration, where this author was present.

[21] U Chang-ch'ang, *Pukp'ung ŭi jinsil* (The Truth about the Northern Wind), *Wŏlgan Chosŏn* (April 1998): pp. 212–24.

Kim Dae-jung campaigning. He was an unsuccessful presidential candidate three times, in 1971, 1987, and 1992, before he finally won the office on December 18, 1997. (Joong-ang photograph)

National Intelligence Service, the second name change since its founding as the Korean Central Intelligence Agency in 1961.

Some 80.7 percent of all qualified voters, more than 26 million South Koreans, participated in the presidential election on December 18; voter participation rates were 89.2 percent in 1987 and 81.9 percent in 1992. Kim Dae-jung received 40.3 percent, Lee Hoi Chang 38.7 percent, Rhee In-je 19.2 percent, labor leader Kwŏn Young-Gil 1.2 percent, and three minor candidates 0.2 percent each, according to the final tabulations by the Central Election Management Commission. If Rhee had not split the ruling camp, Lee would probably have been the winner. When voting returns from various regions were analyzed it became clear that Kim's victory might be attributable in part to the alliance between the two Kims. Put differently, Kim Dae-jung's shrewd use of the longstanding and often pernicious regionalism was a significant factor. He won unprecedented support from the Ch'ungch'ŏng region, the home base of Kim Jong Pil—up to 20 percent higher than in previous elections. Considering that Kim beat Lee by a margin of a mere 1.6 percent, his showing in the Ch'ungch'ŏng region must have contributed to his victory. Another major factor was the IMF-related trauma. It was clear that Kim received more support than the ruling camp candidates from many angry voters in middle-class election districts.

Losing candidates promptly conceded defeat and accepted the outcome. Only ten years before, the military had issued audible threats to veto the election of Kim Dae-jung, one way or the other, but no such voices were heard this time. When Kim was duly inaugurated on a rare smog-free and sunny morning, February 25, 1998, the peaceful transfer of power from an entrenched ruling camp to an opposition leader was accomplished for the first time in fifty years of republican politics in Korea. Procedurally, therefore, the Korean people had now met the basic test of democracy by voting the ruling groups out of office through balloting, conducted free of violence, corruption, and, in the end, fairly.

Kim Dae-jung: The Man and His Ideas

It would be no exaggeration to say that a key factor in the Kim Dae-jung victory was the indomitable man himself. Kim survived six years of imprisonment, sixteen years of forced retirement from political activity, fifty-five house arrests, and two foreign exiles during the period of military dictatorship. Military dictators Park and Chun tried to kill him three times. A rampaging truck tried to crush his car while he was campaigning for opposition candidates in the National Assembly elections in 1971; Korean CIA agents kidnapped him in Tokyo and attempted to dump him in the ocean in 1973; and the Chun regime sentenced him to death on trumped charges after the Kwangju massacre in 1980.[22] In terms of suffering that one man could endure and survive, Kim is probably rivaled by only one other person alive, Nelson Mandela of South Africa.

To say that Kim Dae-jung had humble origins is an understatement.[23] He hailed from a remote and underdeveloped offshore island, Haui, at the southwestern end of Korea. It used to take three hours on a slow ferry boat to reach the Haui island from Mokp'o, the nearest port city in South Chŏlla Province, at the southwestern end of the peninsula. Most people there eked out a living farming or fishing, and the hamlet of Hukwang where Kim was born was the poorest even by Haui standards.[24] He attended primary school on the island and then moved with his mother to Mokp'o, where he finished primary school and graduated from the

[22] Kim Kyung Jae, *Kim Dae Jung: Building Peace and Democracy* (New York: Korean Independence Monitor, Inc., 1987), pp. 246–47.

[23] Kim Su-yŏng, *Kim Dae-jung: kŭ ŭi senge wa chŏngch'i* (Kim Dae-jung: His life and Politics) (Seoul: Tongbang ch'ulpansa, 1986), p. 14; O In-hwan, *Daet'ongnyŏng ka ŭi saram dŭl* (People on the Road to the Presidency) (Seoul: Myŏngjisa, 1992), p. 194.

[24] Kim Dae-jung's pen name is Hukwang; obviously he wanted to remember his roots.

Mokp'o Commercial School. That was the end of his formal education. In a collection of his essays Kim Dae-jung wrote: "I was born in the Chŏlla Province . . . that has maintained a long tradition of *pangol* [literally, 'anti-bone,' or antiestablishment]. . . . The tradition gave rise to *Tonghak* [Eastern Learning], which taught the egalitarian idea that 'men are heaven.' I believe that this was an astoundingly revolutionary idea. The Chŏlla Province led the nation in anti-Japanese movements. Mokp'o never elected a progovernment National Assembly member during the dictatorial periods under Syngman Rhee or Park Chung Hee. My home province has indeed maintained the *pangol* spirit.[25]

Kim's life has been a determined effort at overcoming his disadvantages, opposing unjust authorities, and realizing his populist/democratic ideals as initially taught by *Tonghak*, with which he has repeatedly and explicitly identified himself. All his life he has been tenaciously proving himself so as to rise above his Hukwang origins and realize his goals. Kim had to overcome another handicap: a deeply rooted and irrational disdain elsewhere of people from the Chŏlla region. The discrimination against the people from the southwestern end of the country was intensified during the regimes of Park, Chun, Roh, and Kim Young Sam. Those four presidents hailed from the Kyŏngsang region, which benefited materially from their patronage. Ridiculous as it may seem in such a small country, regionalism has long been a pronounced and pernicious force, particularly among less-educated Koreans.

Because Kim's formal education was limited in a country where learning is highly valued, he compensated for this weakness by voracious reading and intermittent attendance at a number of universities, not top-ranked institutions, when he could afford to do so. It is a well-known fact that he read incessantly while in prison or under house arrest, and during his periods of exile. Kim Dae-jung's biographies highlight his visiting fellowship at the Center for International Affairs at Harvard University in 1983–1984, during his second exile in the Chun Doo Hwan period, after the United States had convinced Chun that he should not execute Kim. It is also well known that Kim's personal library holds more than fifteen thousand volumes, many of which contain underlined pages. Conversations with him reveal an amazing breadth of knowledge, though one often notes soaring rhetorical, as well as logical, jumps. His command of English, largely self-taught with occasional help from tutors, is far superior to that of his four predecessors in office.

Two major turning points in Kim's life were in 1956, when he was baptized a Catholic, and in 1962, when he married Hee Ho Lee. Kim was con-

---

[25] Kim Dae-jung, *Hengdong hanŭn yangsim ŭro* (With a Conscience in Action) (Seoul: Kummundang, 1985), pp. 39–42. This is a liberal translation for Western readers.

verted to Catholicism under the influence of former Prime Minister Chang Myŏn (John M. Chang) of the Second Republic. Chang was a devout Catholic who believed in "Catholic action"[26] to rectify many evils in Korea. He was Kim's sponsor for the conversion and also became his godfather. It is interesting to note that Kim's personal credo and later his presidential campaign motto were "conscience in action," which is also part of the title of his 1985 book. Kim Dae-jung often stated that it was his Catholic belief that sustained him during the worst crises. For instance, he later described the moment when he was about to be thrown overboard from a ship after being kidnapped by Korean CIA agents: "At that very moment, Christ appeared by my right side. I grabbed the left sleeve of his robe and pleaded with him. 'My Lord, there is much left for me to do for my people. This is no the time for me to be killed, so please save my life.' Then I saw a bright flash, even through the blindfold, and heard a loud booming noise. The abductors ran away, shouting that there was a plane. . . . I have come to believe that Jesus accepted my plea, to make me participate in his work for justice."[27] It is difficult to fathom the suffering and survival endured by Kim Dae-jung without taking into account his faith dimension.[28]

The second important turning point came with his marriage to Hee Ho Lee, his second and her first marriage, after the death of his first wife, whom he had married in Mokp'o. Unlike Kim, Lee was born into a comfortable medical doctor's family, in 1922. After finishing her primary and high school education in Seoul, Lee, a Methodist, graduated in 1950 from the College of Education of Seoul National University. She then studied sociology at Lambuth College in Jackson, Tennessee, and received her M.A. in sociology from Scarritt College in Nashville, in 1958.[29] Lambuth is affiliated with the United Methodist Church, and Scarritt was also known as Scarritt College for Christian Workers. At the time of their marriage, Lee was a thirty-nine-year-old secretary general of the Korean YMCA. The union came shortly after Kim's election to the National Assembly had been nullified by the military coup of 1961. Lee wrote: "He was a voracious reader. . . . I was drawn to his convictions, magnanimity, and charm. . . . Despite strong objections from my family and friends, my mind was attracted to him and I decided to marry him because I was con-

---

[26] Han Ch'ang-u, *Hanal ŭi mil'i jukchi ank'onŭn: Chang Myŏn paksa hoegorok* (Unless a Grain of Barley Dies: The Recollections of Dr. Chang Myŏn) (Seoul: Catholic ch'ulp'ansa, 1967), pp. 26–28.

[27] Kim Kyung Jae, *Kim Dae-jung*, p. 237.

[28] Conversations with Donald Gregg, then the U.S. CIA station chief in Korea, New York, September 26, 1997.

[29] Lee Hee Ho, *Naŭi sarang naŭi choguk* (My Love, My Motherland) (Seoul: Myeong Rim Dang, 1992), p. 31.

vinced that I should help him. . . . No wedding invitations were sent. He was imprisoned (by the military authorities) only nine days after our life as a newly married couple began in a rented house."[30] Ever since, she has been his closest confidante, an unfailingly supportive wife, a dedicated mother to their three sons—two from his previous marriage—and his unshakable moral anchor.

Given his unquenchable thirst for knowledge, extensive reading, and exceptional diligence, it is perhaps not surprising that Kim authored several books. In terms of the sheer number of printed words he has written, Kim stands head and shoulders above all former presidents of Korea, including Rhee, a Princeton Ph.D. in political science who spent some thirty-three years in relatively free exile. It would be safe to say that some of Kim's publications reflecting decades of careful thought, as distinguished from many books[31] that were obviously written partly for the purpose of public relations for the perennial presidential candidate, adumbrate the highlights of President Kim's policy directions. The two most important at this time, after his election are *Kim Dae-jung's "Three-Stage" Approach to Korean Reunification*[32] and *Mass-Participatory Economy*.[33]

According to a preface written by Lim Dong-won, former vice minister of the Ministry of National Unification and currently diplomatic and security advisor to President Kim, The "Three-Stage" Approach represents the crystallization of Kim's "evolving ideas of more than two decades"[34]: "The formula posits three main principles of unification: self-reliance, peace, and democracy. Under the principle of 'self-reliance,' that all national issues including unification ought to be solved by ourselves based on the spirit of self-determination without relying on outside forces. Guided by the principle of 'peace,' we ought to settle all national issues not through violence but by means of peaceful negotiations. The principle of "democracy" requires that the unification process be democratic in that they ought to be based on national consultation and consensus."[35]

---

[30] Ibid., p. 37.

[31] For example, Kim Dae-jung, *Naŭi gil naŭi sasang* (My Path and my Ideology) (Seoul: Hangilsa, 1994). This book does not exactly elaborate on his "ideology." Instead it looks at "the great transformation of world history, and the strategy for national unification," as indicated by the subtitle of the book, *Segaesa ŭi daejŏnhwan kwa minjok t'ongil ŭi pangryak*. The volume lists seven other books in Korean authored by Kim. The English translations of the selected titles are indicative of their contents: *Dictatorship and My Struggles, On the Future of the Nation,* and *For a New Beginning,* among them.

[32] Kim Dae-jung Peace Foundation, ed. (Los Angeles: The Center for Multiethnic and Transnational Studies, University of Southern California, 1997). Hereinafter cited as *"Three Stage" Approach.*

[33] Kim Dae-jung (Cambridge, MA: Center for International Affairs, Harvard University, and Lanham: University Press of America, 1996).

[34] *"Three-Stage Approach,"* p. xii.

[35] Ibid., p. 1.

The principle of self-reliance had been a cardinal credo of the North for decades and, notably, Kim suggested that principle as his first point. There could not be any disagreement on peaceful negotiations as an approach. Democracy is posited in regard to the unification "process," not as the substance for a unified government, which ought to be based on national consultation and consensus. These are not strident or bellicose principles. On the contrary, they would cause the least possible resistance. "The first of the 'three-stage' formula is that of a confederation between the two Koreas; the second is federation composed of the southern and northern regional autonomous governments; the third and final state is either a centralized government or several autonomous governments, as in the case of the federal systems in the United States and/or Germany."[36]

The formula is simplicity itself, and Kim was evidently treating the North as a partner to be worked with, not an entity to be overwhelmed or absorbed. This stance, taken in his 1997 book, was reflected in his inaugural address on February 25. President Kim stated "we do not have any intention of undermining or absorbing North Korea."[37] It is clear that his three-stage approach is far more amicable and open than the haughty and self-righteous stance that South Korean governments had taken in the past. The military-dominated regimes and the Kim Young Sam government were arrogant and hostile toward the North, endlessly repeating the litany of aggressive and barbaric acts it had committed, all undeniable facts. The new South Korean president appears open and conciliatory toward the northern regime. Kim stated in his inaugural address: "I earnestly appeal to North Korean authorities. Numerous members of separated families have grown old and are passing away. We must let those separated from their families in the South and the North meet and communicate with each other as soon as possible. On this point, I take note of some positive signs North Korea has shown of late. I also hope that the two sides will expand cultural and academic exchanges as well as economic exchanges on the basis of separating the economy from politics. . . . I propose an exchange of special envoys."

In view of the serious economic cataclysm South Korea is facing today, his *Mass-Participatory Economy* is an important indicator of Kim's thinking on the economy. The central ideas of this volume also evoked over time, since his 1971 presidential campaign, in which "mass-participatory economy" was an election platform. An English version of *Mass-Participatory Economy* was written in 1983–1984, when Kim was a fellow at Harvard. It should be noted that Kim is the only Korean political leader, now a pres-

[36] Ibid., pp. 1–2.

[37] The text of President Kim Dae-jung's inaugural address was distributed to ceremony participants.

ident, who wrote a book dedicated to an economic topic. Park Chung Hee published a number of books under his name, but none was specifically on the economy. In the introductory chapter of his 1996 version, "My Vision for the Korean Economy," Kim makes a sweeping declaration:

> [A] new age of economic nationalism and economic regionalism has already begun, and the post–Cold War world is now witnessing a different kind of world war—economic warfare.
>
> To succeed and win in this new competitive environment, genuine and complete democracy is an absolute necessity. If Korea can implement genuine and complete democracy under a new government with competent and effective leadership, and address a host of urgent problems now paralyzing it, it will be able to elevate its national economy to the level of the eighth largest economy in the world, joining the ranks of the industrialized Group of Seven by the end of this century or soon thereafter. . . . To achieve this, I propose the Korean government take the following steps . . . for economic democracy, it must guarantee self-regulation of business activities with maximum restraint from intervention in the business area. It ought to protect the freedom of legitimate labor movements. Maintain absolute neutrality in management–labor relations. . . . It must also legally ensure the independence of the central bank (the Bank of Korea) and liberalize the nation's financial service industry by relinquishing the nasty habit of government control and interference. It must exert greater efforts to realize a just and fair distribution of wealth and income, and protect and promote the long-neglected small and medium-size business and agriculture.[38]

His agenda for far-reaching structural reforms in the economic sector was outlined in this book, published in 1996 with considerable prescience, in view of the reforms compelled by the IMF in 1998. Many of the policy-level features of the IMF's reform programs are akin to what Kim wrote in *Mass-Participatory Economy*, including self-regulation of the economy with minimal government interference, the autonomy of the Bank of Korea, and the financial sector reform. His stance on labor–management relations constitutes a fundamental departure from the high-handed practice of many past regimes of throwing in the so-called *kongkwŏnryŏk* (roughly, the force of the public authority), concretely thousands of riot police to break up some strikes. Kim has been friendly toward labor ever since he was backed by a labor union to run, unsuccessfully, for a seat in the National Assembly in 1954. His special attention to small and medium-sized enterprises has been longstanding, as has his commitment

[38] Ibid., pp. 2–8.

to an equitable distribution of wealth. Having elaborated on his themes, he summed up his ten-point economic policies as follows:

> First, we must establish a market economy driven by private-sector initiative, within a system of fair, equitable, and orderly competition. . . .
>
> Second, sustained economic development is not possible without price stability. . . .
>
> Third, the Korean economy can be reinvigorated if rent-seeking land speculation is eliminated. . . .
>
> Fourth, operating under the three basic principles of equity, efficiency, and simplicity, we ought to reorganize the fiscal structure to enhance the government's ability to redistribute income. . . .
>
> Fifth, we ought to devote our national energy to strengthen our competitiveness. For this, our manufacturing facilities must be modernized, and we must increase our investment in research and development. . . .
>
> Sixth, for the entrepreneurs and workers to coexist in prosperity, productivity must be enhanced through cooperative labor–management relations. . . .
>
> Seventh, there ought to be a new division of roles between large enterprises and small and medium-sized firms. Special favors for the *chaebŏl* must end, and government efforts should be concentrated on building up small and medium-sized enterprises. . . .
>
> Eighth, it is urgent that we greatly expand social overhead capital. . . . Weaknesses in our road system, port facilities, and other transportation infrastructures not only restrict our economic activities in general, but also cause price inflation by increasing transportation costs. . . .
>
> Ninth, investment in agriculture and the rural economy must be increased. . . .
>
> Tenth, all forms of life must be protected under the new humanitarianism, and this embraces both environmental protection and economic development.[39]

It is clear that Kim, more than any other president of South Korea, has considered economic matters in concrete detail for decades, with a distinctly populist, egalitarian, and humanitarian bent. His stance on no "special favors for the *chaebŏl*" is noteworthy, and is diametrically opposed to positions by some presidents, who actively encouraged their formation and growth. A few presidents colluded with and exploited the *chaebŏl* to extract huge "slush funds" from them, corrupting both the government and the economic sectors, and contributing to the pervasive and systemic corruption of South Korea. In his inaugural address President

---

[39] *Mass-Participatory Economy*, pp. 223–34.

Kim stated that he felt "limitless pain and anger" when he thought of "the innocent citizens" in "this IMF period," the citizens who were "bearing the brunt of the suffering over the consequences of the wrong-doings committed by those in leadership positions" in the past. In correcting the past wrongs and turning "today's crisis into a blessing," Kim declared, "I will take the lead."

✪

Conclusion

The end of the Second World War witnessed a tidal wave of Western democracy on many shores including those of Japan, where American occupation authorities hurriedly wrote a "model" democratic constitution in the name of the Japanese people. A small group of Koreans, whose backgrounds indicated little familiarity with a democratic system of government, likewise drafted a constitution that declared "Korea shall be a democratic republic," under a not-so-subtle nudge by the American military government in South Korea. Thus "democracy" became the founding ideology for the Republic of Korea, when it was inaugurated as the American military occupation there ended in 1948. Meanwhile, in North Korea, then under Soviet occupation, Communism was dictated as the ruling ideology. Thus began the trial of democracy in the South, which was desperately poor and constantly concerned about her security in her precarious geopolitical position. The Korean War followed two years later, making South Korea a garrison state.

Prior to the establishment of the republic, Korean politics had hardly been democratic. A long dynastic past was succeeded by a militarist occupation by Japan, which in turn was replaced by the American military occupation. Traditional political culture in Korea was essentially feudal, elitist, and authoritarian, albeit not without some populist, protodemocratic elements such as the *Tonghak* ideals. These spread rapidly and widely among numerous peasants toward the end of the nineteenth century and left an indelible imprint on the political consciousnesses of numerous Koreans. The principal legacies of the traditional political culture, therefore, were largely authoritarian and elitist on the one hand, and populist and protodemocratic on the other. At the risk of overgeneralizing, the former, which lasted for a much longer period than the latter, may be called the Confucian tradition and the latter the *Tonghak* tradition. Tension and frequent conflict between the two traditions continued to unfold throughout the life of the Republic of Korea, sometimes perhaps giving the impression to outsiders that a Korean is at once an authoritarian and a democrat. Examples of just that abound, including Syngman Rhee who apparently became a "Confucian" autocrat surrounded by *yangban* officials as he was elected the first president of South Korea, and President Kim Dae-jung who has repeatedly and explicitly identified himself with the *Tonghak* tradition. One might add that a Korean citizen is at once a Confucian and a populist, among other things.

From another perspective, a fundamental problem has been the huge gap between the elaborate "republican" superstructure, which was hurriedly erected in 1948, and the largely authoritarian and underdeveloped substructure of Korean politics. On the morrow of the establishment of the republic, this abysmal gap was to occasion numerous tragicomic incongruities. For decades it caused painful dislocations and necessitated drastic adjustments in South Korean politics and government. This gap, however, has narrowed considerably in recent decades. In the past fifty years the legal–institutional features have been modified, partly through constitutional amendments and changes in institutional structures and procedures. At the same time, the increasingly better-educated people have become gradually familiar with many democratic processes while learning to abhor dictatorial practices.

It is striking that democracy has remained for the past half a century a persistent and strong aspiration—initially among intellectuals and elites but gradually spreading to the expanding middle class and beyond. Historically Koreans have manifested a tendency to intensify what they acquire and choose to believe in. For instance, many Korean Confucianists were more Confucian than Confucius, and many Korean Christians today may be more Christian than Christ. Likewise, numerous Korean "democrats" in recent decades have fought for democracy, arguably with more determination than did Thomas Jefferson. The quest for democratization continues in South Korea, and that drive has resulted in the recent peaceful transfer of power to an opposition presidential candidate who opposed authoritarianism for nearly fifty years.

Economically, a vast majority of Koreans led a life of genteel poverty for generations. Japanese colonial domination left the Korean economy debilitated and disjointed after the Pacific War. The American occupation barely kept South Korea alive, and two years after the establishment of the Rhee government, which was largely indifferent to economic matters while preoccupied with nation and state building, came three years of the devastating Korean War.

The war and persistent security obsessions left South Korea with the fourth largest standing army in the world, and so it was not surprising that disgruntled or reform-minded elements would plot the overthrow of the civilian regimes that became harshly autocratic in the case of the Rhee regime and dysfunctional in the case of the Chang Myŏn government. The 1960 "righteous student uprising," that toppled the Rhee administration was spontaneous, somewhat like the *Tonghak* peasants' rebellions, against an autocratic and oppressive regime that had lost its legitimacy in the eyes of the people. It set a precedent of successfully overthrowing an unjust or ineffectual regime.

The military coup d'etat of 1961 led by Park Chung Hee was the first military putsch with the cynically twisted justification of restoring "democracy," assuring national security, and reviving the economy. What turned out to be a thirty-year military-dominated authoritarian rule thus began, justifying its legitimacy and prolongation of the military rule in the name of rapid but colossally unbalanced economic growth. It is an undeniable fact, nevertheless, that the strong developmental state led by Park triggered spectacular economic growth, giving rise in time to a large middle class and, with it, an energized civil society. Thus the unprecedented economic growth that was generally sustained under another former general contained the seeds of the destruction of military dictatorship and of the structural distortions and problems rooted in government–business collusion.

Ordinary citizens seemed to accept, almost fatalistically, a great degree of government control and even oppression in the name of economic growth and national security. However, when the various governments became overly arrogant and dictatorial, intellectuals, many religious leaders, opposition leaders and their parties, educated middle-class citizens in numerous urban centers, students largely from middle-class backgrounds, workers, and other members of the increasingly active civil society repeatedly and valiantly struggled to protect and reassert their democratic rights. Until very recently they were practicing "protective democracy."[1] While they were struggling against dictatorships their slogan was "Fight for Democracy!" and soon they became self-professed believers in democracy, although the concept itself was seldom carefully analyzed beyond the textbook level by these "democracy fighters." Political parties remained ephemeral. Individual political leaders, including Kim Young Sam and Kim Dae-jung among others, courageously and single-mindedly led these struggles for democracy for decades. Initially democracy had been a "gift" of the American military occupation in South Korea. However, millions of Koreans demonstrated all over South Korea intermittently for decades to defend the country against dictators, both civilian and military. The student uprising of 1960, the Kwangju uprising of 1980, and the mammoth people's march of 1987 are but the most spec-

---

[1] Held, *Models of Democracy*, pp. 36–71.

tacular examples. Hundreds of democracy fighters even gave their lives for the cause. Numerous others were wounded or suffered in some other ways. For instance, Kim Young Sam fasted for about three weeks, and Kim Dae-jung, who was almost killed by military dictators three times, was imprisoned for six years and exiled twice. What the South Koreans fought for and retained is genuinely their own.

The United States, the "prime mover" of Korean democracy and the principal defender along with South Koreans of the republic during the war, usually sided with those Koreans who struggled to retain and nurture democracy. However, during the cold war era the primary priority of the United States was security in and around Korea. Much anti-Americanism there was due to the perception by young Koreans that the United States was supporting dictatorial regimes in Korea, where tens of thousands of American soldiers are stationed even today to contribute to the country's security.

In a relatively secure and stable Korea, civil groups and ordinary voters participated in politics with increasing sophistication. For instance, when three political leaders merged their parties in 1990 in a Machiavellian marriage of convenience and created a superruling party in the National Assembly under President Roh, the people in effect nullified the merger by defeating the ruling party in the 1992 National Assembly elections. The election of a "civilian and democratic" president in 1992 finally marked the end of the military domination of politics. However, when that government became self-righteous and arrogant, the outcome of the 1995 local government elections, in which the government party was decisively defeated, once again proved voter sophistication and adumbrated a transfer of power to an opposition camp. In time the Korean nation has made democracy—at least procedural democracy—its own by regularly electing freely and fairly its representatives and presidents. The election of an opposition candidate as president in 1997 clearly marked an historic turning point in the evolution of Korean politics.

In this evolution, however, political parties remain the weakest link. Fifty years after the establishment of the republic political parties are still essentially loose coalitions of politically active individuals organized around strongwilled and identifiable political leaders or bosses. They still do not articulate, with any degree of consistency, political principles or action plans. Parties are largely based on patron–client relations and they form, merge, split, and disappear with the movements and political fortunes of these patrons. Though the number of these groupings has definitely shrunk in recent decades, and some intraparty procedures, such as candidate nomination processes, are gradually regularized, South Korea still does not have anything approaching a stable two-party system. Until political parties become stable and predictable, the South Korean political arena will probably remain volatile.

In sum, despite fluctuations and setbacks, the political and economic transformations of South Korea have been extraordinary. The transfiguration of the past fifty years has been far more revolutionary than the changes that took place in Korea for thousands of years before that. Democracy is showing sufficient vital signs today to indicate that it is not only surviving but taking root in the southern part of the divided Korean peninsula and has met the test of attaining procedural democracy by "kicking the rascals out" of office and installing a genuine opposition group. Democracy has passed the stage of being merely a founding and legitimizing ideology and an aspiration. Indeed, the turbulent, zigzagging, and sometimes bloody quest for democratization has recently experienced a constrained transition and movement toward consolidation.[2]

The Korean economy, largely agricultural until the mid-1960s, has become essentially a manufacturing and a capitalist economy and experienced unprecedented and generally sustained growth under the direction of a developmental state until the late 1980s. However, the economy has recently suffered from long-accumulated structural problems and systemic corruption, and is facing the urgent needs of drastic structural readjustments and the elimination of corruption largely attributable to government–business collusion. For too long the state remained authoritarian, and the top leadership positions of most *chaebŏl* were occupied by the original, and sometime legendary, founders of these conglomerates, Confucian patriarchs or veritable "monarchs" of huge manufacturing and business empires. Business tycoons colluded with political leaders and created what might be called a *"chaebŏl* republic," whose tangled webs of power and money could not be broken until a powerful external force, the IMF, urgently intervened days before South Korea faced sovereign insolvency. Business practices and state–business collusion precluded accountability and transparency, the phenomenon that created the illusion of invincibility in the Korean economy among the top government bureaucracy, *chaebŏl* executives, and investors, both foreign and domestic—until shrewd international speculators began withdrawing their investments from South Korea. The state–economy interplay, which once had created a thriving "Korea, Inc.," rapidly degenerated as both sides became authoritarian, unaccountable, greedy, and corrupt.

The state–business interplay was continuous, significant, and often interactive—both positively and negatively. When economic activities lacked sociopolitical recognition and rewards during the Rhee era, for instance, the economy remained inactive and anemic. It took a determined military-led regime to trigger rapid economic growth, and another au-

[2] Linz and Stepan, "Toward Consolidated Democracy." Diamond, "Rethinking Civil Society."

thoritarian-bureaucratic regime to sustain it. For nearly two decades, beginning in the mid-1960s, the interaction was generally positive and productive, strictly in economic terms. However, from the perspective of democratization, political development and economic growth were often inversely correlated. In other words, political development in terms of democratization and the advancement of human rights suffered severely under the strong developmental regimes, with the dreaded intervention of the ubiquitous Korean Central Intelligence Agency, subsequently called the Agency for National Security Planning—and now in the Kim Dae-jung administration, the Agency for Intelligence Service. Most recently, political democratization has reached a high point while the economy is experiencing a catastrophe, again in an inverse pattern, for the present. Just as the evolution of democracy elected a president from the opposition camp, the economy was shaken to its foundations due to long-accumulated problems. While the new deadlock-prone government, business conglomerates, and labor are responding sluggishly to the economic cataclysm, it was remarkable symbolically that the "free" citizens, largely of the middle class, voluntarily responded under the aegis of civil society groups to the economic crisis, as in the gold collection campaign and various voluntary belt-tightening measures.

However, it appears that the worst may be yet to come. When large-scale restructuring and the survival of only the fittest enterprises occur, they are bound to produce wave after wave of unemployed citizens in a society with sparse safety nets. The quest for economic development has been frustrated in catastrophic proportions, and the crisis might last for years. The economic position of the middle class, an element of stability and often a liberalizing force during the last decade, may be seriously eroded. The unemployed and angry might suffer in relative silence for a while, as they have in the past under political suppression; however, they also have a history of taking to the streets, sometimes violently. Social and political consequences of such disturbances might be far reaching, particularly if the newly installed government were to come under a seize mentality and overreact against, for instance, labor strikes. Much of the political gains in terms of democratization might be quickly wiped out, and the limits of democracy in Korea might yet be exposed in an unfortunate interplay of the economy and politics. Such are the challenges that the Kim Dae-jung government, essentially a coalition regime with an unstable legislature, faces at this writing.

Political and economic turning points have been reached almost simultaneously. It will take all the genius and resources of the Korean leaders and the people alike to overcome the worst national crisis since the Korean War. It is evident that the quest for democratization, beyond the stage of procedural democracy, and the quest for sustainable and equitable economic development, remain real but somewhat distant and idealized goals for the Republic of Korea.

⚙

SELECTED BIBLIOGRAPHY

This bibliography is not meant to be exhaustive. The author regrets very much that many sources, even those listed in endnotes, are excluded from this *selected* bibliography.

Books

Abelmann, Nancy. *Echoes of the Past, Epics of Dissent: A South Korean Social Movement*. Berkeley: University of California Press, 1996.

Adelman, Irma, and Cynthia Taft Morris. *Economic Growth and Social Equity in Developing Countries*. Stanford, CA: Stanford University Press, 1973.

Amsden, Alice, H. *Asia's Next Giant: South Korea and Late Industrialization*. Cambridge, UK: Cambridge University Press, 1989.

Cho, Soon. *The Dynamics of Korean Economic Development*. Washington, DC: Institute for International Economics, 1994.

Choi, Jang-jip. *Hanguk hyŏndae chŏngch'iŭi kujowa pyŏnhwa* (Structure and Changes in Contemporary Korean Politics). Seoul: Kkach'i, 1989.

Ch'ŏndogyo Central Headquarters. *Ch'ŏndogyo kyŏngjŏn* (The Ch'ŏndogyo Scriptures). Seoul: Ch'ŏndogyo Central Headquarters, 1973.

Chōsen kenpeitai shireibu ([Japanese] Military Police Headquarters), ed. *Chōsen san-iche dokuritsu sōyō jiken* (The Incident of the March First Independence Disturbance in Korea). Tokyo: Reinando shoten, 1969.

Cole, David C., and Princeton N. Lyman. *Korean Development: The Inter-Play of Politics and Economics*. Cambridge, MA: Harvard University Press, 1971.

Cumings, Bruce. *The Origins of the Korean War*. 2 vols. Princeton, NJ: Princeton University Press, 1981, 1990.

Dahl, Robert A. *Poliarchy: Participation and Opposition*. New Haven, CT: Yale University Press, 1971.

———. *A Preface to Economic Democracy*. Cambridge, MA: Polity Press, 1985.

Deuchler, Martin. *The Confucian Transformation of Korea*. Cambridge, MA: Council on East Asian Studies, Harvard University Press, 1992.

Deyo, Frederic C. *The Political Economy of New Asian Industrialism*. Ithaca, NY: Cornell University Press, 1987.

Eckert, Carter J. *Offspring of Empire: The Koch'ang Kims and the Colonial Origins of Korean Capitalism, 1876–1945*. Seattle: University of Washington Press, 1991.

Eckert, Carter J., et al. *Korea Old and New: A History*. Seoul: Ilchokak. 1990.

Fukuyama, Francis. *Trust: The Social Virtues and the Creation of Prosperity*. New York: Free Press, 1995.

— Han, Woo-keun. *The History of Korea*. Honolulu: University of Hawaii Press, 1970.

Hankook Ilbosa. *Hanguk ŭi chungsan ch'ŭng*. (The Middle Class of Korea). Seoul: Hankook Ilbosa. 1987.

Held, David. *Models of Democracy*. Stanford, CA: Stanford University Press, 1987.

Henderson, Gregory. *Korea: The Politics of the Vortex*. Cambridge, MA: Harvard University Press, 1968.

— Henthorn, William E. *A History of Korea*. New York: Free Press, 1971.

Huer, Jon. *Marching Orders: The Role of the Military in South Korea's "Economic Miracle," 1961–1971*. New York: Greenwood Press, 1989.

Johnson, Chamlers. *MITI and the Japanese Miracle*. Stanford, CA: Stanford University Press, 1982.

Kang, Wi Jo. *Christ and Caeser in Modern Korea: A History of Christianity and Politics*. Albany: State University of New York Press, 1997.

Kim, Ch'ol-su. *Hanguk hŏnpŏpsa* (A History of the Korean Constitution). Seoul: Taehak ch'ulpansa, 1988.

Kim, Dae-jung. *Mass-Participatory Economy*. Cambridge, MA: Center for International Affairs, Harvard University; and Lanham, MD: University Press of America, 1996.

———. *Three-Stage Approach to Korean Reunification*. Los Angeles: Center for Multi-ethnic and Transnational Studies, University of South California, 1997.

Kim, Eun Mee. *Big Business, Strong State*. Albany, N.Y.: State University of New York Press. 1987.

Kim, Un-t'ae. *Hanguk chŏngch'i non* (On Korean Politics). Seoul: Pakyongsa, 1982.

———. *Ilbon chegukchui ŭi hanguk t'ongch'i* (Japanese Imperial Rule of Korea). Seoul: Pakyong-sa, 1985.

Kim, Yong Choon. *Oriental Thought*. Springfield, IL: Charles Thomas Publishers, 1973.

Lee, Chong Sik. *Materials on Korean Communism, 1945–1947*. Honolulu: Center for Korean Studies, 1977.

Lee, Hee Ho. *Naŭi sarang naŭi choguk* (My Love, My Country). Seoul: Myeong Rim Dang, 1992.

— Lee, Ki-baik, ed. *A New History of Korea*, trans. Edward W. Wagner. Cambridge, MA: Harvard University Press, 1984.

Legge, James, trans. *The Four Books*. Taipei: Culture Books, 1970.

Linz, Juan J., and Alfred Stepan. *Problems of Democratic Transition and Consolidation*. Baltimore: Johns Hopkins University Press, 1996.

Mason, Edward S., et al. *The Economic and Social Modernization of the Republic of Korea*. Cambridge, MA: Council on East Asian Studies, Harvard University Press, 1980.

McNamara, Dennis L. *The Colonial Origins of Korean Enterprise, 1910–1945*. Cambridge, UK: Cambridge University Press, 1990.

Merrill, John. *Korea: Peninsula Origins of the War*. Newark: University of Delaware Press, 1989.

Moore, Barrington, Jr. *Social Origins of Dictatorship and Democracy*. Boston: Beacon Press, 1966.

Nahm, Andrew C. *Korea: Tradition and Transformation*. Seoul: Hollym, 1988.

O'Donnell, Guillermo, Philippe C. Schmitter, and Laurence Whitehead, eds. *Transition from Authoritarian Rule*. Baltimore: Johns Hopkins University Press, 1988.

Ogle, George E. *South Korea: Dissent within the Economic Miracle*. London: Zea Books, 1990.

Oh, John Kie-chiang. *Korea: Democracy on Trial*. Ithaca, NY: Cornell University Press, 1968.

——. *The Dilemmas of Democratic Politics with Economic Development in Korea*. Seoul: Korea Development Institute, 1990.

Paek, Se-myong. *Tonghak sasang kwa Ch'ŏndogyo* (The *Tonghak* Ideologies and the Teaching of the Heavenly Way). Seoul: Tonghaksa, 1956.

Pak, Ki-hyuk. *A Study of the Land Tenure System in Korea*. Seoul: Land Economic Research Center, 1966.

Pak, Tong-so, and Kim Kwang-ung. *Hangukinŭi minju chŏngch'i ŭisik* (The Democratic Political Consciousness of the Korean People). Seoul: Seoul National University Press, 1989.

Robinson, Michael E. *Cultural Nationalism in Colonial Korea, 1920–1925*. Seattle: University of Washington Press, 1988.

Rossiter, Clinton L. *Constitutional Dictatorship: Crisis Government in the Modern Democracies*. Princeton, NJ: Princeton University Press, 1948.

Rostow, W. W. *The Stages of Economic Growth*, 3rd ed. Cambridge, UK: Cambridge University Press, 1990.

Samil undong osip chuyŏn kinyŏm nonmunjip (Collected Essays on the Fiftieth Anniversary of the March First Movement). Seoul: Dong-A ilbosa, 1969.

Shumpeter, Joseph. *Capitalism, Socialism, and Democracy*. London: Allen and Unwin, reprint, 1942.

Song, Byung-Nak. *The Rise of the Korean Economy*. Oxford: Oxford University Press, 1990.

Sorensen, Georg. *Democracy and Democratization*. Boulder, CO: Westview Press, 1993.

Tewksbury, Donald G., ed. *Source Materials on Korean Politics and Ideologies*. New York: Institute of Pacific Relations, 1950.

Woo, Jung-en. *Race to the Swift: State and Finance in Korean Industrialization*. New York: Columbia University Press, 1991.

Yang, Sung Chul. *The North and South Korean Political Systems: A Comparative Analysis*. Boulder, CO: Westview Press, 1994.

Yi, Ton-hwa. *Ch'ŏndogyo ch'anggan-sa* (The History of the Inauguration of the Teaching of the Heavenly Way). Seoul: Ch'ŏndogyo Central Headquarters, 1933.

Yu, Chin-o. *Hŏnbop kich'o hwoegorok* (Recollections of Constitution Drafting). Seoul: Ilchogak, 1980.

Articles and Chapters

Cho, Lee-Jay. "Ethical and Social Influences of Confucianism," in *Economic Development in the Republic of Korea: A Policy Perspective*, Lee-Jay Cho and Yoon Hung Kim, eds. Honolulu: University of Hawaii Press, 1991: 559.

Diamond, Larry. "Rethinking Civil Society: Toward Democratic Consolidation." *Journal of Democracy* 5, no. 3 (1994): 4–17.

Dong, Wonmo, "University Students in South Korean Politics: Patterns of Radicalization in the 1980s," *Journal of International Affairs,* 40, 2(1987): 233–55.

Inglehart, Ronald. "Trust, Well-Being and Democracy." Paper presented at Conference on Trust and Democracy, Georgetown University, November 1996.

Kim, Chang Rok. "The Characteristics of the System of Japanese Imperialism in Korea from 1905 to 1945." *Korea Journal* 36, no. 1 (Spring 1996): 20.

Kim, Dae-jung. "Is Culture Destiny? The Myth of Asia's Anti-Democratic Values: A Response to Lee Kuan Yew." *Foreign Affairs* 73, no. 6 (1994): 192.

——. "Asia sik minjujuŭi" (Asian-Style Democracy). *Sin Dong-A* (December 1994): 230.

Kim Sunhyuk. "Civil Society in South Korea." *Journal of Northeast Asian Studies* (Summer 1996): 81–97.

Kim, Tscholsu, and Sang Don Lee. "Republic of Korea: The Influence of U.S. Constitutional Law Doctrines in Korea," in Lawrence W. Beer, ed. *Constitutional Systems in Late Twentieth Century Asia.* Seattle: University of Washington Press, 1992.

Linz, Juan J., and Alfred Stepan. "Toward Consolidated Democracies." *Journal of Democracies* 7, no. 2 (1996): 14–33.

Lipset, Seymour Martin. "Some Social Requisites of Democracy: Economic Development and Political Legitimacy." *American Political Science Review* 53, no. 1 (1959): 75.

Pak Chŏng-hŭi (Park Chung Hee). "Naui sonyon sichol" (My Boyhood), in *Pirok: hangukŭi daet'ong nyŏng* (Hidden Records: The Presidents of Korea). ed. Wolgan Chosonbu. Seoul: Choson Ilbosa, 1993: 512.

Pak, Won-sun. *Kukka Poanbŏp yŏngu* (The Study of the National Security Law). Seoul: Yoksa bip'yŏngsa. 1992.

Putnam, Robert D., and Eric M. Uslander. "Democracy and Social Capital." Paper presented at Conference on Trust and Democracy, Georgetown University, November 1996.

Shin, Susan S. "Tonghak Thought: The Roots of Revolution." *Korea Journal* (1983): 205.

Steinberg, David I. "Residential Elections and the Rooting of Democracy," in *The 1997 Korean Presidential Elections,* ed. Chaibong Hahm, Robert A. Scalapino, and David I. Steinberg (New York: Asia Society, November 1997): 25–35.

Weathersby, Kathryn, trans. with commentary. "From the Russian Archives: New Findings on the Korean War." Woodrow Wilson Center *Bulletin* (Fall 1993): 14.

Yi Ki-bong. "Pukhan chŏmnyŏng soryŏngun sunowe hwoego" (Recollections of a Soviet Occupation Chief in North Korea). *Sin Dong-A* (July 1995): 380.

Official Documents

Headquarters, U.S. Army Forces in Korea. Official Gazette. (April 15, 1948): 1.

"Laws and Documents," *Korea Annual,* various issues.

Republic of Korea, *Kwanbo* (Official gazette), various issues.

Secretariat, House of Representatives, Republic of Korea, "The National Security Law" (December 1, 1948).

U.S. Department of State, *American Foreign Policy: Current Documents,* various issues.

INDEX

ABOUT THE AUTHOR

John Kie-chiang (K. C.) Oh is currently professor of politics at the Catholic University of America. His study of law at Seoul National University was interrupted by the Korean War, and, having served with the United Nations Command delegation to the Korean armistice negotiations, he came to the United States in 1954. He studied political science at Marquette, Columbia, and Georgetown universities, receiving his Ph.D. in international politics from Georgetown University in 1963. He has served as dean of the Graduate School of Marquette University and was academic vice president of the Catholic University of America.

Oh has published books, articles, and reviews on Korean, Japanese, East Asian, and international subjects. *Korean Politics: The Quest for Democratization and Economic Development* (1999) and *Korea: Democracy on Trial* (1968) are both published by Cornell University Press.